MY JOURNEY TO LIFE!

TO LIFE!

BIOGRAPHY/MEMOIR

Dr. Sabelo Sam Gasela Mhlanga

WESTBOW
PRESS®
A DIVISION OF THOMAS NELSON
& ZONDERVAN

WestBow Press books may be ordered through booksellers or by contacting:

WestBow Press
A Division of Thomas Nelson & Zondervan
1663 Liberty Drive
Bloomington, IN 47403
www.westbowpress.com
844-714-3454

Scripture taken from the New King James Version® Copyright © 1982 by Thomas Nelson. Used by permission. All rights reserved.

Scripture taken from the King James Version of the Bible.

Scripture quotations taken from The Holy Bible, New International Version® NIV® Copyright © 1973 1978 1984 2011 by Biblica, Inc. TM. Used by permission. All rights reserved worldwide.

ISBN: 978-1-6642-3724-7 (sc)
ISBN: 978-1-6642-3725-4 (e)

Print information available on the last page.

WestBow Press rev. date: 06/22/2021

Mabutho Gasela
UCCSA Evangelist & Missionary-Died 1958

Hope Fountain Mission Church Built-1870

CONTENTS

This book is dedicated to my late father Joseph Gasela, my late mother Josephine (née Nyathi) Gasela, my grandfather Mabutho Gasela and grand-mother MamKhwananzi Gasela. To my aunt, the sister of my grandfather, Maphico MaMhlanga and her daughter Anna Hlongwane. The dedication also goes to my siblings, the first born of my father, Ernest Gasela, followed by Margaret Siphelile Gasela, Alexzander Gasela, Joshua Gasela, Gladys Gasela, the late Adwell Gasela, the late Mavis Gasela, Senzeni Gasela, Sithabile Gasela, Sabelo Gasela, Zenzo Gasela, Sipho Gasela and Duduzile Ellen.

This book is also dedicated to the siblings of my father, Amos who married MaThebe and six children, Noel, Alfred, Sibonile, Simanga, Betty, Daisy, and Lillian. The other siblings of my father were: Ethie, Dan, Esther who bore Hebert Masina, Mayaya who was married to Gumede the President of Zimbabwe-Rhodesia the government of Abel Muzorewa in 1979, and Matthew who married MaSibanda and they had two daughters, Nompilo Gasela and Sinikiwe Gasela and the whole of Gasela Clan.

INTRODUCTION

LIFE is a special gift from God, the very essence that we exist in and the reason we were protected in the conception, birth and longevity its mind blowing for the love God bestowed on us. What is life? Life is the passing of time. What is time? Time is the passing of life. Time is categorized into two facets, *Chronos*, which means the ordinary time, determined and calculated within our solar system and *Kairos* is God's divine timing, the perfect time. I was born on 14 August, 1965, at Hope Fountain clinic in Matabeleland North, although this is not my official birth date as my birth certificate got lost after the family disintegrated after the death of my father, Joseph Gasela and my mother, Josephine Gasela, could not hold all things together alone. My mother, Josephine Nyathi Gasela, told me the true birthdate years later after much inquiry. I was the seventh child from my mother's side to be born and my father named me 'Sabelo'. The meaning of my name is "My Portion" because when I was born, my father told his sister who was living in South Africa that he had another son, instead of congratulating him, she scorned him saying that he had too many children. My father told her that it was God's portion that He had given him, thus "Sabelo" means my portion. I have a faint idea about my father. This book narrates the life that was preserved, protected and unleashed into the world with a special purpose to change the world and human limitations. This book articulates the journey and adventure of my life into a broken and unfriendly world yet to the world with kind, compassionate and loving people who overcome evil with good.

The purpose of this book/autobiography is to show God's hand in my life, His guidance, His protection and sailing through the challenges and hurdles of life but yet it calls for patience, perseverance, resilience, faith, staying focused and pushing on regardless of the situation one encounters and confronts. Sit back, relax and buckle-up as we prepare to take off on my life journey and enjoy the ride! My hope and prayer are that this memoir/autobiography will inspire you and compel you to keep moving and believing regardless of your circumstances or situation. The book documents the genesis of the Gasela-Mhlanga family tree, the disintegration of my family, my departure from Hope Fountain, my life in Tsholotsho, my departure to Botswana, then to Zambia and my return to Zimbabwe in 1980 after independence. My life journey in Zimbabwe after independence, my education, my service in the church, United Baptist Church, my struggles and my challenges. The last chapters detail my departure to the USA, the pursuit of my education and my second commission as a missionary in the Northwest. Let me begin at the beginning.

CHAPTER ONE

Tracking and Tracing my Roots

The Gasela-Mhlanga family lineage dates back to the 18th century in KwaMhlanga, Mpumalanga, Pretoria in South Africa. The place was named after Mhlanga. KwaMhlanga is a town in Mpumalanga Province, in the district of Nkangala South Africa, the home of the Ndebele tribe who settled in the 18th century, a Nguni, an ethnic group. They are two kraals, the Manala Royal Kraal and Ndzundza Mabhoka kraal. Mhlanga in Zulu/Ndebele means *Reeds*. The Mhlangas were part of the Ndebele tribe under Mzilikazi KaMatshobana who was the lieutenant of Tshaka in 1823. In 1822, Tshaka had sent Mzilikazi to invade and loot the regiment of Sotho chief Ranisi. After pounding and defeating the Sotho regiment, Mzilikazi herded the cattle away; however, he decided not to surrender the loot to king Tshaka. He decided to keep them for himself and to form his own kingdom. He had no choice but fled from Tshaka, instead of facing execution. He decided to head northwards in pursuit of a new and free land. He was tired of a life of subservience. Tshaka ruled with iron-fist and he brought his subjects under brutal submission. As a result of his autocratic rule, Mzilikazi fled Zululand under the rule of Tshaka in 1823, refusing to surrender to Tshaka, (https://en.wikipedia.org/wiki/Mzilikazi, accessed, November, 23, 2020).

Mzilikazi was born in 1790, the son of Mashobane kaMangethe in the neighborhood of Mkuze, Zululand. When he fled, he first headed to Mozambique but then he moved to the west to Transvaal as his enemies kept attacking and pursuing him as a runaway fugitive. Along the way, he invaded some smaller kingdoms and absorbed his subjects into his growing kingdom. He eliminated all his opponents to a new Ndebele kingdom. Anyone who resisted was crushed, hence the *"Mfecane"* crushing period. In 1836, Mzilikazi with his people were forced out of Transvaal and he headed northwards. The Boers who had occupied Transvaal had constant battles with Mzilikazi regiments. In the north, he settled in Botswana with his people but constant attacks did not give him peace as one time in 1836, Dingane's Zulu regiment, attacked him as he took the opportunity of his loss with the Voortrekkers battles. However, Mzilikazi's regiment annihilated Dingane's regime with umph. He was further pushed to move northwards again. Fleeing his enemies and tsetse flies in parts of Zambia, he headed southeast, crossed Limpopo River and settled in Matabeleland in 1840, (https://en.wikipedia.org/wiki/Mzilikazi, accessed, November, 23, 2020).

After settling in Matabeleland in Zimbabwe, he amalgamated the local tribes and any kingdoms that became part of his kingdom. He organized a militaristic regiment similar to that of Tshaka, using tough military training techniques, a short stabbing spear that was used in the close range of the enemy rather than a long spear. His warriors trained bare-footed and they were under the age of 40 years and younger. His regiments were so strong, tough and skillful that they defeated the Boers in 1847-1851 until they agreed to sign a peace treaty in 1852.

Mzilikazi allowed some of the hunters, traders and European travelers in his kingdom in the likes of Robert Moffatt whom he befriended in 1830, a Scottish missionary who was working with the Tswana. During the time when he was forming his kingdom, a section of his people wandered away and they thought they had lost the king. They thought of putting Nkulumane as the heir and a successor of his father, Mzilikazi. That was the biggest mistake the chiefs had made. When king Mzilikazi reappeared and found that the chiefs had installed Nkulumane as the king, they were summoned and brought before the king and were all executed without pity or mercy, including his son, Nkulumani being thrown down a steep hill called Ntabazinduna. However, another account says that Nkulumane was not killed; it is believed that he escaped back to Zululand but did not reach there for fear that he would be killed by the enemies of his father, Tshaka warriors. It is believed that he settled in Bakwena territory, lived there until he died in 1883, (https://www.sahistory.org.za/people/king-mzilikazi, accessed November 26, 2020).

The oral narrative says, king Mzilikazi became so infuriated by the scheme perpetrated by the chiefs so much that he killed his other sons. One of his wives, Fulatha, the daughter of the Swazi chief, managed to hide her son, Lobengula, from being executed. When Mzilikazi had consolidated his kingdom, he moved from Ntabazinduna to Bulawayo, his capital, Matabele kingdom, Mthwakazi. Tshaka had Bulawayo as his capital also in Zululand. Mzilikazi permitted white hunters who had firearms and ammunition. However, after Henry Hartley realized that Mashonaland did not have enough gold he was looking for, he ventured into Matabeleland, explored the north and discovered gold along Mfuli and Tate Rivers. Miners from Europe and Australia scrambled to usurp the gold discovery in 1867. The Europeans flooded the country for gold. Mzilikazi was no longer able to control the invaders, he was overwhelmed, (https://www.sahistory.org.za/people/king-mzilikazi, Accessed, December 5, 2020).

When Mzilikazi was ailing with his illness which is not known or disclosed, he died leaning on the shoulders of his Matabele kingdom at Ingama near Bulawayo on September 9, 1868. His son Lobengula, who had escaped execution through his mother, Fulatha, was installed as the successor. Lobengula was born in Mogesa, Transvaal, South Africa in 1836.

However, the heir did not come easy without a fierce fight. For two years, there was a bitter fight with his elder brother, Mangwane and some chiefs who saw him as not the rightful heir because he was born of the mother from the Swazi origin. The battle between the two sons continued until Lobengula's warriors conquered Mangwane's regiments. Lobengula was installed as a king in 1870. Lobengula managed to repel Ngwane's regiments in 1872. He was crowned at Mhlahlandlela, one of the principal military kraals.

King Lobengula was confronted with yet another enemy, gold traders, explorers, hunters and the imperialists who wanted to mine gold. In 1888, Lonbengula signed a friendship treaty in which he was hoodwinked into believing that it was a limited mineral concession with Cecil John Rhodes' business team which was led by Charles Rudd which became known as Rudd Concession. The British South Africa Company (BSAC) tried to get access to gold areas but Lobengula refused to give them the access as he was sensing that the British empire was pitching its nose into his kingdom, sarcastically. Pursuing their ambitions, BSAC invaded Mashonaland in 1890 by force. Led by Leander Starr Jameson in 1891 who represented the British South Africa Company, orchestrated the invasion of Lobengula's kingdom, militarily. He promised the settlers, gold, land and cattle as rewards for waging the war. King Lobengula saw that his kingdom was slipping away from him but he waged fierce battles against the settlers and who Jameson was the commander. King Lobengula's warriors were fighting with short stabbing spears while BSAC were using firearms with gunpowder. Lobengula's regiments could not cope with such sophisticated weaponry. When Lobengula saw that the enemy was closing in on him, he burned his city, Bulawayo and fled northwards, crossing the Zambezi River, (https://www.britannica.com/biography/Mzilikazi, accessed December 2, 2020).

He is thought to have died in 1893-1894 across the Zambezi River in Mpuzeni's Ngoni people. However, it is not known to this very day where he went but he is known to have disappeared. His son, Nyamanda succeeded him in 1896. The first Matabele War began in 1893, after the death of King Lobengula. The wars fought against the imperialists and colonialists were to prevent the subjugation of the local people. In response, the Ndebeles and the Shonas waged uprisings against the invaders, first in 1893 and again 1896, rebellions against the British who intentionally, moved in the land through coercion of king Lobengula, the chiefs and also through cooked peace treaties, mineral treaties and warfares, (https://www.britannica.com/biography/Mzilikazi, accessed December 2, 2020).

On Track of my Consanguinity Roots

Missionaries came together with the colonialists and imperialists. At the beginning, it seemed as if these two institutions were the same, the Politicians and the Church. It appeared as if the Church and the state were inseparable. They seemed to have had a razor thin relationship between the two institutions. While the politicians focused on three government branches, Legislative, Executive and Judiciary, the church focused on the three entities, Education, Religion and Health System. The British colonialists were aggressive in pursuing political scores, to subjugate, repress and rule Zimbabwe by all means necessary. The church was careful in advancing the kingdom of God. Robert Moffat's son, John Moffatt had become a missionary. They were three missions that were established to cater for these three entities, the Church, the School and Health. The first mission established was Inyati Mission School which is the oldest mission in Zimbabwe, established in 1859 under London Mission Society (LMS). Christianity never spread to the Ndebele people until the fall of the Ndebele nation in 1893. Inyati Mission School was followed by Hope Fountain Mission, now Tenson Hlabangane High School about 5.6 km away from Bulawayo, established in 1870. They were both established under the United Congregational Church of Southern Africa (UCCSA). (This is the mission school in which I was born). The third mission was Dombodema Mission School in Plumtree which was also established under London Missionary Society, (https://zimfieldguide.com/matabeleland-south/hope-fountain-mission, Accessed December 7, 2020).

They were other mission schools that were established throughout the country in Zimbabwe. When the missionaries came to the unreached virgin lands, they had a strategy that they implemented. Firstly, they wanted the new converts to be able to read the Bible, meditate and apply it, spiritually. Secondly, they wanted the new converts to educate the mind to be able to internalize, analyze, and perceive, mentally. Thirdly, they wanted the converts to do agriculture and animal husbandry for a balanced diet. It does not mean that the indigenous people did not have their form of education, religion or physical education but they wanted to teach them the European or western civilization. They established mission schools to teach new literature, new religion, new European or western cultures. Christianity was purported to replace African Traditional Religion (ATR) which was regarded as a pagan and evil religion. The missions were also designated areas where those who had repented and converted to Christianity were encouraged to leave their villages and be relocated to mission schools where they would receive education, Christianity and medication. These mission schools were also the institutions for training life skills such as building, carpentry, agriculture, animal husbandry, teaching, nursing etc. The Schools, Churches, and Hospitals were the main features of the mission stations.

Hope Fountain Mission, was the second oldest mission in Zimbabwe. It has a beautiful landscape with perpetual streams of springs with clear water undulating along the green forest between the hills. Just a short background of Hope Fountain Mission. Rev. Robert Moffat arrived from South Africa in 1817. He developed a close relationship with king Mzilikazi in 1854, 1857 and 1859. John Moffatt was the son of Robert Moffatt and had become a good assert in translating the Ndebele/Zulu language into English and he became a missionary in Zimbabwe during that period. John Boden Thomson was assisted by Hartley and Baine to find a suitable second location for the second mission and called it Hope Fountain Mission. The land was granted by king Lobengula who retained the rights to repossess it if London Mission Society decided to leave the place for whatever reason, in November 16, 1870. King Lobengula first refused to grant them the land but he finally agreed to grant them the permission to start the second mission but with a condition that the mission will be under him, the king, that no traders should build anything and also that he did not want any more missionaries on the site. Thomson lived at Hope Fountain until 1875 after building his house and other facilities, (https://zimfieldguide.com/matabeleland-south/hope-fountain-mission, Accessed December 7, 2020).

During this period, my family, the Mhlanga Gasela clan was already in the vicinity. My grand-father, Mabutho Gasela was the local man whom John Boden Thompson befriended, and he was the handyman, scouting the land for the second station, Hope Fountain. He was converted, and he became a Christian and an elder in the church, London Missionary Society, with his brother. He later became an evangelist and travelled as far as Nyamandlovu, preaching and witnessing for Christ. The mother of our great grandmother was Nkasana but her father died during the battle. Our grandfather Mabutho Gasela had his brother, the first born in the family who had a son called Fani. They were three siblings. Mabutho's sister, Maphico Gasela-Mhlanga married Hlongwane. They bore Philip, Stephen Sitshotshoto, George, Anna, Khiwa, Philemon and two twins who died when they were still young. Her daughter Anna Hlongwane married Hablya Ndlovu. Our grandfather, Mabutho had seven children, Amos, Eddie, Joseph, Greta, Dan, Esther and Matthew. His son Amos and his wife Esther Thebe bore Noel, Alfred, Sibonile, Simanga Norma, Betty Siphiwe, Daisy and Lillian. Eddie was married to her husband Masina and bore Herbert Masina and other children. Joseph bore Maudie, and Ernest, then he married and had two children, Siphelile Margaret and Alexander. When his wife died, he married Josephine Mankaza Nyathi and they bore Joshua, Gladys, Adwell, Mavis, Senzeni, Sithabile, Sabelo (me), Zenzo and Sipho. Esther married Josiah Zion Gumede who became the President of Zimbabwe Rhodesia in 1979 during the Bishop Abel Muzorewa government. They bore Titus, Mandlenkosi, Mnyamana, Box, and other children. Dan married Maluphahla and they bore Gideon and Bodrick. The last born of Mabutho and Mkhwanazi was a son, Matthew who married Patricia Sibanda and they bore three daughters, Nompilo, Sinikiwe and Sikhanyisiwe. Nompilo married her husband David Nyathi and they bore Nonhlanhla, David Junior, Nathaniel Emmanuel. Sinikiwe got married to Johannes Ndlovu and bore Blessed, Sibonginkosi, Samukelisiwe Sangiwe, Mandlenkosi, and Nomagugu. Sikhanyisiwe had no children.

The children of Amos and Esther Thebe were: Noel, Noel's children were Benjamin and Thutsha. Alfred Mafayithi and MaMguni bore Vusa and Sifiso. Sibonile married her husband Mayibuye Benjamin Mtshayisa and they bore Sithabisiwe, Sibongile Sibusiso,

Mdingi Murphy, Zimema Lenox, Zanele, Mihla, Sokesibonane, Sinini, Lindiwe, Khululani Masawa, Edwin and Fikile. Simanga Norma bore Nothando Dade, Nomusa Mankiza, Sithembiso and Ngqabutho, Makhosazana. Betty Siphiwe bore Njabulo, Bhekani Panther and Nyaradzo. Daisy bore Bekithemba, Donald, Petronella, and Allan. Lillian bore Phumzile with her husband Dube. Greta with her husband Sadomba bore Bob, Sibongile, and Roddie. Siphiwe bore Edna, Huggins and Dumisani. Herbert Masina and MaNdlovu bore Jabulani, Sandile and Sibusisiwe. Mnyamana with his wife Sihle Nyoni bore Mzwandile, Dumehlezi, and Luba. The family expanded, Bishop Gasela had five children, Gconiwe, Kitty, Graham, Zondiwe, and Fanyana. Funny Gasela bore Funisen.

Joseph's children were as follows, Maudie and her children are not much known. Ernest married his wife MaKhumalo and bore Themba, Siramu, Sukoluhle and Thabani. Themba had one son, Mafana Alex. Siramu bore Xolani, Precious Mankri, and Edith. Thabani bore Vanessa. Sukoluhle had no children. Siphelile Margaret married Hlongwane and they had two children, Themba and Cynthia Sikokotshi. Alexander Ngundu married MaMsipha and bore Thina and he married MaNcube and bore Mnumzane, Mhlonipheni, Mthulisi, Mkhululi and Mthokozisi. Joshua Buntu married MaNkomo and bore Nkosikhona and Charity. He married MaDube and bore Thulani, Mjamosana, Nkululeko, Sanelisiwe and Simelokuhle. Gladys and her husband Enock Ndlovu bore Mpekwana, Thembi, Mzamane, Themba and Mthandazo. Mavis married her husband Elijah Moyo and they did not have any children but they adopted Sipho, Sithabile and Agrippa Ncube's grandson. Adwell Nanatsho married MaChirwa and bore Promise and Makhosendulo. Senzeni Khathazile married her husband Isaac Maseko and had one son Mandlenkosi. Sithabile married her husband Agrippa Ncube and bore Nomalanga, Dorcus, Patricia, Siphathisiwe Luluzana, Sandra Girlie, Trust Khuluzana, Trevor Mfanembuzi and Treasure Bhudiza. Sabelo Sam married his wife Judith Kurwaisimba Sithole and bore Qhawelenkosi (Blessing), Sinqobile (Shalom), Thandolwenkosi (Prosper), Nkosilathi (Emmanuel), and Nkosana Joseph Sam Junior. Zenzo married Rosie Gwebu and bore Thembani Crag, Anna, Ntombi, and Thando. Sipho married Siduduzile Sikhosana and bore Polite, Prince and Pinky. Duduzile Ellen, had a daughter with Alex Gumbo and bore Ledwin Magumbanyana Gumbo.

Anna Hlongwane with her husband Habiya Ndlovu bore Gladys. Gladys bore Bester, Marko, Thenjiwe, Moses, John Tshiwawa, Sikhumbuzo, Thembekile, Nomthandazo and Pumulo. Agnes bore Caroline, and Pearl. Jester bore Maxwell, Sithembile Mangcungcu, Lindiwe and Washington. Timothy bore Lihle, Trust, Sukoluhle, Limuka, Lizwe. David did not have any children. John Tshiwawa married MaGwebu and bore Tracy, Booker, Duduzile and Nozipho. Jane bore Patricia Mtize. Philp Hlongwane and his wife Alice Hlongwane bore Canaan, Enock, Vetl, Christopher and a twin sister. George Hlongwane had no children. The next in line was Stephen who went to live in South Africa. Stephen's son married Nelson Mandela's daughter, Zinzi Mandela. Philimon Pearl bore Yeolanda, Godfrey, John, Brian and the twins who died while they were still young.

Grandfather Mabutho Gasela who was now a fully fletched evangelist under United Congregational Church of Southern Africa (UCCSA) contracted malaria while he was doing evangelism outreach in Nyamandlovu, using his motorbike. He was admitted at Memorial Hospital in 1958 and he did not recover from malaria and he died in 1958. He was laid to rest at Hope Fountain cemetery. The hero of faith joined others who had laid the foundation of the gospel in both Matabeleland South and Matabeleland North. His death was a blow to the family and the church at large. He had chartered Christian life in his family, the community and to the church. He left a legacy of Christian faith to his children, grandchildren, and great grandchildren to follow and to believe in the Lord, Jesus Christ. If they abandon the life of faith in Christ Jesus, it is up to their futile and peril. Life without Christ is doomed and miserable. We salute our grandfather who showed us the Way, the Truth and the Life, in Christ Jesus, (John 14:6, NKJV). We honor him and love him for his sacrifice, his faith, his caring and for carrying the torch of the gospel to give light to the dark world. Let me address my grandfather for his sacrifice in bringing the gospel to our family and other families: "Thank you my grandfather, Mabutho

Gasela, for answering the call to preach and to witness for Christ. Your labor was not in vail. Although your sons and your daughters did not take after you to be preachers, your grandchildren have. I personally have answered the call as you did and I went to Theological College and Universities got the training and I became a Pastor. I was ordained and I continued to do my Masters, and my Doctorate and I answered the call to be a missionary in the Northwest in America, following your steps. You planted the seed and here I am in your footsteps, grandfather. We will meet you in heaven in the presence of our Lord Jesus Christ. We love you grandfather, Mabuto Gasela." After resting in eternal peace, his sister Maphico Gasela-Mhlanga, lived for some few years after. She was a devoted Jehovah's Witness member. She is known for reading the Bible all the time and praying. I lived to see her when I was six years old. She lived to see her great grandchildren. She was known for making creamy cultured milk (Izankefu) which was the best in the area. She was often called, (Ugogo uMaMhlanga) grandmother, Nee Mhlanga.

She lived at least seven more or so years after her brother Mabutho Gasela had died. She eventually gave up the ghost and joined her family at Hope Fountain cemetery. Mabutho's children also died one after another. The most painful death I witnessed was of my father, Joseph Gasela. I was five years old and I have a faint idea about my father. I remember, when they took us away from our home to go and stay with my uncle, Dan for some days. They did not want us to know that our father had died. He died at Inyati Mission Hospital. They discovered that he had some throat infections without knowing the cause. I saw my mother throwing herself on the ground and mourning bitterly and I did not know what was happening. I saw a lot of people flocking to our home, sobbing and mourning. Some of them were crying so loud that you could hear them from a distance. My mother Josephine was made to wear black clothes immediately as the Ndebele culture and tradition when one's husband dies. Husbands/men were required to wear a black ribbon on their shirts and jackets if their wives had died or a sibling or a relative to show that they were in grief. The woman was required to wear a black dress and a black head gear to show grief for the whole year. The complete black clothes and headgears for women and a small black ribbon for men were to be worn for twelve months. After one year of grief had been completed, they were cultural rituals to be performed for cleansing and to release them from a one-year vow.

During the funeral proceedings of my father, I never saw anything else after that. We were kept away from the scene and ignorant of what had happened and we discovered later that we were not seeing our father any more. Mom used to tell me when I asked her that he had travelled without more explanation. The next chapter narrates what happened after the death of my father Joseph Gasela.

CHAPTER TWO

The Fallen Heroes and the Beginning of Family Despair

Joseph Gasela had the first son, Ernest, born of Mangwenya. Ernest married his wife MaKhumalo and bore Themba, Siramu, Sukoluhle and Thabani. Themba had one son, Mafana Alex. Siramu bore Xolani, Precious Mankri, and Edith. Thabani bore Vanessa. Sukoluhle had no children. The other daughter was Maudy Gasela born of a different woman. Joseph got married to the mother of Margaret Siphelile and Alexander Ngundu Gasela. Siphelile Margaret married Hlongwane and they had two children, Themba and Cynthia Sikokotshi. Alexander Ngundu married MaMsipha and bore Thina and he married MaNcube and bore Mongameli, Mnumzana, Mthabiseni and Muziwabo. Joseph Gasela then remarried, to Josephine Mankaza Nyathi, my mother. According to Josephine's narration, her father, Bafana, who was living in the vicinity, arranged the marriage to my father. She was just sixteen years old when they wedded. Her father, Bafana, liked and admired Joseph Gasela's home and his lifestyle and wanted her daughter to be married to him. This is the story my mother told me. My father was a builder /constructor. He had built a beautiful homemade of stones and cement. He had cattle, orchards with apples, pitches, oranges, grapes and lots of fruit trees. It was a beautiful home-stead. Tourists used to come and take photos of the house and admired the home. My father was born in 1912 and my mother was born in 1938. The age difference between Joseph and Josephine Gasela was twenty years. It actually means that my father married a teenager who was not yet mature to be a mother but she was able to manage her family and bore children.

Joseph and Josephine bore Joshua Buntu who married MaNkomo and bore Nkosikhona and Charity. Joshua remarried MaDube and they bore Thulani, Mjamosana, Nkululeko, Sanelisiwe and Simelokuhle. Joseph and Joseph bore Gladys and Gladys married her husband Enock Ndlovu who bore Mpekwana, Thembi, Mzamane, Themba and Mthandazo Joseph and Josephine bore Mavis, Da who married her husband Elijah Moyo and they did not have any children but they adopted Sipho, Sithabile and Agrippa Ncube's grandson. Joseph and Josephine bore Edwin Nanatsho who married MaChirwa and bore Promise and Makhosendulo. Joseph and Joseph bore Senzeni Khathazile who married her husband Isaac Maseko and had one son, Mandlenkosi. Joseph and Josephine bore Sithabile she married her husband Agrippa Ncube and they bore Nomalanga, Dorcus, Patricia, Siphathisiwe Luluzana, Sandra Girlie, Trust Khuluzana, Trevor Mfanembuzi and Treasure Bhudiza. Joseph and Josephine bore Sabelo Sam who married Judith Kurwaisimba Sithole and they bore Qhawelenkosi (Blessing), Sinqobile (Shalom), Thandolwenkosi (Prosper), Nkosilathi (Emmanuel), and Nkosana Joseph Sam Junior. Joseph and Josephine bore Zenzo who married Rosie Gwebu and bore Thembani Crag, Anna, Ntombi, and Thando. Joseph and Josephine bore Sipho who married Siduduzile Sikhosana and bore Polite, Prince and Pinky. After Joseph died, Josephine remarried Jonas Dzonzi and bore Duduzile Ellen, who had a daughter with Alex Gumbo and they bore Ledwin Magumbanyana Gumbo.

I remember when my father used to come from work, I would go outside the home gate to wait for him almost every day. He would put me on the back of his bicycle and push it until we got home. He had a motorbike too that he used to go to work with as a builder/constructor. He enjoyed cultivating his orchards daily when he was from work even if it was dark, he would use a gas lamp. I enjoyed a deep relationship with my father and he used to favor me in many ways. I was always close to him at five years old. However, he used to be tough on my older siblings, spanking them if they disobeyed the family chores and rules. He used to have a gumtree stick close to him for spanking. In the same vein, my mother Josephine used to discipline the children too. Myself, Zenzo and Sipho we were never spanked because we were younger. When my father Joseph Gasela died, it threw the family into chaos. As the breadwinner and the pillar of the home that held our home it became difficult to put things together. My mother Josephine being a housewife, she could not provide us with food, education, and other necessities. My father had written a will to distribute his wealth to his children. Each one was given a cow or a bull or he designated something for everyone. He wrote a will for my mother to have the house/home and all the property in it. He really was smart to write a will so that his sons, his daughters, the uncles and relatives would not fight over what he left behind.

For the next three and four years after the death of my father, my mother was able to put food on the table and send us to school. It was a great challenge to my mother to put the puzzles together for all the children. She continued to send us to school but it was becoming tough for her to manage without relying on what my dad had left. Soon, the wealth was diminishing months after months. She provided and led the family for at least four years but with more challenges, my mother started to look for a job in the white suburbs as a maid. She finally got the job to do laundry, cook and clean the houses. Her work place was a bit far away from home, about 20 km away. It was quite a distance from home. Instead of commuting every day to work, she was offered a cottage to live in. My siblings got scattered and I really don't know where they went but I remained at home living with my brother Alexander with his wife MaMsipha. I did my preschool, grade one, two and three but did not finish my grade three at Hope Fountain Primary school. I still remember my first teacher was Mr. Elikhana and my sister Gladys used to take me to preschool carrying me on her back and I cried bitterly when she left me behind. The teacher gave me some car toys to play with and I started to like the school. At home I used bricks as bus toys and enjoyed playing with bricks. I used to build small houses with mud and my aunt, Anna used to say that I would be a constructor just like my father, Joseph but later in life, I never wanted to be a constructor/builder.

The question was, who was going to manage the home and the children while my mother was away? My older brothers had left home to look for work in the nearest town, Bulawayo. My sisters were also taken away by some uncles and aunts to live with them. Our home was deserted. Our elder brother Ernest had got married and went to live in Bulawayo with his family at Old Pumula Suburb. Our sister Maudy got married and went to live in Harare. Margaret Siphelinile got married and went to live in Bulawayo with her husband Hlongwane. Joshua left home to look for a job and got married to MaNkomo. Alexander got married to MaNsipha and lived at home. Edwin Nanatsho went to live in Bulawayo. Mavis went to live with my uncle Dan Gasela and went to school of nursing but she did not finish the course. She later got married to Elijah Moyo and went to live with him in Bulawayo. Senzeni Khatha went to Tsholotsho to live with our aunt, the sister of my mother, NaMpilo. Sithabile went to live with my mom at her workplace at a cottage. Zenzo had run away from home when Sipho was born as he was scared of him because he was very bright in complexion. So, he had gone to seek refuge from gogo Maphico Mhlanga Gasela, the sister of our grandfather Mabutho Gasela. He never came back since. Sipho later went to live with mom's sister. NaMpilo was sent to join Senzeni Katha in Tsholotsho. I am the only one who remained at home living with my brother Alexander and his wife MaSipha.

I was still going to school when my brother Alexander left home with his wife, leaving me alone to take care of our home. I was living alone in this big home because everyone had left. My uncle Dan and his wife Maluphahla persuaded me to go and live with them, which was a stone throw away from our home. We used to play with Edina, Mangwiro, my uncle's niece and nephew and others in the area. However, I did not want to abandon our home with no anyone taking care of it. This did not go too long before I realized that this was unbearable to live alone in such an environment. I left home reluctantly, to live with my uncle Matthew with his wife Patricia Sibanda with two of their daughters, Nompilo and Sinikiwa. I went back home to live alone and I would go and eat at one of my uncles and aunts around the homestead but at night I would go and sleep alone. I went to live with aunt Ann Hlongwane with her grandchildren, Mangcungcu Sithembile, Lindiwe, Trust, Limuka and Sukoluhle but I went back to live alone, taking care of our home. We used to play also with Jabulani, Sandile, and Sibusisiwe, the children of Herbert Masina and MaNdlovu, our cousins. The relatives hatched a plan to force me out of my home because they were now concerned that a child cannot live alone in a home. One day when I was sleeping, someone came into my room where I was sleeping through the window. I heard him opening the window slowly at midnight. He opened it, climbed through the window, put his feet on my bed and I screamed at the top of my voice, calling uncontrollable. After five minutes, David, one of my cousins, came and asked me what was happening. I told him that someone had come into my bedroom and stepped on me. I really panicked that night and David took me and I never went back again.

When my mother heard of the incident, she came to take me to live with her at the cottage together with my sister, Sithabile. The employer of my mother did not want her to bring any person to live with her including her children. My mother had no other option but she sneaked us into her cottage and we lived with her, though it was illegal. She was warned by the employer that if they saw any person living with her, they would fire her immediately. She lived in fear and we were locked inside the cottage every day. She made sure she would pull the curtains and close them so that no one could see us inside. We lived for almost three months in hiding and it was like a prison. One day, I opened the curtain a little to view outside and to see the sunshine, the birds chasing each other. The wife of the employer saw me through the window. She was very angry and infuriated and she called my mother immediately to ask her about what she had seen. She asked her who it was that she saw in the cottage through the window. My mom told her that it was her son. She sternly warned her that she did not want any small monkeys around her house, scratching and looking through the windows. She told her that her house was not a zoo for monkeys or baboons. My mom was so shocked and saddened by the incident. She told my mother that she does not want to see any monkeys again and that it was the last warning or she would be fired immediately because she and her husband did not want her to live with anyone, not even her children. When my mother came after work, she was crying and saying that her boss saw me through the window and that she called me a monkey and threatened to fire her. My sister and I joined her crying and I apologized to my mother and promised her that I would never open the curtain to look through the window again. My mother wasn't harsh on me nor did she scorn me. I loved my mother. She was kind and a caring mother. My mother was no longer at peace seeing us going through such trauma. You cannot keep the young ones in a cage for too long. Young people need space to run around and play in a large space. Here I was with my sister, imprisoned in a cottage day and night in fear of being noticed and or else, our mother would be fired from her job.

Our mother had to make a plan to ease the situation between Mesisi and herself to avoid losing her job. She consulted her brother, Solomon Nyathi who was born after her and he was the last born of his family. The uncle, Solomon, agreed to take us and live with us and that he would send us to school. In a few days, our mother sneaked us out from the cottage not wanting her employers to see us in the evening and took us to her brother, uncle Solomon in Bulawayo City. When we arrived at my uncle Solomon's house in Mzilikazi Township, he was happy and welcomed us with a happy smile. He promised my mother that he would take us on the following weekend to Tsholotsho at his village, Bindane Village where he had built his homestead. He promised my mother that he would send us to school and we would receive a high quality of education. He promised her that he would take care of us just like his children. My mother left and she went back to her work knowing that her brother would take care of us. We did know anything but we were excited that we were going to start a new life in a different environment. However, my heart was still thinking back at our original home, Hope Fountain Mission.

We did not have large suitcases with my sister but we had all our clothes in our respective suitcases/bags. The weekend came, on a Saturday, we went to Rankin/Bus station to board a bus to Bindani village, in the southwest of Bulawayo more than 200 km away. The bus left around 10:00 am and it traveled the whole day. At Tsholotsho Center, the bus was parked there for almost one hour and thirty minutes. The driver, the conductor and other people were drinking liquor, including my uncle, Solomon. They were all friends. He did not pay the bus tickets for us and for himself. We discovered that they were friends and he used not to pay for bus tickets the rest of his life. We were exhausted and tired from the journey because the journey was very long. The bus continued the trip, through narrow and dusty roads, through the jungle, crossing rivers and seeing wild animals including lions, zebras, elephants along the road. We finally arrived at Bindani village, which was infested with wild beasts, tsetse flies, mosquitos and diseases such as malaria and typhoid fever. We arrived around 9:00 pm at the village. The bus stop was a distance from the village, about 10 km. We walked to the village in the dark, afraid that we might encounter and be devoured by the wild animals. However, uncle Solomon was not afraid or scared because he was used to the road and the environment and he was drunk. We arrived at his homestead. We were welcomed by his wife, MaNdlovu or NaSinikiwe, their children, Sinikiwe and Bonani plus his brother's wife MaMoyo. The first wife had fled the home with her children to her home because of some misunderstanding with my uncle. We were introduced to his family. The homestead was big with six huts built with mud and thatched roofs. We were given a place to sleep with his son, Bonani and my sister with his daughter, Sinikiwe. It so happened that my uncle Solomon had gone to his first wife NaThina's home previously, to appeal for her to return home. She for sure, came back on Saturday with her children.

In the morning we were introduced to the whole family. His first wife, MaNcube had six children, Thina, Sithobekile, Silibele, Lutho, Lwazi and Nobayethe. The second wife had two children, Sinikiwe and Bonani. These were lovely and friendly children. He had adopted a middle-aged man, Philemon to herd his cattle but then as I came, he handed the cattle to me to herd them. Uncle Solomon had promised my mother Josephine his sister that he would send us to school together with his children. I was immediately introduced to the cattle, how I would herd the cattle in the jungle, he taught me how to milk the cows, how to use the oxen to till the fields and how to care for the cattle. I was taken to the green pastures where the cattle were usually, grazing and it was in 1974. That was the shock of my life! Of course, we raised cattle at my original home at Hope Fountain but I was not fully responsible to take care of them in that way at that young age. I was quickly handed over the task to take care of the cattle. My sister also was introduced to the chores of home on how to pound millet and corn using a manual pounding equipment to make a mealie meal and to pound it until it was flour to make thick porridge (Isitshwala) the stable food in Zimbabwe. She was introduced to where to fetch water for the homestead, where to gather firewood for cooking, and warming during the winter time or the fire to light up the night in the homestead, and also how to wash kitchen utensils and the chores for the girls. Surprisingly, my uncle's children went to school and we were not allowed to go to school. My mother thought we were going to school as uncle Solomon had promised her.

I started to herd cattle from 1974 to 1977. Every day, I would milk the cows in the morning and take the cattle for grazing pasture every day at 9:00 am and come back at 6:00 pm. I did not have anyone to exchange with and I did not have any rest, year in and year out. That went on for five years and without attending school. I had no shoulder to lean on or a person to cry to or to be heard. I was the cattle herd boy and my sister was the maid of the homestead. It was painful to see my sister working like a slave and me too as a slave. We had no one to tell or to ask to rest, all was on us. However, the wife of our uncle, MaNcube was a kind, generous woman, soft hearted and loving. She did not have any power to make a decision except her husband Solomon and she was loyal to her husband although some of the things he was doing she did not condone or agree with. Life in Tsholotsho was not fun, it was the same routine every day. My day in summer would be waking up early in the morning around 4:00 am, preparing the oxen and walking about 15 km with oxen to till the field using four oxen drawing the plough and the women would follow behind putting some seeds.

After coming from the field, I would milk the cows, eat and head out to the green pastures to graze the cattle around 10:00 am and I would come back home with the cattle at around 6:00 pm. This kind of routine would continue for at least a month and half until the field was completely ploughed and planted with corn, millet, sorghum, sweet reeds, pumpkins, groundnuts, monkey nuts, beans. okra, sweet potatoes and other seeds. We became so close to my sister, Sithabile comforting and consoling each other. My uncle Solomon's children were so friendly and we lived together as one family. We were living with his first wife, MaNcube, often called NaThina. His second wife MaNdlovu or NakaSinikiwe was also nice. The other uncle, Moses, lived and worked in Bulawayo City and he used to come home at the end of the month. His wife, MaMoyo was also nice but she did not have children. The two uncles used to share the homestead, one with his children on one side of the homestead and the other on the other side. They lived together peacefully with their wives and the children although the children of uncle Moses from his previous wife did not live in Tsholotsho with us but lived in Bulawayo because they were older. My sister and I were now part of the big family but our home duties were different from other children as they used to go to school. They were some social games that we used to play with other children in the village for entertainment.

My closest friends were my cattle. There were about 25 cattle I used to look after them daily. I would spend the whole day with them. I gave each of them their names, Jamluthi, Hlavukazi and my great bull was Buffalo. It used to fight with other bulls in the village and it would come victorious. Some of the names I gave to the goats were Gugandele, Bluesky, Thokazi. I came to love my cattle dearly and they loved me because I spent more time with them. I would go with them to good grazing pastures and take them to the dams and rivers to drink some water. I would take them once a month to the village dip-tank to treat and prevent ticks on their bodies. I knew each of them their hoof prints, their sounds when mowed or bellowed and their behaviors. When they got lost, I would follow their hooves prints until I found them. It was not that I loved to herd cattle but I had no choice; my uncle forced me to do that. Young as I was there was no way I could escape to go back to my original home, Hope Fountain. I was more than 500 km away and the bus came to our area, Bindani village twice a week. I actually never thought of escaping back home. I was between the devil and the deep blue sea deep sea. I had left all my relatives back at Hope Fountain and there was no means of communication. I was cut off completely with my family. I missed my mother and all my siblings, Zenzo, Siphu and my sisters, thank God I was with my blood sister, Sithabile at least. We used to sit down and chat together, remembering our mother, our relatives and our upbringing in our home land. We had to start a new life in Tsholotsho with new people, my relatives of course, from my mother's side and the new environment was populated with wild beasts like lions, elephants, hyenas, wild dogs, and warthogs. The nights were decorated with wild animals' sounds, screaming and wandering in the neighborhood. They would come closer in the dusk in the neighborhoods, looking for domestic animals that were straying at night. If they did not find their prey outside the kraals, they sometimes sneaked and would snatch some domestic animals within the kraals. It was dangerous to walk at night. Sometimes they would invade homes. Elephants used to eat the grass of the thatched huts while people were sleeping. Sometimes the elephants would trample people sleeping in their huts.

The goats and the sheep were vulnerable to the lions, hyenas, wild dogs and other carnivorous animals roaming around, especially at night. I used to cut and curve knob carries that I kept for hunting and defending my cattle and goats. I had almost twenty of them and I used to keep them in one of the barns. One night some hyenas invaded my goats and I heard the noise in the middle of the night. I came out well armed with five knob carries, my spear and an axe. I found one hyena in goat kraal, killing one of the goals. I killed it with the spear and it was a nightmare. The goats panicked and got confused as to what was happening. Fortunately, I was able to kill the hyena and dragged it out of the kraal and I buried it outside the homestead in the forest. One day when I was grazing my cattle in a jungle about 25 km away from home, I found two ostrich eggs. I took them home but while I was driving my cattle home almost in the evening, carrying the ostrich eggs, when I looked back, I saw two ostriches coming fast after me because I had taken their eggs. Fortunately, I was already close home, so I left the cattle and ran home as fast as my legs could carry me. My cousin Philemon was able to fend those ostriches from harming me. My uncle's wife, NaThina welcomed me with the ostrich eggs and she decided to put them in the sitting room in the cabinet display. After a week, they exploded and shattered the glasses and plates. She regretted having put them in the cabinet to display and decorate the sitting room with them.

In 1975, one of my cousin's brother, came to live with us in Tsholotsho. My cousin came to Tsholotsho to live with us, family in the homestead. At first, he looked like a good cousin-brother but as time progressed, his true colors came out. My older cousin Philemon had left to look for work in the city, Bulawayo. My uncle's wives saw what was happening but they had no power to stop him. But to the rest of the family, he would pretend to be nice. Sometimes I would sleep in the kraal of the cattle and not go home for several days until I found the cattle that had been lost. One time, I could not go home for one week because I was afraid. I could not eat or drink water for several days and I was found lying on the side of the road not able to walk. I was so weak that someone picked me up beside the road and he asked me my name and he carried me on his back and took me home. They apologized and promised him that this would not happen again.

In the village, I had some friends whom I used to play with. Usually, they used to bully me because I was not able to fight anyone. I was very afraid to fight. So, the boys in the village used to send me to look for their cattle and donkeys and to bring them to them. I was very meek and timid. My cousin was in the vicinity and the other boys were no longer messing up with me. Other boys told him that they could fight me in boxing and could send me to look for their donkeys and cattle.

He told them that I was able to fight them in boxing and they told him that I was a coward and timid boy. He arranged for me to fight with our neighbor, William Stedana Ndlovu who used to bully me. It was a boxing contest. I beat William in the first round and with the first punch. He bled and cried and went out of the ring. The next boy entered the ring, Velempini and in the first round I beat him once and he fell down and said that he doesn't want to fight me anymore. I could not believe that I was that strong and a good fighter. The rest of the week, he moved with me to the village and made me fight with all the boys and I would beat them and become a champion at Bindane village. I beat Nene, one of the strongest fighters in the village but I beat him too. I fought against six more boys and I beat them all. I became a hard puncher and no one could ever mess up with me and I was feared by all the boys in the village. I broke my thumb while boxing and I continued to fight to the end. I told my cousin that I had broken my thumb but he wanted me to continue fighting many boys even in the next village. I fought not because I liked it but because I was forced to fight even the bigger boys. It became an entertainment to do boxing while in the jungle, herding the cattle.

After being warned by my uncle's wife MaNcube, NaThina, he left for the City Bulawayo where he had come from and he never came back. It was a big relief and I was so happy that he had left and there was new peace and tranquility without his presence. I continued to be a hard puncher in the area and the boys in the village feared me. One of my friends was Vungwana, the brother of William, Sitedana. Vungwana loved school and went to a high school away from the village, waking up in the morning and walking about five times to school from Monday to Friday. He really inspired me because he was resilient and hardworking and loved school, walking a distance of about 20 km one way. The boys around the village used to laugh at me including William saying I am uneducated; I only know how to fight boxing. For sure, I would admire them speaking English, showing me their homework and their drawings. I could not redeem myself from this misery and mockery of the village experience. My other friends such as Muhle Moyo, Themba Ndlovu, Vungwana, William and others were a strong force in the village. Herod's young brother, Stephen Makoni, visited us in Tsholotsho for a week. I thought he would behave like his brother Herod. But he was totally the opposite of my other cousin. He was a loving, caring and responsible cousin. He brought me good stuff from the city and he was so friendly and kind. I could not believe that he was the young brother of Herod. When he left after a week, I was very sad because I liked him for his tender spirit. The other young brother of cousin was Amon. He was as well friendly, loving and caring. His sisters Judith, Thoko were friendly and loving people too. I really don't know how Herold was totally opposite to all his siblings.

CHAPTER FOUR

An Encounter with the Divine

Meanwhile, my sister told me that there was a Zion church in a neighboring village at Tshibizina. Back home at Hope Fountain, we used to attend church at United Congregational Church of Southern Africa (UCCSA), a family church under London Missionary Society but I never knew what the church was for. This is the very church that my grandfather Mabuto Gasela was a missionary. I was younger and I never heard about Jesus Christ. My mother and my siblings used to sing the church songs at home when we were having our devotions but I didn't know what it was all about. When my sister and I went to visit that church at Tshibizina village, a Zion church, referred to as a cultic church composed of indigenous congregants but we were welcomed by the Pastor Manjinqela Tshuma. They are called cultic because they do a lot of syncretism i.e., mixing Christian doctrines with African cultures and traditional beliefs and practices. In that church, there are three time periods for prayer, to dance, sing with drums and preaching. We looked at them with admiration when they were dancing, round and round in their white uniforms. We enjoyed the whole dance. When Pastor Tshuma preached about the birth of Jesus Christ, born of Virgin Mary through power of the Holy Spirit, that He lived and died a gruesome death, was crucified and on the third day, He rose from the dead. That God demands everyone to repent from his/her sins because God overlooked their ignorance, (Acts 17:30, NKJV). If people can invite Christ in their lives and call upon the name Jesus, they will be saved. It was my first time to hear about the name of Jesus Christ. I went back home pondering who Jesus was. The following Sunday, we went back again. The Sunday services were in the evenings. After driving my cattle into the kraal, we would go with some of our neighbors. We went as a group on Sundays. I was enjoying the preaching most, followed by dancing and then singing and praying. Months went by and the Pastor in his sermons would always talk about Christ's coming to die for sinners and that God was calling people to repent from their sins. One day, he called an outer calling for those who wanted to give their lives to Jesus. I was one of them who went, kneeled and prayed for Jesus to forgive my sins. It was 1976. But I did not understand all about Jesus fully and I loved to understand that He is my Savior, God's Son and that God is my Father too. God is my Father too! My father had died and I was taught that God is my Father, what a replacement! I heard about God's love, His Grace and His Mercy just struck me. I really fell in love with Jesus Christ and He indwelled in my heart. Remember, there was no one I could lean on, my uncle could not embrace me and my cousin Herod could not embrace me. The only person who could embrace me was Jesus Christ, and God the Father. I really embraced God as my Father and Jesus Christ as my Savior. This love for God grew day by day. I did not have the Bible and I did not know how to read the Bible even if I had it. I believed what I heard and treasured in my heart. There was another church in the other village and my uncle's wife NaThina occasionally went with us to Seventh Day Adventist Church. I kind of liked it too. The congregants always dressed articulately, and they sang good and melodious songs without instruments. I admired them and I enjoyed the church services on Saturdays.

I had a new perspective of life and my faith grew day by day. I became a devoted Christian and I would pray out in the jungle, while herding my cattle. I would pray and pray all the time alone in the jungle and I would dance around and round the shrubs until there were some marks around the shrub. When I would be out there herding my cattle, prayer and dancing became my daily moto. Now it was between me and my God and of course my cattle. My faith grew to the extent that other boys when they lost their cattle or donkeys, they would seek me and ask for prayers. God was so faithful that they usually found the donkeys and their cattle. I asked them to forgive me for fighting against them in boxing. They were now seeing me as their pastor because they would constantly come to me if they had some problems. God turned my life upside down and I started to recognize my purpose in life. I began a new life in Christ but it was clouded with the dominance of my uncle Solomon's dark life on ancestral worship. Even if I found a new life in Christ, uncle Solomon believed in the spirits of the departed ancestral spirits. Every year, he would tell us to join him to appease the ancestral spirits through worshipping and praying to the bull, called Buffalo. He would mix herbs, and other things I did not know and made us drink. He would let us kneel while he would pour some herbs on the bull, mentioning his great grandfather's names and all those relatives who had died before to ask them to protect us and guide our lives. I did not understand what I was doing and my new found faith in Christ wasn't explained to me that I should not participate. I was a young Christian who did not know about my faith and the worship of the idols. I never had any Bible and I did not know how to read the Bible because I was not educated.

It became a struggle to understand if I could worship God only or to mix to worship God and the ancestral spirits. Thank God, the traditional rituals with my uncle were done once a year and the rest of the time, I was worshipping God. Well, it was not a serious thing, I thought. It was just like playing games. No one took it as seriously as my uncle Solomon. My faith in Christ was very strong and my God was my Father and I believed in Him for everything. From this time onwards, my life started to change gradually. I could see the hand of God in my life but I did not know about my future. I had peace and joy in my heart. My uncle Solomon was still controlling me and my future. I was just living life without knowing any future. I used to pray but I didn't know what my prayers were. My prayers were mainly focused on God, His mercy, sovereignty, grace, loving kindness, His Son Jesus Christ for dying for my sins. I imagined how Jesus died in the hands of the soldiers and I would cry and sob for sympathy for Christ. I never prayed for my life because I did not know what to pray for. In the next chapters, the hand of the Lord was upon me even though I did not notice oftentimes. Even if I don't mention God in the following chapters, know that His hand was directing and guiding my path and creating my future and also. He was putting the puzzles together.

The most painful thing I ever experienced was when my mother visited us in Tsholotsho. Yes, at first, I was so excited and happy to see my mother after two years of not seeing her. The love I had for my mother was rekindled. The trauma we had gone through with my sister Sithabile made my mother cry and to regret why she had brought us there. It was a real shock to her to hear that our uncle Solomon had lied to her that he would send us to school. For the first time, I had a shoulder to lean on and pour out all of my stress, frustration, trauma I had gone through. My mother was intently listening and trying to understand all the saga. When our mother heard about all the suffering we had gone through, she decided to take us with her but it meant that the cattle would be left without any one to take care of them. My mother respected and loved my uncles' wife, NaThina dearly and she did not want to put her in a dilemma. Instead, she decided to take my sister Sithabile with her and said that she would come and take me later. That's why I said that it was the most painful thing to take my sister away from me. She was an encourager, a consoler, a dear sister and everything. For her to leave me behind in Tsholotsho was the most painful experience I had never had.

When my mother came, she had brought me some new shoes, new clothes and good stuff. I was up on the moon with excitement and happiness. After a week, she left with my dear Sithabile, it was as painful as a toothache. When the day came for them to leave, I accompanied them to the bus stop and I took my cattle with me and left them grazing on the green pasture. As we were waiting for the bus to come, my sister Sithabile started crying because she did not want to leave me behind. My mother also cried and I also joined them crying and saying goodbye. My mother promised that she would come to take me. The bus came and they boarded the bus and within a twinkle of an eye, they were gone. I was left standing and crying bitterly, looking at the bus as it disappeared in the dust and the tall trees. I pondered, thinking if I would ever see them again. It was a sad day, weeks, months and years to come. As they headed to the east to the City of Kings, Bulawayo, I never knew that I would head to the west to meet them after five years.

CHAPTER THREE:

The Rise of the Dust

I n 1977, people in the neighborhoods began to talk about the liberation of independence because they were guerillas from Zambia who were recruiting people to cross the borders for training to join the liberation. They would come in the villages to talk to the villagers about why Zimbabwe should be liberated from the government of Ian Smith regime. They politized the villagers as to when the liberation started and why. The Prime Minister Ian Smith of Rhodesia declared a Unilateral Declaration of Independence (UDI) from British on November 11, 1965. He divorced Britain politically and wanted to be independent from the British Protectorate so that they could be independent Rhodesia with the minority white population without any influence from any other countries including Britain. But the world did not recognize his government and it was declared as an illegal government. The indigenous people were encouraged to set liberation for independence. The British had named Rhodesia after the British colonizer and industrialist, Cecil John Rhodes. The native Africans were under suppression rule by white minority. In the 1960s, the nationalists envisioned freedom. In 1960, the National Democratic Party (NDP) was formed with the objective of gaining freedom, independence and to rule themselves. The NDP was banned in 1961 by the Rhodesian government.

After the ban, the group emerged as the Zimbabwe African People's Union (ZAPU) in 1962. Its leader was Joshua Nkomo. They wanted the freedom to vote, one-man-one-vote, to unite and for liberation against imperialism and colonialism, retract all forms of oppression and dehumanization and to develop African values. ZAPU was banned by the Rhodesian government in 1963. However, ZAPU remained intact but underground. In 1963 there was internal conflict within the party and there was a split in which another party was formed, Zimbabwe African National Union (ZANU) led by Ndabaningi Sithole. As the same nationalists with the same goals, ZANU shared the same goals as ZAPU. The split was based on ethnic lines, ZAPU being Ndebele and ZANU being Shona. They were now two fractured groups, not united. ZAPU remained in Zambia and waged liberation from the south and west of Zimbabwe. ZANU waged the war from east and north of Zimbabwe both beginning in 1964. Both wanted a political and military unit. Still desiring to have a united front from both ZAPU and ZANU, in 1976, they formed Patriotic Front Party and it was led by both Joshua Nkomo from ZAPU and Robert Mugabe from ZANU. When Rhodesia had lost a severe defeat and saw their end coming closer than they anticipated, they allowed the British to facilitate negotiations between the Patriotic Front Party and Rhodesians at the Geneva Conference, 1976. Rhodesians objected to the term for the peace negotiations that were going to culminate for independence on December 1, 1977. After realizing that Ian Smith with his government was not yet prepared to give up, the liberation of independence continued but now with intercity.

It was in 1977 that the wave of going to Zambia for the liberation of Zimbabwe was in the air and everyone wanted to go and join. The guerillas came and gathered everyone in the villages to recruit and to help people to cross over to Zambia for training. They took a group of young people both women and men, to travel to Zambia via Botswana. They took another group, and another group and another group. They continued week after week. They wanted boys and girls, men and women above 18 years old. I did not qualify to be recruited because I was young under 18 in 1977 so I did not meet the qualifications. I talked to the leadership that I wanted to join them too but they said that I was too young. Another group came but they did not have the liberation cadres, as I was so desperate to leave the cattle behind and find a new better life, I joined them by telling my uncle's wife NaThina that I was leaving. I just left the cattle and joined the group. The group was composed of about 8to 10 young people. We just travelled, herding to the west without knowing the directions. We walked by foot for three days without food or water. Every village we passed by, they showed us the directions, gave us food and water. We went to the last village, Phelandaba, before Hwange Game Park/Reserve. We were told that it was a no-go area because it was a game park/reserve full of all kinds of wild animals and that we would be devoured before we got nowhere. We missed the road and we were lost. It was not the way. After traveling for three days by foot, we were now at the end of the world. Everyone was exhausted, hungry, some of us had swollen feet and not able to walk back home any more. That was a frustrating and disappointing journey. There were no other options but to go back home by foot again. What a waste of time and energy. I thought of going back to herd the cattle again. We all decided to go back home. Others who had swollen feet stayed behind and were not able to walk, we left behind waiting for the bus that came once or twice a week in the village.

Going back, we took two days, not three because we were mostly men, because the rest of the women were not able to walk back. They had to wait for the bus in two or three days to come. When I arrived home after five days away, I found out that my uncle Solomon was home, it was a month end. When he saw me getting in the gate with a limp on my foot, my mouth dries with thirst and hunger, he stopped me right at the gate and he did not allow me to get in. He told me to go back where I had gone. I had left the cattle on their own and he said that I was posing danger for his family as the Rhodesian soldiers would annihilate his family because of what I had done. He told me that he did not want to see me again in his homestead. That was a devastating scenario to handle. I prayed to God to help me. I had nowhere to go. Where would I have gone? There were no other relatives in the village. I just went to one of my friends, Muhle Moyo's home. His step mother was nee Mhlanga and she took me as her brother because of her madam's name. The whole family welcomed me, his father was also very good, Makhanda Khanda, Moyo. They had four children, Muhle, Thandi, Peninnah, Vusa and Thembekile. I stayed with them for a week. My uncle never checked me where I was. When he went back to the city, in Bulawayo, my uncle's wife MaNcube, NaThina came to take me back home. I thanked MaMhlanga with her husband Mr. Moyo with Muhle who played a pivotal role in bringing me to his home and told his parents the ordeal and the predicament I was in. When I went back, I resumed to herd the cattle again and I was no longer at peace. I thought that if my uncle came at the end of the month-end and he would find me here, he would kill me. He arranged to bring one of my younger brothers, Sipho Gasela, to come and herd the cattle. He had seen my intentions and never trusted me anymore.

At the end of the month, my uncle came and found me at his home and warned me strongly never to go away anywhere again without his knowledge. He came with my young brother Sipho to join us and to herd the cattle. My young brother Sipho was the same age as one of his sons, Lutho. While his son Lutho was going to school, Sipho did not. We took some turns to send the cattle to the green pasture. There was at least a relief for me. Lutho would join Sipho sometimes to take the cattle to the grazing land. The liberation for independence cadres continued to come to the villages to politicize the villagers and persuaded young people who were 18 years and older to go and join the liberation of independence in Zambia. I really wanted to go too, to leave this miserable home which did not longer add any value to my life. I just wanted to leave but my age could not allow me to and the cadres had refused several times to add me to the groups. I was really frustrated and did not know what I would do. My uncle's wife NaThina understood my frustration and my situation, to continue to live in such an environment where my uncle was always harassing and scolding me. She sympathized with me and empathized with me but she had no suggestion as to what to do.

CHAPTER FIVE:

The Escape and The Dark Episodes

One morning, at dawn, a group of cadres passed by our village with a group of youths and adults taking them to cross to Botswana. An hour later, at around 6:30 am, my uncle's wife, NaThina came to my hut and woke me up and she told me that the group of youth and the cadres had passed by and they were gone. I did not hesitate I just got out of my blankets and ran after them. Running and walking long distances was my favorite as a cattle herd boy or an African cowboy. With my experience to track the hoof prints of my cattle, I knew how to track human footprints easily. I walked and ran for a long time. They had really gone for one and 30 km.

They had passed three villages and I asked the villagers and they told the directions they had taken. They went through the bush, not the roads because they were afraid that they would be spotted by the Rhodesian army. After walking for about one and half hours, I finally heard the voices in front of me. I posed to listen carefully to what they were saying. They were resting and giving them, instructions and I was about 50 meters, in the jungle in the thick forest and tall grass. I sat down and my heart was pounding, knowing that when they would see me, they would be very mad at me because they did not want me to join the group because of my age. It was in October, 1977. While they were still talking, I gained my strength and courage and approached them, walking slowly towards them like a cat. When they saw me, they got into action and they were about to shoot towards me, thinking that it was their enemy. When they saw it was me, they scolded me and shouted at me why I had come and that I was too young to join the group. They also warned me that they usually planted some land mines where they walked so that the enemy could be blasted by them. I apologized to them and told them how I wanted to join them. They actually debated whether to send me back home or to allow me to join them. There were three cadres who strongly argued that I should go back home because I was too young and the journey was too long, a four to five days walk to reach Botswana. However, some cadres argued that I had traveled a long distance and to be sent back home, it would not be fair to me. Well, they welcomed me and we started the long journey together. We walked in the bush, day and night. When we were hungry, we would go through the villages to get food and the villagers were always ready to cook for us.

The villagers in the whole of Tsholotsho province in Matabeleland north and Matabeleland south and the whole country at large were encouraged to provide food, clothes, medical and any assistance necessary for freedom fighters as a part of participating and supporting the worthy cause of the liberation of independence. Everyone had a part to play in supporting those who were crossing over. We walked for five days towards Botswana and I was the youngest. At some point, we heard that the Rhodesia army had camped in one of the villages near the dam. We hid in the bush and the villagers brought us some food and water. The cadres who were leading us told us that they were going back because they didn't have to confront the soldiers for our safety. We were divided into a group of fives so that in case we met with the Rhodesian army, they would not suspect us that we were going to cross to Botswana. So, we spent the whole day hiding in the forests and the cadres were instructed to go in even when it was dark and not to use the road ever. At around 9:00 pm, we departed but we took different directions. We were five of us, the boys only and we informed each other with other groups that we would meet ahead after avoiding the villages. We walked towards the northwest in the jungle, avoiding entering into the two villages which were ahead of us.

It was pitch dark and it was raining heavily with lightning and thunderstorms, as a result, we got lost in the jungle. We did not have any means to measure out directions. The moon was there but because it was cloudy and raining, we found ourselves back where we had started three hours ago. The lightning bolt struck the tree that we were hiding under into halves. It was scary but no one got hurt, fortunately. It was now midnight and we calculated the directions and we walked on the road that went to the next village. When we started to see homes, we turned to the right to avoid the village. We walked until it was about 2:30 pm and we were very tired. We were wet all over, and I did not have some shoes for the past four years since I was at my original home at Hope Fountain. Since I came to live with my uncle Solomon, he never bought me any shoes or any clothes for that matter. To walk barefooted was very normal to me and my feet had developed a thick skin acting as if they were my shoes. Some of the people were also barefooted. To sleep on the muddy ground was impossible. One of the men decided to command us to stand over him covering him from the rain. He sat on a stone and all of us covered him with our hand to protect him from the rain. It was as if I had gone back home to what I had experienced with my cousin, Herod. It seemed like the devil was following and haunting me wherever I went to torture and to confuse me. It was a tough night. Some of us who were used to the jungle, climbed on the trees and slept for a few hours and we proceeded to travel at dawn.

We walked to cross the Tegwane river and it was flooded but the local villagers showed us where we could cross which was less dangerous. We managed to cross safely. That was the border between Zimbabwe and Botswana. After crossing Tegwani river, we walked for a long time and slept on the way. The soil was muddy and stuck on our feet and it was difficult to lift up our feet. It slowed our walking progress. We slept again in the bush. In Botswana, we were now free and we were no longer afraid of Rhodesian soldiers anymore. Early in the morning, we woke up and continued with the journey. We were now walking along the dust road and along the way, we got a lift, a lorry/truck which was going to the place where we were told to go. The driver left us in the small camp where people were on transit to Francis Town in Botswana. There were about 80 to 100 people waiting to transit to Francis Town. There was not enough food for all these people. It was a pathetic situation. People spent much of the time sleeping because of hunger and some went around to local homes in Botswana, looking for food. The rumors circulated to us that the Botswana local people loved to drink liquor and partying day and night and did not like working hard.

Well, that's what we were told but we could not substantiate whether it was true or false. While waiting for transit, some people looked for part-time jobs to work in the yards to clear the grass and trim their trees in the homes of the local people. It gave them some money to buy food. We spent a week in that small town and there was a big hall where everyone slept. Every night, there was a boy who always had convulsions and it was really scary. After a week, a lorry/truck came to pick us up. It was my first time to leave. They took us to some two townhouses in another town and stayed there for another week. However, the place had better facilities and enough food. After a week, we were sent to Francistown where there were hundreds of people. It was a shock because I had never seen such a large number of people living together in dormitories. We were assimilated into groups according to age groups in companies, platoons and sections. Every morning, we would wake up around 5:00 am to do some exercises, stretching, judo, toitoi, and then we would be taught Marxism, Leninism, democracy, capitalism and their differences in terms of their ideologies. Well, I was so happy to be in a different environment than to be in Tsholotsho herding cattle. I was no longer missing anyone, not even my mother, not my sisters or brothers. It was another environment, everyone a sister or brother. My focus was on what I was doing now, not the past. I did not want to view my rear mirror but the big picture of my future before me although I still did not know what the future held for me. In Francistown, the instructors were impressed with my strength. I was stronger, more resilient, and with positive aptitude because I had herded cattle for five years and I understood what toughness was all about. Some of my village boys and older arrived too while I was there such as Sijabhe.

I stayed in Francistown for about three months and we were transferred with about 80 others to Dukwe camp populated by young people, women and a few men. Dukwe was a difficult place to live. There was not enough food, not enough water and it was over populated. Dukwe camp was not as organized as Francistown camp. We did not have organized programs, no exercises, but people were just milling around aimlessly which made people think about their problems. It seemed as if life was dull and my hope to go to Zambia was slowly clouding on me. The group of instructors used to come after two weeks to select those who were fit, eighteen years and above and those who were strong. It was a painful process to watch and because of age, I was too young to be included. I did not have hope anymore. My cousins, Thina, and Silibele, two of them being the siblings, arrived too. I was thrilled to see them join me. The bathing shower facilities were very few and the males and the females exchanged times to take showers. Food was so scarce that I used to share my small portion with my cousin, Silibele, because she was like my sister and I did not want to see her starving to death. She was weaker than I. Months rolled by and some people were being selected and sent back to Francistown where they would be ready to board the Botswana airlines to go to Zambia for training. By logic and the criteria, they were using, I was not qualified by far because of my age.

As I saw people being selected, I had an urge within me when they called thirty people to go in the line. They had wanted twenty-five people but thirty-five to forty people rushed into the line. I was one of the thirty people who scrambled to the line. The instructors said that the number was too much and they said that they would scale it down to twenty-five. They said that they would start from the last people at the end of the line where I was, they stopped. They told us that we should go and register our names. It was unbelievable that I was selected too regardless of my age. Actually, they never asked any age of the people that day. I was so excited to be in the next group going to Francistown and then to fly to Zambia for the first time in my life. My cousins, Thina and Silibele, congratulated me and wished me well. They were crying seeing that I was leaving them. I was glad to leave that miserable place, Dukwe camp. I really never prayed that time but God intervened in my life. That time, it was as if I had left God back in Zimbabwe because of the political teachings we got about communism, Marxism and Leninism and socialism and they condemned Christianity, alluding that the imperialists and colonizers were hiding behind the Bible. They taught us how they would teach about God's love while they were taking away our land, making us slaves, dehumanized and hating our people. I was now confused about God and my belief in Christ. I actually had no strong discipleship and teachings about God, Christ, sin, redemption, soteriology and eschatology.

The following day, we left, heading to Francistown camp that I had left some months ago. It was as if I had some wings to fly and I had anticipated so much to go to Zambia. We arrived in Francistown and we received bad news that they were no longer taking people to Zambia because there were some incidents in which the Rhodians jet fighters courted a Botswana airline which was carrying Zimbabweans on board and they gave them a severe warning with their maneuvers signaling that they had spotted that the Botswana airlines were taking the Zimbabwean people to Zambia for training. The Botswana airlines suspended the trips to Zambia with that purpose in. That was another setback. We were told that we would be sent back to Dukwe camp again for some time until everything had been cleared. I was very disappointed and very sad. After a week, when they were preparing to send us back to Dukwe camp, we were told that the air space was cleared and trips to Lusaka Zambia could resume. However, they needed to scale down the number once more. In a hall, they called the names for those who were selected to go to Zambia. I was glad to hear my name being called. We prepared our small bags and the plane was to depart the following morning. The truck that took us to the airport was scheduled to leave at 6:00 am and the plane was to depart at 9:15 am. I went to take a shower at 5:45 am to prepare for a long flight to Lusaka, Zambia. While I was bathing, with the soap on my head, one of my friends came into the bathing room, calling my name saying that the truck was leaving. I quickly dressed up with soap all over my body including on my head and my face and ran out. People were laughing as I ran towards the truck which was, for sure, leaving and waved my hand running like a made horse. The truck stopped for me and I jumped into the truck with hands waving high and thanking the driver for stopping. I don't know how I missed the correct time for the truck's departure. I always thank that friend of mine, I have even forgotten his name, but he was my hero. I could have missed going to Zambia, my dream destination at that time. This friend of mine was not even chosen to go to Zambia yet he tried by all means to see me succeed and triumph in life. He remained in Francistown and I always think of him with his good heart. He was a real a good friend, indeed.

We drove to the airport in Francistown and the Botswana airline was waiting for us to board. I was so excited to get into the plane for the first time! It was as if I was dreaming. I looked around the plane inside it, admiring and scrutinizing the windows, the seats, and everything. Everything was beautiful, even the air hostesses were friendly and kind to everyone. The flight was about one and sixteen minutes to Lusaka, Zambia. It was too short for me, because I wanted to enjoy the flight some more. I used to see the planes when I was herding cattle in Tsholotsho and they looked tiny above my head with the white tails of smoke, streaming behind them. Now I was inside one of them, unbelievable! God is amazing, no one could have imagined and thought of a wretched boy like me, without education, knowing nobody important in life but see, within a twinkle of an eye, there I am, sitting in a plane, of course, with others who were almost like me. But the fact that I was in a plane, it was the greatest achievement ever.

When we landed in Lusaka, Zambia, we were led to beautiful glassy rooms with red carpet, galaxy walls and it was mind boggling. I thought, yes, I had arrived in paradise. Well, after registering our names, about three trucks were waiting for us outside, big green trucks which looked like those of soldiers. The trucks had high tires almost my height and were called Zili. We were told to get in and we drove through Lusaka downtown and headed west. I admired the big city with all its vehicles crossing and honking and the glittering skyscrapers of the buildings. Off we left Lusaka city and drove through the bush where you could not see the buildings but forest along the road. The trucks maneuvered in undulating roads, ascending the steep hills, crossing the rivers, and small bridges. No one told us where we were going and, in my mind, I was thinking where on earth were we really going? Everyone was quiet and I think that in everyone's mind flashes of thoughts were racing posing questions where were we going?

After about three to four hours, in the middle of nowhere, the three tucks stopped in the jungle and we were told to get out quickly. There were no buildings around, no lights, not even a torch. It was pitch dark. We were taken one by one into a ten and each one was instructed to take off all clothes and to surrender everything we came with. Each one was searched thoroughly because they said some sell-outs may be amongst us. After a thorough search and investigations, we were given Russian camouflage. We were welcomed and we were told that the place was called Nampundu camp. We were given tents to pitch and we were allocated five of us for each round green tent. We had last eaten some snakes in the Botswana airline in the morning and we were very hungry but we were not given any food. We were told we would wake up early in the morning at 5:00 am to exercise and to be introduced and assimilated into various companies. Early in the morning, the instructor woke up with a terrifying voice threatening to beat anyone who was found sleeping. We were told to line up and to be introduced and initiated into various companies. It was startling to be in such an environment. I never expected it to be like this.

We were taken in a company, to run, march and exercise, such as push-ups, judo, kung-fu, karate, frogs exercises, finger and arms exercises. After two weeks of those exercises, we were given some logs and we were told that they represented AK 47. They initiated us by backpacks filled with stones and ran steep gorges, valleys, crossing deep rivers. Three weeks had gone by doing the same routine developing muscles, physics, tough spirit and understanding the mindset of being ready for the next level of training. After four weeks in Nampudu camp, they screened us for all those who were under 18 years of age to step aside and I was one of them. The instructors told us that they were not going to train boys from 18 years and younger but only those who were above 18 years of age. It was arranged that a camp for young people, Khijana, was opened at Jason Ziyaphapha Moyo's farm west of Lusaka. In a week's time, four Zilli trucks came to pick us up and sent us to J.M. Moyo farm. This was in early 1978. It was a long distance from Nampundu camp to J. Z. Moyo camp which consisted of boys of 18 years old and under.

They had started a school for the young boys who were envisioned as the leaders of tomorrow. The Leader of ZAPU and ZIPRA, Dr. Joshua Q. Nkomo had a strategic plan to put all boys and girls to school to be part of the elite after independence. The young girls had their own camp in VC camp not far from Lusaka City. Instead of training the young people for military training, they decided to open schools both at J. Z. camp and VC camp. The J. Z. The camp continued to train the boys in preparation for the liberation war. If one turned 18 years old, he would join the other cadres to be trained and cross the border of Zambia into Zimbabwe to fight against the Rhodesian regime. Meanwhile, the school was given the first priority to all young people. The training was done especially, every morning, daily, from 4:30 am to 7:30 am. The training was mainly running in uniform, singing in unison the songs hailing the ZAPU leaderships, praising them for taking the armed struggle against Ian Smith and discrediting Ian Smith regime, marching in the form of companies, platoon and section. The company consisted of 24 cadres, a platoon consisted of 12 cadres and a section consisted of 6 cadres. In each company, there was a commander, and a commissariat. Each platoon had a commander and each section had a commander and commissariat. The commander was responsible for military action, if there was any attack and the commissariat's responsibility was to politicize, teach the ideologies of communism, Marxism and Leninism that were against capitalism.

The brainwash is very intensive to make all cadres to hate all forms of imperialism, colonialism and Christianity. We were intentionally indoctrinated with Marxism and communism. Communism is a political and economic philosophy that seeks to create a classless society, advocating that the major means of production must be owned and controlled by the public. The main production such as mine, factories, industry, land and agriculture are owned and controlled by the public in terms of production and distribution. The opposite of communism is capitalism which stipulates that the political and economic philosophy or system of the nation's trade and industry are controlled by private owners for profit. It is a free-market and trade, "survival of the fittest in the economic and political systems." Communism was so ingrained in my mind that I started to question Christianity for its teaching of love, forgiveness, caring, and sharing fairly one's possession with others. Christianity started not to make sense anymore because it was individualistic because capitalism did not care about others but it was egocentric and selfish in its nature. In contrast, Socialism was more for the collective and population centered and sharing the production. To me it looked like socialism was closer to the Biblical principles where it teaches to share our wealth equally if one could reflect on what the earth church advocated to share with those who are in need, (Acts 4:32, NKJV).

We would start classes at 8:00 am and end the classes at 12:30 pm, Monday to Friday. Every afternoon, after lunch at 2:00 pm, we would go out of the camp into the jungle to dig our trenches in preparation for any attack from the Rhodesian armed forces. We used to have our trenches ready and we knew how to get to them as fast as we could. Our camp was guarded by the trained cadres with sophisticated weaponry from Russia and Cuba. There were about seven anti air missile weapons to shoot down jet fighters and the ground force at the same time. They were trained cadres who guarded and patrolled our camp 24/7. We were trained physically, with schemish tactics, judo, karate but we were never taught or trained to shoot with a gun. We were not allowed to hold a gun or use a gun because we were not yet trained to be militants. Our concentration was physical fitness and to learn to be the future leaders after gaining independence.

The leadership of Dr. Joshua Q. Nkoma and all his cabinet was really amazing for upholding the international law that scorns child soldiers. It was like a family who would not allow the children under age to hold and to be taught how to shoot. We were trained physically and mentally but we were not introduced to operating the guns.

I started my first grade in J. Z. camp and the teacher chose me to become a class monitor. Sometimes the teacher would leave me to teach other students. I quickly adapted to the environment and I knew what was required to pass the examinations, tests and homework and I began to pass. We were so close to each other and we were taught to care for each other as brothers with supreme trust. However, we used to make some jokes about one another, sarcastically. One day, in the evening, in our tent when we were about to sleep, Philip and I were making some jokes about each other sarcastically, and then it intensified and we began to fight. I was still having the skills to box taught by my cousin, Herod back in Tsholotsho. I beat him with a hard punch and his eye got swollen. We were both afraid that if the commander learned and discovered that we were fighting, we would be in trouble and we would receive the harshest punishment and severe discipline. So, we hatched a plan to say that if Philip was asked what happened to his eye, he would say that he fell in the dark on top of a stone. In the morning, he was asked what had happened to him and he said that he fell on the stone in the dark, that's why his eye was swollen. The plan worked! I now realized that we could connive on such silly things and get away with it.

The war of liberation back in Zimbabwe was intensifying in 1978 and Ian Smith was trying by all means to bomb camps outside Zimbabwe. He bombed Nampundu camp where I was when I first came from Botswana. He bombed the Mayeba camp of the cadres. He bombed Mkushi camp and VC camp for women and young girls. The ZAPU leadership were becoming vigilant that Rhodesians armed forces could bomb our camp, J. Z. camp which was near VC near Lusaka. Our camp was not very far from VC camp where they had bombed and many people died. We were very alert that any time he could attack us. We were no longer staying in the camp during the day.

We went to live in the trenches in the jungle and we were eating only in the evening when we came out from the trenches, daily. It was the rainy season and it rained for weeks without stopping and we were always wet, hungry and cold. That was the time when I thought of Jesus Christ and my mother. I prayed in my heart that Jesus was my Lord even if they had told and taught us that Jesus was for colonizers and the imperialists and that it was a false and fake ideology. However, I was convinced deep down in my heart and convicted in the midst of indoctrination that Jesus Christ was the truth. I was basing my conviction on what I had heard not what I read because I did not have any Bible ever and I was not able to read or write. One time, I got very sick with malaria and there was no hospital. That was really difficult to cope with. I could not get any help anywhere. One had to be strong and fight to survive not to die in the foreign land. I survived by God's grace but malaria nearly took my life. It was cerebral malaria. I recovered without any medication. Some of our people died of malaria, typhoid fever and dysentery.

The Rhodesian jet fighters bombed Chimoio camp and several camps in Mozambique owned and run by ZANU. At the beginning of 1979, our camp, J. Z. camp was moved from Lusaka City to the outskirts of Solwezi town further northwest of Zambia, near the border with Angola. The move was massive. It took almost two months to relocate to Solwezi. The buses were sent to ferry us at night to disguise any plot against us by the enemy. The buses travelled the whole night and arrived at dawn in the middle of the jungle and left us there. We walked in the forest to the destination but we crossed the rivers, thick forests, and it was raining for many weeks. Before we arrived at the new J. Z. camp in Solwezi, we had to temporarily camp for a week before we proceeded because it took us some days to arrive at the new camp. Finally, we arrived with our backpacks but our tents were ferried by lorries ahead of us. We pitched our tents in the jungle and it was safer than old J. camp, although it was reported that Rhodesian planes had bombed another camp nearby but many of them were shot down by the cadres using the anti-missiles weaponries. It was reported that one of the cruel and fierce commanders of Rhodesians air force,

Green Leader's plane was shot and it crashed in the open kitchen at the camp.

We were now living far away from the enemy. We were able to do open training, marching, running and toitoi freely and with loud voices, exercises, judo, karate and we had well organized schedules for training, classes and other entertainments such as soccer, music, choirs. It was more like home compared to old J. Z. camp, where we used to be on our toes, running and hiding in our trenches in fear of attacks from the Rhodesian forces. The food supplies were better and we had formal education. There were no buildings but we used the tents to cover classrooms and we did not have desks and chairs, instead, we used logs to sit on and used our laps as desks. I got sick with malaria again and this time it was severe. At J. Z. Two, there was a camp clinic with a doctor, Dr. Maphosa and some nurses. I was treated with chlorophyll that treats malaria although It took time for me to fully recover. There were many mosquitoes, especially anopheles' mosquitoes, the female mosquitoes that cause malaria and the area was swampy because of continuous rain.

There was an attack on the nearby female camp by the Rhodesian armed forces, through air-force. The female cadres were displaced and some of them escaped to the direction of our camp, causing chaos and anarchy in our camp. We thought that the Rhodesian air force had invaded our camp and we took covers and we ran to our trenches. It was after an hour that the camp instructor, Blue Stone, and Makanyanga called a parade and told us that the female camp was attacked. That was the reason we had witnessed the female cadres crossing our camp in panic. Everything was brought into a standstill but eventually, the situation calmed down and the situation normalized. We received constant updates from the commissariat about the current situation.

We used to listen to Zimbabwe news through radios about the situation and how the liberation for independence was progressing. The war intensified in Zimbabwe and Ian Smith had a deal with Bishop Abel Muzorewa, a leader of the United African National Council (UANC), thinking that Dr. Joshua Nkomo the leader of ZAPU and ZIPRA and

Robert G. Mugabe, the leader of ZANU and ZANLA would lay down their weapons and join them. But Dr. Joshua Q. Nkomo and Robert G. Mugabe rejected that offer, vehemently. At the election on May 28, 1979, Bishop Abel Muzorewa was appointed to be the Prime Minister of Zimbabwe Rhodesia and Josiah Zion Gumede, my aunt's husband was elected as the first President of Zimbabwe-Rhodesia, (https:// en.wikipedia.org/wiki/Lancaster_House_Agreement, Accessed on December 10, 2020). Rev. Ndabaningi Sithole and Chief Chirau became part of Bishop Abel Muzorewa government. The Rhodesian Front members served under the Prime Minister, Bishop Abel Muzorewa. The government of Bishop Abel Muzorewa, a United Methodist Church Bishop and a nationalist leader, was short-lived in 1979. Dr. Joshua Nkomo and Robert Mugabe refused to recognize that deal, (Wikipedia, https://en.wikipedia.org/wiki/Abel_Muzorewa, Accessed on December 13, 2020).

We heard about the negotiation of the deal which was intended to transfer power, peacefully, from Ian Smith's government, a white minority to black majority. However, it was perceived to be a sinister deal and the Patriotic Party did not become part of the deal. Instead, they continued to wage the war of liberation of independence despite an offer. The internal settlement was also condemned by the United Nations Security Council Resolution 423. There was a Lancaster House Agreement to renegotiate a peaceful deal of independence. Dr. Joshua Nkomo and Robert Mugabe attended the conference under the "Patriotic Front" (PF). It was at Lancaster House Agreement in 1979 negotiation that led to full democracy which ushered parliamentary and Presidential elections and Robert G. Mugabe emerged as a winner on March 24, 1980. He became the Prime Minister of Zimbabwe in 1980 to 1987 and the President until 2017. It was at that time in the 1980 elections that as ZAPU and ZIPRA, we were anticipating that Dr. Joshua Mqabuko Nkomo would be elected as the President of Zimbabwe. The news shocked us to the core when we heard the news that it was Robert G. Mugabe who had won the elections and had become the Prime Minister. We thought Dr. Joshua Mqabuko Nkomo was well known and loved by all Zimbabweans across the country.

The elections in 1980 set tribal wars and divisions between the Shona and the Ndebele people to this very day, (https://www.britannica.com/topic/Robert-Mugabe-on-Zimbabwe-1985189/The-Lancaster-House-Negotiations, Accessed on December 15, 2020).

The whole camp was in great silence with great disappointment. It was as if someone important had died. Some cadres were crying thinking about all the years they had spent in the bush, fighting for the liberation of Zimbabwe but to end with such failure and disappointment. The tantalizing beauty of Zimbabwe had been dashed to the other direction, that's what we thought. Many of us were anticipating to take key leadership positions and build Zimbabwe we wanted but now all was in vain. We knew that we were not going to participate in the cutting and eating of the cake, I mean Zimbabwe land, economy and all its beauty. We had fought through thick and thin for all the years, being hunted by Rhodesian forces, day and night, having sleepless nights, without enough food, medication, formal school and having left our families back home. It really was a big disappointment to everyone in the camp. It was like a great failure in life to end up being the loser. Counting the cost was gracious and very heart-breaking. Introspection, analyzing and aging with so many years spent in the jungle fighting, reminiscing about all the colleagues who had died through being bombed, shot, hanged and tortured because of the love for Zimbabwe to liberate it. The future looked blared and dim. We could not imagine what life would become in a ZANU-PF government under Robert G. Mugabe. We knew for sure that we would never enjoy and be part of the building of Zimbabwe. We knew their characters and policies that were focused on developing Mashonaland and not of Matabeleland.

It took some weeks to come to reality and to believe what had happened. While ZANU-PF was celebrating in Mozambique, and in Zimbabwe, we were mourning in Zambia at J. Z. Moyo Two camp. I could imagine that other camps scattered in Zambia were boiling with anger, regret, frustration, depression, stress and anxiety. We were thinking about how our loved ones would welcome us with such a dismal failure, how our mothers, sisters, brothers, aunts, uncles, and all our consanguinity and our neighbors would think of us. Time heals! After some weeks, Dr. Joshua Nkomo visited our camp because our camp was composed of vibrant youths who were eager and had high hopes of a new Zimbabwe that held their future and visions. When Dr. Joshua Nkomo came to J. Z. Camp Two, he found us not as enthusiastic as usual but with low morale than we used to be. But Dr. Joshua Nkomo spoke with eloquence assuring us that all is well even if he did not win. He told us that we had won because ZANU-PF and Mugabe we had fight together with one purpose and mission, to bring about the change and to usher a new error of black majority rule and removing Ian Smith government regime that had perpetrated brutality, torture, murder, atrocities, dehumanization, and which had orchestrated discrimination laws, color bars, racism, land tenure act pushing the indigenous people to poor arid land while the minority whites grabbed the most fertile land. He said that all the bad things that had happened were now in the past and we should focus on the future with boldness, ready to bring Zimbabwe back to the global stage. He injected high morale to the whole camp. He talked as if he had won and we regained our strengths and energy and we came back to our senses again and realized that we were not enemies with ZANU-PF but we were one family and one Zimbabwe. It takes a great and a good leader to encourage, inspire and to give hope to the despondent followers.

Dr. Joshua Nkomo's speech was galvanized with the new President of Zimbabwe, Robert G. Mugabe in his independence speech on April 18, 1980 when he called for reconciliation with all those who were enemies in the past. He assured everyone that there would be a room for everyone in the new Zimbabwe. With that assurance and hope, Dr. Joshua Nkomo informed us that we were going to be repatriated back to Zimbabwe in months to come as returnees. He told us that we are going to continue with school because our future depended on education. J. Z. Moyo Camp would continue to be J. Z. High School in West Nicholson near Gwanda and another school would be created, George Silundika High School in Nyamandlovu. Both schools would be boarding schools for all of us starting from the primary schools to the secondary schools. We began to attune our minds to return to Zimbabwe and continue with our education. That was a big deal and proper planning to invest in education. I spent more than four years in Zambia from grade one and now I was in grade three. I could not imagine my return back to a free Zimbabwe. Flashes of home started racing in my mind and I asked myself what was home and where? My home would be my original home, Hope Fountain, at Esigodini or it would be Tsholotsho, my uncle Solomon's home, Bindane village again with those cattle, honestly? I had to reset my mindset, thoughts, fantasy to reality. Well, I just toasted away all those thoughts that wanted to imprison me again. Nevertheless, I was getting ready like others to go back home. We started packing the few belongings we had, actually, not much.

CHAPTER SIX

The Return and The Pursuit of Future

The time arrived when the camp instructor Cde. Mpofu and Blue Stone assembled us and instructed how we were going to be repatriated back to Zimbabwe, starting with oldest and higher grades in descending orders. It was to avoid any harm to the younger ones not being victimized if ever there was a conspiracy plot against the returnees. It was strategically planned to start with older ones to travel by buses from the deep forests of Solwezi to Ndola, then to David Livingstone. Then we would disembark from the buses at the border of Zambia and Zimbabwe and then cross the border by foot to the Zimbabwe border. We would board the trains from Victoria Falls to the city of Bulawayo. The first group departed on about ten buses, from Solwezi town to Ndola and then to Diving Livingston which was about 634 kilometers plus the distance from the camp to Solwezi town. It took two days for the buses to come back to the camp to ferry some more returnees. My group was the third group to be ferried. You could observe that the population in the camp was dwindling, gradually. The news came that the first group had diarrhea and the trips were suspended for about two weeks as the health experts were inspecting the food that they were supplied. We were able to avoid the outbreak of the infectious disease chlorella. It was quickly managed and eradicated before the next group. There was fear that it could have been poison put on the food to kill the returnees but it was not verified that it was poison. It was discovered that it was simply hygiene. After putting the hygiene protocols in proper places, they resumed ferrying of the returnees back to Zimbabwe.

My group's turn came and we were excited to get into the buses with our bags and you were allowed to have one big bag only. We boarded the buses early in the morning around 3:00 am and travelled through Solwezi town, Ndola town up to David Livingston town. It was a long trip/journey and we arrived in David Livingston, disembarked from the buses to cross the border by foot. My liberation of independence name was Samson Mzingeli because we were instructed to give ourselves new names so that the enemy would not be able to trace and identify. All the past four years, when I got to Zambia, I was known as Samson Mzingeli. After going through Zambian immigration processes, we walked to Zimbabwe immigration and we were repatriated and now I started to write my name as Sabelo Sam Nyathi Gasela. We boarded the train the following day to Bulawayo City from David Livingston town which took almost the whole day because the goods-trains are slow and they stop almost at every station. In my mind, I was thinking what I would do when I arrived in Bulawayo. I thought my uncle did not know where I was, my mother or my siblings did know where I was because I had left them a long time ago. Well, I just thought, things will happen on their own. In Zimbabwe, the news was broadcasted both in the TVs and Radios that the returnees from Zambia were coming back and the government encouraged parents, relatives and friends to go to those designated places to check if ever their children, siblings or friends returned safely back to Zimbabwe. Whenever the group would arrive, parents, relatives and friends would go and look for their children or siblings. I did not know that my mother had been checking the groups that arrived every time.

The love of the mother endures forever and it lasts. We arrived in Luveve township, Bulawayo in the morning and the buses came to pick us up to a designated school in Luveve, close to the railway line. The facility had some bedrooms, kitchen, and a big yard. It was like a training center for adult children. There were many people and you could see hundreds of parents, siblings, relatives and friends coming to pick up their loved ones. It was sad to hear others being told that their siblings, children or relatives did not make it who had died in Zambia. Some of them who had been bombed, shot or murdered by Ian Smith's regime or through illnesses did not make it. You could hear the screams and mourning that saturated the air as their beloved ones did not make it back home. So, what they would do is, when a relative came to check their children, siblings, relatives or friends, they would ask the name of whom they were looking for and their names would be called in public. I was mingling among my colleagues when I heard that my name was being called. It was a shock to hear my name being called because I could not imagine who would have come looking for me. I thought I was no longer known and not on the world map, having been forgotten, no relatives or anyone knowing where I was. I was now fifteen years old in 1980, still with a small voice and a tiny body not because of the statue but because of lack of food, good health, and under nourishment. All the food for a fifteen-year-old boy to eat and for growth I was lacking. I did not fully develop and grow because of those challenges I faced in the jungle.

Someone came to me in the crowd and told me your name is being called. I just ran towards the front maneuvering among the people. Suddenly I saw my mother, Josephine Gasela, and she called me, "Sabelo Gasela!" and I responded and said, "I am here mama!" My mother embraced me and kissed me several times on cheeks, neck, head and tried to lift me up with her tears streaming on her soft cheeks. I also shed a lot of tears of joy and gladness, hugging my mom. She had come with her friend, a neighbor, MaNgwenya. She introduced me to MaNgwenya, a lovely woman, indeed, and my mom told me that they had been coming to check on me in every group that arrived. She did not miss even one group. I saw the love of a mother in action. I love my mother so dearly. It was unbelievable to be reunited with my mother after such a long time. It actually means that my uncle had told my mother that I had left and crossed over to Zambia. But he did not waste time to check on me if I returned. I really thank my mother Josephine Gasela for coming to look for me. If she did not come, I don't know what would have happened to me. I was going to remain in that facility until we were taken to one of those schools that they had promised us that we were going to continue with our education. I sympathize and empathize with those who remained in the facilities, whose parents, siblings or relatives did not come to look for them either because they were in the villages out of town or they had lost the connection with their loved ones.

My mother and her friend took me home, we walked to Pumula North, that's where her house was. It was a long distance between Luveve and Pumula North. She bought me donuts and muffins and Fanta in the stores along the way. I had missed such tasty stuff and devoured them like a hungry lion and drank with the Fanta. It took us about an hour to reach home. Walking was my hobby and I just felt for my mother and her friend but they were very strong and they were used to walking too. There were no buses connecting Luveve and Pumula North or lifts. You had to board a bus to the city, downtown and then board another bus to Pumula. So, walking was easier and faster. When we arrived home, I was thrilled to see my siblings, Edwin Nanatsho, Joshua, Sithabile, Sipho, Duduzile Ellen, Gladys, Senzeni Khatha, Mavis except Zenzo who was still living at home, at Hope Fountain. All my siblings were not staying with my mother but they had their own homes except Sipho and Duduzile. My older brothers and sisters came to see me when they heard that I had returned well and sound. They came to meet me and it was a great reunion and I was glad to be reconnected with my consanguinity. That's when I heard that my two brothers Edwin Nanatsho Gasela and Alexander Gasela had also gone to Zambia for training and because they were older and mature when they went, they were trained as cadres and actually crossed over the board to Zimbabwe to fight the war of liberation of independence against Rhodesian Army.

We were only allowed three days to meet with our parents and relatives, only three days and then we would report again at the facility. After three days, I returned to the facility and saw my friends and we were asking each other about the reunions with our beloved ones. It was all good stories and sharing memories and experiences with our relatives. We stayed at the facility for about two months while the government, especially PF-ZAPU, was allocating the schools where we would be going as the schools we were going to live in as school borders and these were still empty and simple farms without building facilities. The government allocated a farm in Nyamandlovu where a boarding school would be built and become George Silundika High School and Jason Ziyaphapha Moyo High School at Major farm in West Nicholson, near Gwanda. They were two opposite directions, one in the northwest of Bulawayo and another one in Southeast of Bulawayo. We could go to those two respective places because there were no buildings and they started building those schools as fast as they could. Meanwhile, we were located in smaller facilities or temporary schools to stay while the schools were being built at Nyamandlovu, George Silundika High School and J. Z. Moyo High School at West Nicholson.

At the Luveve facility, we were only allowed to go to visit our parents and relatives on weekends, Fridays and we came back on Sundays. Basic school started informally. I used to enjoy going home to see my mother and my brothers and sisters on weekends. I would sometimes take my friends especially, those whose parents and relatives had not yet come to claim them. My brother, Edwin Nanatsho promised me that he would visit me at the facility to bring me some clothes and good stuff. I was so excited when he told me that. I was anticipating seeing him come to visit me with the clothes that he had promised me. He was still drafted in the Zimbabwe army together with my other brother Alexander. They were still being formed and assimilated into one Zimbabwe army from the ZIPRA wing, ZANLA wing and Rhodesian forces. There were some clashes among themselves, the forces who were fighting against each other before, especially ZIPRA and ZANLA cadres against the Rhodesian forces during the liberation war of independence. It was a boiling pot and complicated. I did not know that it was my last time to see my brother Adwell, Nanatsho. I saw Adwell Nanatsho only one time after independence when I visited my mother and other siblings and I never saw him again.

We were relocated to Fatima Mission School in Lupane, north of Bulawayo about 209 km away. It was a Catholic Girls boarding School but was reserved for boys for a year in 1981. At the end of 1981, we were sent to George Silundika High School although it was still under construction and we lived in tents as if we were back in Zambia. In 1982, few of us were chosen to go to Ntabazinduna, near David Livingston High School because George Silundika High School was crowded. It was a training center facility. We were about one hundred and about one hundred students. We stayed there from 1982 to mid-1983 and then we were sent back to George Silundika High School in Nyamandlovu. We were still learning under the trees and sitting on rocks without classrooms and desks. Food was not enough just as it was back in Zambia. Our predictions that we would not enjoy the fruits of our supreme sacrifice for participating in the liberation war of independence back in Zimbabwe were correct. Here we were, still struggling in our soil because ZANU-PF had won elections and Robert Mugabe the President had taken grip on the government and led it to the dungeon and that had become a reality. We were never safe again. There was fighting against the cadres and from ZIPRA and ZANLA. The civilians were being killed in cold blood. It was as if we were in war zones and more vulnerable than while we were in the jungle in Zambia. ZIPRA cadres were discriminated against in the formation of the Zimbabwe army. Some of them were shot point blank and were told they had no portion in the Zimbabwe army. Tribalism in the Zimbabwe army became a heated debate and contrition among the army commanders. As a result of the ill treatment by ZANLA forces within the Zimbabwe army, some ZIPRA opted to leave the Zimbabwe army forces and some were even threatened with death if they remained hanging around. The ZIPRA forces, most of them left the Zimbabwean army or they were forced to leave. From 1981 to 1985, the Zimbabwe army hunted the ZIPRA forces who had left the Zimbabwe army and had assimilated into villages as civilians. Demobilization of the ZIPRA forces was rampant and they were mistreated.

The 5th brigade was formed and trained by the North Korean army with the sole purposes to stem out the so called "Dissidents" who were former ZIPRA cadres and Zimbabwe Defense forces who were now living among the villagers and in towns such as Bulawayo, Gweru, Gwanda, Tsholotsho, Plumtree, Lupane, Hwange, Victoria Falls. They went around villages and towns searching and persecuting and killing people, asking if anyone knew where the dissidents were. During that time, I received a letter from my sister Sithabile Gasela, informing me that my brother Adwell Nanatsho was killed at Entumbane battle between ZIPRA forces and ZANLA forces, mixed with bombardment that happened in Bulawayo. My heart sank. A spell of killings in Matabeleland North, Matabeleland South and in the Midlands led to genocide of more than twenty thousand people. There was chaos in the country, especially the Ndebele territories. They went village by village, smoking out all men and the youths, killing all those they found. They came to George Silundika High School where I was and searched in our tents, took some of our teachers and other students, put them in their truck and they were never found. It is reported that they went with them to some mines and they dug holes and shot them dead and threw their bodies. It was a horrible situation. They took many teachers in our school and one of my favorite teachers were Mr. Sibanda, and Mr. Mpofu. They all disappeared never to be found and known where they were buried. Many of the friends that I grew up with, Muhle Moyo, Phikelela, were dragged out and shot in the villages and they even went to towns and searched house by house. I survived because during the school breaks/holidays, I went to Bulawayo City. They came to our house in Pumula North and searched our house by house. They asked me what I was doing and I told them that I was at school and I showed them my school reports. That's how I survived but another youth friend, my neighbor was taken away and disappeared forever. The experience was traumatic and painful.

Going back to school at George Silundika High School was frightening. The first School Headmaster/Principal who was a graduate, Ndlukula, resigned and went away. The next Headmaster/Principal was Mr. Muthobe who did not lead the school very long.

He was taken by the 5th Bridget soldiers and he disappeared, never to be seen again. When the massacre was reported to the international community media and many voices from the SADC and International Community, Human Rights, Catholics, who condemned the genocide, the government changed the strategy, not to eradicate the suspects in public but in secrets by nights. They hunted and eliminated thousands of people. It is estimated that 20 thousand Ndebeles were massacred during this period of genocide. One of the brothers, Alexander Gasela, when he was at home, the 5th Brigade soldiers came and interrogated him. They took him with others and put them in the truck to kill them. They drove them far away and he said that when they were taking them to the place of massacre, he pondered his sacrifice for Zimbabwe and now he was led like a sheep for slaughter. Then the 5th Brigade went through the shopping centers and they stopped the trucks to buy liquor. My brother and others were left inside the trucks while the 5th Brigade army went out to buy liquor and other stuff. My brother Alexander decided with one of the men captured, to escape. They jumped out of the truck and started running to the jungle and the 5th Bridget soldiers fired shots at them and his colleague was shot and one of the bullets bruised his head but he was not fatally shot. He escaped, bleeding until he was helped by the Good Samaritans in the next village. He travelled until he crossed the border to Botswana to seek refuge. That's how ugly the 'Gukurahundi' was perpetrated by the 5th Bridget under Robert Mugabe. Women were raped and some were skinned alive. This is not a myth, but firsthand information about what happened. Most of the Shona people don't believe this period. They take it as a conspiracy theory meant to tarnish Robert Mugabe since 1980 to this day. They have not apologized or brough Truth and Reconciliation like what the South Africa government did under President Nelson Mandela which was chaired by Bishop Desmond Tutu.

The leader of PF-ZAPU, Dr. Joshua Q. Nkomo was also hunted and he was nearly killed when the 5th Brigade soldiers invaded his house at Number Six in Bulawayo, near the White City. They shot his house and Dr. Joshua Nkomo narrowly escaped murder and he travelled and crossed to Botswana and ended in Britain to seek refuge. He survived the murder plots. If you were a Ndebele during that period between 1981 to 1987, you lived in constant fear. The international community intervened and warned President Robert G. Mugabe and his regime that if he was pursuing that path of genocide of the Ndebele people as he was doing, he would suffer the international wrath of law. The Catholics and Anglican Churches and other churches and human rights started raising voices against that madness of killings. Through talks and negotiations, Dr. Joshua M. Nkomo was persuaded to come back home from Britain. They tried to reconcile with President Mugabe and to negotiate a peace deal but the damage had been done, thousands and thousands of the Ndebeles were dead, women were raped and had children of the 5th Brigade forces, and not accounted for. Some people were maimed, some disabled, some traumatized, some imprisoned and some left to suffer emotionally and psychologically for the rest of their lives. The killings stopped on December 22, 1987, when the two, President Robert Mugabe from ZANU-PF and Dr. Joshua Nkomo from PF-ZAPU signed the peace agreement. Dr. Joshua Nkomo was made the second Vice President of Zimbabwe and he entered the agreement to stop the annihilation of the Ndebele Tribe. Peaceful environment prevailed and the reconciliation paid off. It was the wisdom of Dr. Joshua Nkomo to stop the atrocities of Robert Mugabe's government. No harassment and killings publicly from then except secretly adaptions and killings that have continued to this day. Those who had fled the country were given amnesty to come back home and to surrender all their weapons and they were assured of security and protection by all means.

Now ZANU-PF has changed its form, the killings of the opposition parties through adaptions and eliminating the opponents in secret. After 41 years of ZANU-PF rule, now most Zimbabweans start to understand the ideologies of ZANU-PF to suppress and eliminate the opponents, using the Russian and Cuban strategies and banning all the media that support a different view or opposition parties. By the same token, the main opposition Party, Democratic Movement Party (MDC) has erred many times. They have called for sanctions against the government of Zimbabwe. That was a grave mistake because with the sanctions imposed on Zimbabwe, their relatives, friends and the general population, have suffered economic slump since 2000. They invited the European Unions and American to impose sanctions. Now more than twenty-one years, they cannot reverse those sanctions themselves. It's like they shot their own foot with a gun and they are also experiencing economic hardship as the general population. Although there was a short-lived government of National Unity in 2009, with Morgan Tsvangirai as the Prime Minister and Robert Mugabe still being the President, crafted by Thabo Mbeki, the former South African President backed by the SADC. It brought a break of both political and economic leverage, but it did not go far. The government of National Unity collapsed and plunged the country back into severe political and economic polarization once again, even worse.

CHAPTER SEVEN

The Pursuit of Education

During all this chaos and anarchy in the country, I never quitted school. I had realized that education is power and that my future hung on education nothing else. I remained in the boarding school at George Silundika High School in Nyamandlovu, pursuing my studies. I did not go to grade four and grade five but I went straight to grade six. I wrote my grade 7 examination at the end of 1983. I had become involved in the school club of Journalism, reporting school events and sports. It was a great experience. I also joined the Seventh Day Adventist Church group through a student called Lawrence who persuaded and witnessed Jesus Christ to me. As I was a Christian before but having been brainwashed with Marxism and Communism while we were in Zambia, I had to rededicate my life to Christ once again. That love for God rekindled once more. I started to participate in the Seventh Day Church within the school and joined the school choir, singing during the school assemblies. I admired a young man, Newman Kolobe who used to preach in the open air at the front of dormitories and he was like an evangelist. He was moving around in the dormitories, in the classrooms and anywhere, preaching and calling people to repent and to receive Christ as their personal Lord and Savior, just like John the Baptist. Journalism club made me popular because I was always reporting about sports, school events every Friday at the school assembly. I was also acting in a drama club and I was almost known by everyone in the school.

We also started singing Imbube music with Jupiter and Lucky Dube (Not the South African one), Bernia Khuphe and others and we formed Black Umfolosi group. Jupiter was the lead singer and he was the founder of the group and we joined him. He was a close friend of mine and he was a Rasta. I did not stay long in that group, I quitted later and concentrated on the Seventh Day Adventist Church Choir instead of being with friends who did not want to join the church. Other friends who refused to join me in the church were Benedict Moyo, Qhawe Dube, Big-boy Moyo, Gibson Ncube, Austin Mabhena, Godfrey Ngwenya, Quickson Ndlovu, Vusumuzi Ndlovu, and many others. Jason Ziyaphapha Moyo High School was opened at Majoda farm in West Nicholson, near Gwanda. Some of the students were taken from George Silundika High School. They first selected students who were notorious and rude, to get rid of them at George Silundika High School. It was like a cleansing process to start to eliminate the bad ones. The school advised the teachers to select the troublesome students and to dump them in a new school, J. Z. High School in West Nicholson. I was not selected because they regarded me as one of the cool and loyal students at George Silundika High School. I was chosen as a School Prefect/Monitor by teachers at the school.

In my journalism club, I was assigned to go to J. Z. High School with a soccer school team as they had a game to play with J. Z. High School soccer team. I was very excited to go with the soccer team. When we got there, I was very impressed with the beautiful and modern buildings at J. Z. High School. The school soil was not as red and dusty as that of George Silundika School. At George Silundika High School, it had red and dusty soil. I did not like the red soil. One's shoes were always dirty and had dust and if it rained, it would be muddy everywhere. When I got to J. Z. High School, it was grey soil, no dust at all and the school was so beautifully built and I fell in love with it. We stayed at J. Z. from Friday and the soccer teams played on a Saturday and on Sunday, we headed back to George Silundika High

School in Nyamandlovu. When I reported about the outcome of the soccer game at the school assembly and we had won, I also added about the beauty of the school. I felt that I would be happier to be at J. High School than at George Silundika High School. I now started to look at how I could be transferred to J. Z. High School.

Every year, whenever Form Four classes would graduate at J. Z. High School, they would take form one student from George Silundika High School to J. Z. High School. I decided to persuade my teachers to join the other students to go to J. Z. High School. My teachers discouraged me and said that those who were selected to go to J. Z. High School, were those who were not smart, rude and arrogant and that I was not the type. They tried to refuse me to be registered but I insisted that I had wanted to go to J. Z. High School. My problem was not about other students they had described but it was about my desire to be in a different and better environment. I knew that I would handle those students whom they were said to be mean, not smart, rude and all the names they were given. I had fallen in love with J. Z. High School at West Nicholson. In early January, 1984, the buses came to ferry us but the teachers still insisted that I should not be allowed to get into the bus. I brought my bag with me to get in the bus but they refused me entry and took my bag away. I had a strong conviction to get into the bus without my bag and I said that I could go without my bag. Finally, the teachers gave up and they put my bag into the bus and told the driver that it was okay for me to go. However, they told me that they would miss me and said a bid farewell. It was a bittersweet to leave George Silundika High School and I knew that I would miss many of my friends and the teachers. The bus departed around 10:00 am and arrived at J. Z. High School at 6:30 pm. The dormitories were well prepared and the teachers and the students were waiting to welcome us, including the Headmaster, Mr. Matshaka Nare and the Deputy Headmaster was Mr. Sibanda. Mr. Matshakatshaka was a scholar and a diplomat by profession and very kind yet very tough in his leadership. I liked him very much because he led the school to greatness. I was allocated to Impala House dormitory. I already knew how the school looked and I just loved every part of it. The school was tidy, with beautiful buildings, classrooms, dining room, fewer students than at George Silundika High School, the soil and the grounds were pretty, for my taste for that matter.

We arrived on a Friday at J. Z. High School and the weekend gave us ample time to assimilate into the system, get used to the routines and schedules for everything and we checked out our classrooms. I had left almost all my friends, such as Qhawe Dube, Big-boy Moyo, Benia Khuphe, Lucky Dube, Jupiter, Gibson Sibanda, Benedict Moyo, Lawrence, Newman Kolobe and many more friends. This was the beginning of a renaissance and being aware of myself of who I was and where I was going. Doing my Form One was the beginning of a long academic journey and life. To be in a place where you like best and to be among the people whom you love is a conducive environment where you can stride so well. I started to work hard in my studies but also enjoying the school environment and making friends. I started attending the Christian choir that had been started by some Christian students, but predominantly, Seventh Day Adventist. I joined the choir. The school was for boys only from its inception but in 1987, they started to allow girls also to be enrolled and the local students. In the choir, I began to have friends such as Elvis Tshuma who was a great singer and, Quickson Ndlovu, Austin Mabhena, Godfrey Ngwenya, Joshua Masebe, Julius Ncube, Christopher Moyo, Ngiyekeleni Kololo, Joel Gama, Lovemore Ncube and many others. Most of these fellas were seniors to us and they soon graduated before us. They left the school for various carriers and professions. In that group, Godfrey Ngwenya, Austin Mabhena and I remained in the school choir and we continued, recruiting some more new students in the choir. I had become a devoted Christian and I was elected as the Impala dormitory prefect, making sure that the four dormitories had discipline, clean and monitoring the behaviors of all the students in Impala House Dormitory. I was also in charge of the students' wellbeing and for the sport activities. That was the first time to hold a bigger position among the students at J. Z. High School.

In 1985, there was a missionary, Jerald Haadsma who visited our school to show films to all students who were interested. He came with

Rev. Jealous Manyumbu who was a local Pastor at West Nicholson, pastoring African Evangelical Church. They used to come every Sunday afternoon around 6:00 pm. It was good entertainment for many students because we had no entertainment except soccer on weekends. Showing films was a big deal and there were Christian films only and there were no options. We all loved Sunday's entertainment. Many of us became devoted Christians and Rev. Jealous Manyumbu and Jerald Haadsma, a missionary from Grand Rapids, were now leading the school church which was interdenominational. Jerald's wife Florence Haadsma, was always coming with her husband for the new ministry which they had started in the school. They organized to start a church at the school because before showing the films, Rev. J. Manyumbu and Jerald Haadsma would preach the gospel to the students for repentance and many students repented. They later changed to start the church services at 3:00 pm at school and we got involved in inviting students to come to church. It was at this time in 1985 that I really rededicated my life to Christ and I repented from all my sins and I asked Christ to forgive me. After Jesus' film was shown, depicting his gruesome and scogging and painful death, it dawned to me that Christ is my Savior. When Jerald Haadsma explained about the salvation, justification, sanctification and glorification, and also quoted some verses from the Bible such as "For all have sinned and come short of the glory of God," (Romans 3:23, NIV), "If you declare with your mouth, 'Jesus is Lord,' and believe in your heart that God raised him from the dead, you will be saved," (Romans 10:9, NIV). It became clear to me that Jesus is the Savior of the world. I was thoroughly convicted and convinced that for sure I needed Jesus in my life.

In November 1985, I sat for my junior certificate examination in Form Two and that's when I got baptized also at West Nicholson by Jerald Haadsma with many other students. In 1986, Jerald Haadsma and Rev. Jealous Manyumbu had trusted me and gave the authority to keep the film equipment in my dormitory for them for the following Sunday. I used to invite many Impala students to go to church with me on Sundays but many of them resisted. I used to sleep next to Austin Mabhena. Our beds were next to each other in the dormitory. One day,

I asked Austin Mabhena to iron my tie and he burnt it. I used it as a bait to ask him to go with me to church because he had burnt my tie. He refused several times because he did not want to go to church. With my persistence to compensate for burning my tie, he eventually agreed to come with me. He later repented and became a strong member of the school interdenominational church and African Evangelical Church of West Nicholson. The rest is history. He is now a Bishop at United Baptist Church of Zimbabwe. Meanwhile, I was elected as the chairman of Scripture Union, the chairman of interdenominational church and Impala dormitory prefect. I used to take the Christian students out in the rivers and jungle to pray and fast, (*Enhlane*). Austin Mabhena and Godfrey Ngwenya were part of the group I used to lead and pray with them. People were now calling me a Pastor. I drew more respect from both students, teachers and school staff because of my Christian beliefs, conviction and character. I had close friends who were not Christians such as Ndondela, Alfa Ncube, and many who overheard that there was a conspiracy plot to attack me by some of the students because of popularity at school and of my Christian life. As a Christian group, we went out of school in the jungle as Christians to pray and fast for my protection from the evil during the weekends and that rumor just dispelled in the thick air. We saw the hand of God at work and His protection. Jerald Haadsma enrolled me and others in Bible Correspondence School courses and I completed all the levels required to graduate with a diploma. Mr. Jerald Haadsma was very impressed with my determination and hard work. He advised me that when I completed my school, I should consider going to Bible College to study Theology, at Theological College of Zimbabwe in Bulawayo.

When the class of Austin Mabhena graduated in 1986, J. Z. High School started to recruit both girls and boys from the community and far and wide. George Silundika High School had stopped bringing students from George Silundika High School to J. Z. High School. We were the second last to have come from George Silundika High School. I used to go to Scripture Union camps during the school breaks. In August school break in 1986, I went to a Scripture Union camp at Matopo Hills, in South of Bulawayo. During the camp, at break time,

I picked up a pamphlet which was written about the dilemma of Sarah and Abraham who did not have a promised son, at their advanced ages, Sarah at 90 or 91 years old and Abraham was 100 years old. The pamphlet continued to say that if you know a neighbor, a sister or an aunt who cannot have children, you have to pray for them. Maybe God can open their wombs. I took it to my heart. One of my sisters, Senzeni Khatha, was happily married to Amos Maseko but she always had multiple miscarriages at four or five months pregnant. I earnestly asked God to help my sister to have at least one child. I vowed to God that if God would give my sister Senzeni and Amos Maseko a child, I would serve Him for the rest of my life. God honored my prayer for my sister and my brother-in-law, they had a handsome baby boy in 1987 and they named him Mandlenkosi (The Power of God). I kept my vow in my heart. I did tell them that I had prayed for them to have a child but they did not understand it. But it was my secret with my God and I kept the vow and treasured it in my heart.

Then J. Z. High School began to enroll both boys and girls from the community and beyond, starting from Form One in 1987. Our school was now mixed with boys and girls. In the school choir, we invited some students who actually liked the choir and the girls' voices too. It was a beautiful environment. We were joined by young boys and girls such as Douglas Mangena, Xolani Nxumalo, Benziwe Dube, Thokozani Maseko, Siluzile, Jelitha, Zibusiso Ncube, Sikhanyisiwe and many others. The school choir was vibrant and jovial to the envy of everyone. We sang in the School Assembly on Mondays, Wednesdays and Fridays. Academically, I was an average student and I scooped four awards in midterm Prize Giving Day in 1987 in my Form Four, for the highest grade in English, the highest in Agriculture, third highest in O'level class and the Smartest Boy in School. I had invited my mother Josephine Gasela and my sister, Senzeni Khatha Gasela to witness the occasion and they were so proud of me. I felt as if I had wings. I had defied all the odds especially for my Metal teacher, (I have forgotten his name) who used to scold me for being a Christian alluding that Christians were not smart people. He used to mock me in front of the class because he was an atheist and made fun of me all the time in a

Metal Work Class and outside the class. It was a surprise for him to see me getting the awards. I knew that God was fighting for me, not with my own strength. He did not understand God's Kingdom Matrix. In contrast to that mean teacher, I had a science intern teacher who was a devoted Christian, Victor Nhaka. He became the Scripture Union advisor and I was the President of Scripture Union. We became very close and I observed that he had a calling in the ministry. When I told him that one day, he would be called to be a Minister in the church, he vehemently refused that he would be. However, he denied that discernment and said that he would take a different career. I discerned in his preaching and teaching gifts. It was very pleasing to have Victor Nhaka as a Christian teacher at school. He was our liaison teacher to the teaching staff and students.

My final years at J. Z. High School was a great challenge as I was busy preparing for examinations. I was also a student leader, Deputy President of Student Union, and Frank Sibanda was the President. In the Scripture Union, I was the President too, I was in the school choir, I was also in an Imbube group led by Sipho Maphosa. I knew where to go when I faced difficulties in decision making and facing life challenges, to Christ. My time at J. Z. High School was coming to an end and I was to seek the face of the Lord and ask for His direction for my future. I decided to pray and fast for seven days for my future career and profession. I had decided on two things for my life. My supplication to God was that if God could direct me to be a Minister/Pastor. That was my first priority and my first calling. My second priority was that if God was not calling me to a full-time ministry, I would want to be a businessman, to support the church at large with my businesses. Those were the two requests that were submitted to the Lord before I wrote my examinations in November, 1987. I fasted for seven days, pleaded with the Lord to show me the way. After classes, I would go into the jungle to fast the whole day and I would break with dinner for seven days. After seven days, I did not hear any answers from the Lord. I wrote my exams and waited for the results at home. While I was waiting for my examination results at home, waiting for God's answer and pondering what I would do next. Come January, 1988, I enrolled in Business Courses at Zimbabwe Commercial College in downtown, Bulawayo. I enrolled to study Business and Office Practice, preparing to start a business when I completed my studies and I took it as a confirmation that God had wanted me to do that as he did not confirm the calling of being a Pastor. I enjoyed the classes and in a different environment. My home was at Pumula North but I wanted to be closer to Bulawayo downtown for a walking distance to the College as I did not have money to get to the buses every day. So, I asked my uncle Moses' son who had a house at Makhokhoba Township very close to downtown where the college was. I lived with him for a year studying Business. He graciously agreed to take me in. I lived with him with his other cousin, Christian Nkabinde and his elder brother and his wife. We had a very good relationship with Christian Nkabinde and his brother. I used to wake up early in the morning and walked about two to three kilometers to college. The government paid for my education through a scholarship that we were granted as returnees. The scholarship covered books, small stipend but not accommodation.

While I was studying my Business and Office Practice, God spoke to me strongly that this was not where I was supposed to be. There was a College at Lobengula Street called Theological College of Zimbabwe where most of my friends I was at J. Z. High School and George Silundika High School, who were studying Theology. They heard that I was studying Business and Office Practice courses at Zimbabwe Commercial Collage. They visited me and they told me that they were studying Theology at Theological College of Zimbabwe (TCZ). I told them that God had not called me yet and I was following my second passion. I continued my studies the whole of 1988 at Zimbabwe Commercial College. At the end of year in 1988, God convicted me so strongly that I had to go to Theological College but I did not want to just jump on it without His confirmation. I was intending to continue with my course of Business Studies and Office Practice. In 1989 during the night, I heard a voice calling me. I woke up and asked my mother if she was calling me but she said that she had not called me. I went back to sleep. The same voice called me for the second time and I asked my mother if she had called me, but she said that she had not called me. I was now wondering who the person who was calling me, audibly, was at midnight. The third time, the voice called me again and this time I remembered Samuel who was called by God three times, (I Samuel 3:10, NKJV). I started praying and telling God that I was accepting the call to serve Him. I remembered the vow I had made when I was praying for sister Senzeni and her husband, Amos Maseko who did not have a child with several miscarriages and finally, God gave them a son, Mandlenkosi and the vow that I had made with God if He would answer my prayer, He did. I was now on board to go to Theological College of Zimbabwe. When the schools opened in January, I still went back to pursue Business Studies and Office Practice although I had agreed with God to go to a Theological College to study Theology but the question was how. The government was not going to pay for any religious carrier. If one took that route, it was the end of government scholarships.

While I was in the class, I heard that there was someone who was calling me outside. I got out and who do I see, it was Newman Kolobe, an old friend of mine at George Silundika High School who was a student evangelist at the school. Newman Kolobe did not mince his words but told me that I was not at the right place at that College. I explained to him that I was waiting for God to provide for the school fees. He told me to go to the Theological College to talk to President Molly. After class, I went to Theological College of Zimbabwe and when a group of students saw me, especially those who knew me, they welcomed me and directed me to Molly, the Principal of the Theological College of Zimbabwe. In his office, he asked me about my calling to the ministry. I did not know that Rev. Jealousy Manyumbu and Jerald Haasdma had mentioned my name to him long before. Within 30 minutes, I was admitted to Theological College of Zimbabwe to study Theology and I was granted a full scholarship for three years from 1989 to 1991. The ways of the Lord are different from our ways. I was told to go and get my belongings and start my studies in August, 1989.

When I told my mother and my siblings that I was going to Theological College of Zimbabwe in Bulawayo city at the Lobengula Street and that I would be boarding. They were very happy and thrilled for me the opportunity was given. They told me that they knew that I would eventually train as a Minister as my character and my passion were evident. It was good for me too to be in a boarding school again and pursue my studies. I was granted a full scholarship for tuition, boarding and living expenses. I was glad to meet once again Austin Mabhena that I had led to go to church while we were students at J. Z. High School and that he was now being trained as a minister of the Gospel. Some of the students whom I knew who were with me in high school were, Quickson Ndlovu, Godfrey Ndlovu, Christopher Moyo, Reuben Chapasuka, Newman Kolobe from George Silundika High School. I quickly made more friends like Letters Mukoyi, Christopher Nxumalo, Simba, Radman Matanda, Stanley, Dube, Ben Shiri, Motsi, and many others. My lecturers were awesome such as Dr. Burgess, Dr. Heaton, Jenny Smith, Rev. Mabhena and many others. As I got assimilated into the TCZ system, I was appointed to be an Assistant Librarian with Adamson Nyoni and Jenny Smith was the senior Librarian and also a Lecturer. We used to have shifts with Adamson Nyoni and when he graduated, I became a Librarian with Jenny Smith helping me but she was concentrating more as a lecturer. The TCZ was looking for a librarian to fill the position as for a full-time librarian.

Pursuing my studies at Theological College of Zimbabwe (TCZ) was a blessing. I used to earn my salary as a Librarian and also the stipend that the college used to give us. The college had some chores for all the students as an appreciation for the scholarship. We washed utensils, cut the grass, cleaned the college inside and outside and on weekends, took turns to cook. We had some duties but during the week, we had cooks, and garden and swimming pool caretakers, Mr. Nyoni. On Sundays, we used to go to United Baptist Church at Matshobana suburb to worship with others from the local vicinity. The Pastor was Rev. Punungwe with his wife and children, Shepherd, Grace, Miriam, and others. Rev. Punungwe used to live with his family at the same College where we lived, Theological College of Zimbabwe. We used to pray and go for evangelism outreach. He had a great passion for evangelism. The elders and deacons such as Sengwayo, Sigauke, and others who had founded Matshobana United Baptist

Church in Bulawayo having moved to work in Bulawayo in their earlier years from their hometown, Chimanimani district. During the school vacation or breaks, the college connected us to work at RSP, a factory which used to produce and print papers, postal cards, checks, books etc. I also worked at Matopo Book Center across the College which was organized by one of my lecturers who was a member of Brethren in Christ which was their Church Bookshop but he was from the USA.

I was always busy during school and also during the school vacation. My home, at Pumula North, was not far from the College, and I used to have a permanent room at the College during term and during the school vacations. At TZC, for the first time in my life, my friend Christopher Nxumalo organized my birthday on August 14, 1991. What an experience to be the center of the occasion! I really appreciate Chris who organized my first birthday celebrations ever. My friends came to my birthday celebrations including one of my young brothers Zenzo Gasela with his wife, Rosie Magwebu Gasela and she was expecting their first son, Thabani Craig Gasela. It was a great honor to have the first birthday ever. My younger brother Zenzo had already married before me. Marriage was not on my agenda that time and I did not have any pressure from anyone. I wanted to work and put everything together before I got married.

CHAPTER EIGHT

The Church and Family Development

I enjoyed studying Theology for three years at Theological College of Zimbabwe (TCZ). I completed my studies in 1991 and graduated in June, 1992. When I was at TZC for my graduation, I entered the classroom and who did I see? Victor Nhaka, my former science teacher who was our Scripture Union advisor at J. Z. High School whom I told him that he would be a Minister but he had denied that time. It was a shock to see him sitting at the feet of Christ, studying to be a Minister. I shed some tears of joy to see him, thanking God for His faithfulness. Before graduation, our church, United Baptist Church, especially, the National Committee was responsible to appoint and allocate the graduated students and to assign them to churches, institutions, bookshops or schools. I was told to apply for work six months before graduation. I had studied Business and Office Practice at Zimbabwe Commercial College. The National Committee, the Board that leads United Baptist Church, was consulted and approved for me to be assigned to Manage Christian Bookshop in Mature. Dr. Joshua Dhube was the Bishop of the Church presiding as the Church Chairman of the United Baptist Church (UBC) and the National Committee. The

National Committee is also the body that makes policies and makes final decisions. He was responsible for drafting and assigning the new workers to various churches, institutions, schools, and other ministries. The United Baptist Church has various ministries such as Churches, Two Schools, a Hospital, a Bible College, a Conference Center, Three Bookshops, and many missionary houses across the country.

United Baptist Church was founded in 1897 by the missionaries, under the South Africa General Mission which was founded in 1889 in South Africa's Cape province and town. In 1894, the name was changed to South Africa General Mission and it remained with that name until in 1963 when it was changed to African Evangelical Fellowship (A. E. F.). The S. A. G. originated in South Africa and England as an "evangelical faith" Mission Ministry to the indigenous peoples in Kimberly (North Cape) and Johannesburg (Transvaal). When the missionaries came to evangelize the virgin land, in the eastern part of Zimbabwe, at Rusitu valley in Chimanimani and they opened schools to educate the locals to learn how to read the Bible and to nurture the mind, they built hospitals for medication and the Bible College to train those who had been called to join the ministry. Dr. Joshua Ngoweni Dhube has been a leader for more than fifty decades. He led the United Baptist Church with four major concepts borrowed from Protestants strategically and popularized by Venn with American leader Rufus Anderson. They argued that, "New Testament-style churches should have local leaders. Venn suggested that the native and indigenous churches should focus on **Self-Governing, Self-Supporting, Self-Propagation,"** and in addition, **Self-Teaching,** (Henry Venn & Ruff Anderson, Henry Venn and Ruff Anderson, *Christian missions: A Church for every people and the Gospel for every person,* (https://en.wikipedia.org/wiki/Henry_Venn_ (Church_Missionary_Society, Accessed on December 30, 2020). This is just a synopsis of the United Baptist Church where I was going to serve for more than twenty decades.

The National Committee through Dr. Bishop Joshua Ngoweni Dhube, appointed me to go and manage Christian Bookshop in Mutare, in Manicaland Province. There was a General Manager for the three bookshops in the country, Mr. Levi Kombo but each Bookshop had its local Manager. The church had Zvokupona Bookshop in Chimanimani, Tsovane Bookshop in Chiredzi and Christian bookshop in Mutare. I was appointed to Manage the Christian Bookshop in Mutare. It had numerous debts from various companies and it was operating on loss for the past two years. It was well furnished but almost empty. I was both the Bookshop Manager and an Accountant, responsible to balance the ledger books at the end of every month, ordering the Bookshop inventories. There was a sales lady, Mrs. Kombo and some who came to help as volunteers. I was able to pay almost all the debts and close all the accounts which were outstanding with other companies and I ordered the stationary, books, and other inventories. It was a challenge to manage a bookshop which I found bleeding financially, already.

My friend, Letters Mukoyi, whom I graduated with was also assigned and located to be a Pastor at three churches in the district of Mutare and other preaching points, small churches. It was good to have a close friend in the same area because we would discuss our different jobs and challenges. I lived in a cottage while Mr. Kombo the Manager lived with his family in the main house, a beautiful house. Mukoyi lived in a cottage also of one of the members of his church, Mr. and Mrs. Siyekhaya Mutisi. They were a loving family and Mr. Mutisi was a godly man. The cottage I was living in was so bad that I started to be frustrated with the work and the place where I was living. I started to question God if it was his will for me to work in the bookshop. I started in 1991 after my graduation in June. I prayed to God to give me another place to live in, better than the one I was living in. I had a blind faith and I asked God as my Father. Letter Mukoyi was in the same situation. He did not want to deal with elders of the three churches who did not understand him and did not accept him because he was young as I was. Mukoyi used to work with Correspondence Bible School under Murray and he started to miss Bulawayo where he used to work. He was very depressed and frustrated about Pastoring the three Churches. I used to console and encourage him to keep on going on and to be patient. He used to walk to the three locations by foot or by buses. It was an overwhelming experience for my friend and I could feel for him. After three weeks of my prayer to God to provide me with better accommodation, the Vice Church Chairman Rev. Alfred Simango visited me in Mutare and I told him about my plight of the accommodation and that I was opting to quit the job.

In God's providence, when Rev. Alfred Simango returned to his office in Harare, he called me and told me that one of the mission houses which was occupied by an Inland Missionary was now vacant. The missionary with his family relocated to Mozambique and the Mission house was vacant. Rev. Alfred Simango told me to relocate and go and live in the mission house. Praise God! God answers earnest prayers. I thanked God for His provision and His faithfulness. I occupied a five bedroomed house alone and I was overwhelmed by the house. Do not ask from God what you cannot manage! I had to call Letters Mukoyi to come and live with me. Another church worker came to live with us, Ngwena. We lived happily with three of us but I was responsible for the upkeep of the house. Letters Mukoyi was now happy with the accommodation he had got but he was not happy and excited with his work as a Pastor. The work was frustrating for him. I continued to work at the Christian Bookshop as a Manager with good accommodation and a good job as a manager. With my friend Letters, it became more difficult to keep up with the Pastoral work and he decided to call it quits and reconnected with Murray in the Correspondence Bible College in Bulawayo. It was painful to see him submitting his resignation letter to the United Baptist Church district committee. It became clear that my friend was going back to Bulawayo. Before he left, we made a vow that whoever was going to wed first, one would be the best man at the wedding. I felt for him but I was now happy in the bookshop as things were becoming better and better although the church was planning to close two of the bookshops, Christian Bookshop which I was managing and Zvokupona Bookshop in Chimanimani. The third Bookshop, Tsovane Bookshop in Chiredzi, was the only one to remain open.

Letters Mukoyi's departure from Mutare left a void in my life and I heart because Letters was a really good and close friend of mine. I also decided to leave so I applied for a job in South Africa in 1992 at Mayeno Mission in Dundee, KwaZulu Natalie. Surprisingly, they invited me for an interview. I accepted the invitation and got prepared to travel to South Africa. I went through Bulawayo to attend the wedding of my friend, Christopher Nxumalo and Joyce. It was a wonderful wedding which I enjoyed. The wedding was on Saturday. I went to sleep at home at Pumula North where my mother lived and some of my siblings. On Monday morning, I went to City Hall to board a mini-bus to Johannesburg, South Africa. The trip took almost a day to Johannesburg and I arrived at 6:00 pm. The buses, trains, and mini-buses to Dundee, KwaZulu Natal were all gone by the time I arrived. There was still apartheid in South Africa in 1992. As I was walking up and down with my bags, asking for the transport to Dundee, KwaZulu Natal. While I was walking towards another bus station, the fire-works blew up in front of me and I fell head-long and I got scared to death thinking that it was the shooting. I prayed for my safety and people around me burst in laughter, laughing at me the way I fell. I stood up and continued heading to the bus station. There was one mini-bus going to Dundee, KwaZulu Natal which was the last by chance not as scheduled and I managed to get a seat. I left Johannesburg at around 7:00 pm and we arrived in Dundee, KwaZulu Natal at around 2:00 pm or 3:00 pm. I did not know where the Mayeno Mission was and I asked the driver to take me to the place. He said that he did not know where the place was and I was the only one left in the mini-van. He drove with his conductor round and round looking for the place because they did not want to leave stranded. They were very friendly indeed, however, they lost patience and told me that they had no choice but to dump me anywhere because they wanted to go to their homes. It was already late for them too and I understood.

I was now in the position of Jonah to be thrown out of the boat on my own peril. I agreed to be dumped anywhere. They left me standing in the middle of nowhere. I stood there for a while on the side road not knowing what to do. I said a prayer to the Lord to help me. I was scared of the thugs around who might have robbed me and harmed me. God is so good. I just walked a few meters, and I saw a sign written Mayeno Mission. What? The min-van left me just near that Mayeno Mission without realizing. God is wonderful and amazing. I got to the gate and knocked but a white guard scolded me and told me to get out of the place. He was thinking I was a homeless man trying to disturb his night. I told him that I had come for an interview but he could not believe me. So, I decided to sleep there at the gate because it was a few hours before dawn. I slept at the gate without a blanket and it was very cold. When the sun rose, I knocked on the gate again and the white guard came to the gate and asked me what I had wanted. I told him the same thing that I had come for an interview. He let me in and took me to the waiting room. When the President of the Mayeno Mission heard that I was banished by the guard at night, he sincerely apologized and took me to his office and then took me to the guest house that was prepared for me. The guest house had a kitchen and I made my own breakfast, took a warm shower and slept for at least three hours before the Manager came to knock and welcomed me and took me and showed me the campus. I was introduced to the staff and he showed the whole campus. I was not interviewed that day but I was shown almost everything and shared with me how the Mission was started, what it stood for and its purpose. They oriented me before they interviewed me. It was an awesome experience. It was as if I had got the job already the way they treated me. The Mayeno Mission was all whites. I was being interviewed to take the position to teach evangelism and community interventions for the black community. They needed a black mission liaison person to connect with the black community and the mission.

After the orientation and information about the Mayeno Mission, they scheduled me the following day at 10:00 am for an interview. The guest house was so spacious and stocked it with all kinds of food. They told me that I would have lunch and dinner with each member of staff, rotating their homes for the whole week. I ate my lunch and dinner with various staff every day. They had planned to treat me like a king at their homes. It was an incredible courtesy to be hosted in their homes for the lunches and dinners. It was really an honor and I thoroughly enjoyed every day. The interview started and it was about my Christian life, experience, my views of apartheid and my response to white dominance in South Africa. The breaking point question was what would be my recommendation to give to white men living in apartheid South Africa. My answer was simply, that as Christians, they should do what Christ expected them to do and that they should love every human being as Christ would love everyone, regardless of their race, personality, background or ethnicity. They were very impressed with my reference to Christ and the challenge to act justly, love mercy and to walk humbly with God. I quoted this incredible verse, "To act justly, and to love mercy and to walk humbly before your God," (Micah 6:8, NKJV). They told me that I had passed the interview and I was now a full-time staff member. They told me that they would help me with the work visa and everything needed.

It was a great honor to be part of the Mayeno Mission and I was thrilled to work with them. I had to go back to Zimbabwe and to pack and get ready to return soon to Mayeno Mission. I thanked them and appreciated everything that they had done for me and they told me that they wished they had told me to come prepared to stay and start work only that they wanted to see me first and approve of me. They really loved me and they wanted to help me in everything they could. Their hospitality and kindness really warmed my heart even though apartheid was at its highest peak, but I was treated like a king by those white people at Mayeno Mission. On Friday, one of the staff invited me to sleep at their house so that they would drive me back to Johannesburg the following morning. The following day, they drove me back to Johannesburg. They left me at the minivans station to board and travel back to Zimbabwe. What an experience! I travelled back to Zimbabwe, hoping to come back and join the Mayeno Mission. When I got back home, I told the National Committee that I got a job in South Africa to work at a Mission. The National Committee selected Rev. Alfred Simango and Mr. Muchayi and the other two members talked to me and persuaded me not to go with the specified reasons and that I was being asked to start Pastoring work in Mutare District. I was actually torn in between. Mukoyi the District Pastor had quitted the job and went to Bulawayo and I was then asked to take over from him to Pastor four churches. The Mayeno Mission followed up on me to check to see that I was coming because they were excited to have me while here at home a need had risen to take a Pastoral position. Finally, I decided to take the Pastoring position in Mutare District to Pastor the four churches and as there was a great need because Mutare district would remain without a Pastor. It was with a heavy heart to tell the Mayeno Mission that I was no longer coming. They were really disappointed and they wished that they had not let me go. It was a bittersweet to disappoint them. The position was open, a new Pastoral position as the United Baptist Church Mutare District Superintendent, Pastoring the four churches, Mutare City, Sakubva, Dangamvura and Chikanga on January 1, 1993.

Meanwhile, I enrolled at Mutare Polytechnic College studying Diploma in Business Studies and Accounting while I was working to enhance my business expertise. Education was part of my life and still my focus. The Mutare district requested the Head Office to find a Pastor for them. The National Committee recommended that I should take the position to be a Pastor in UBC Mutare District. I did not hesitate because I had fallen in love with Mutare UBC district and they loved me too. The Head Office advised me that Christian Bookshop was to be closed with Zvokupona Bookshop in Chimanimani. They advised me to wrap up all the accounts, sell the furniture and all that was in it and pay all debts owed by Christian Bookshop. I sold most of the things and I gave away some of the furniture, books, fans and other items to the two churches, Sakubva UBC and Dangamvura UBC. Chikanga UBC and City UBC had not been built yet. I accepted the call and I became the Mutare District Pastor/Superintendent. I was a Pastor of Sakubva UBC, Dangamvura UBC, City UBC, Chikanga UBC and some preaching points such as Burma Valley UBC, Zimunya UBC, and Odzi UBC which we started with my youths of the district. The ironic part of it was that I did not know the local language, ChiNdau, a dialect of Shona language. As a Ndebele, born in Bulawayo in Matabeleland North, I did know how to speak ChiNdau and Shona for that matter. Fortunately, ChiNdau has several Ndebele/Zulu words even though some of the names of people are similar to those of the Ndebele Tribe, the language was different. Actually, history tells us that when Sotshangane escaped Tshaka Zulu's amalgamation of his

Zulu kingdom, Sotshangane passed through the eastern border of Zimbabwe and Mozambique. As he was moving, he left some of his people in Chipinge and part of Rusitu valley. I was able to hear and talk a little as time progressed. The congregates were so friendly to me, loving and caring and the language barrier did not dampen the spirits between us. They enjoyed my broken ChiNdau when I was preaching but most of the time, I used to preach and teach in English with someone translating for me.

Mutare UBC district was full of life. I used to live in Greenside and the UBC City was in town, northeast of the city. This was the church I was a member of although I Pastored three more churches including the preaching points. UBC City was composed of a few older and young people, basically their children. The notable leaders and elders of UBC City Church were Mr. Matyanga, Mr. Piteri, Mr. Mutisi Maga, Mr. O. Charlie, Mr. Machekano, Mr. Bonnie, Mr. Masango, Mr. Chisoro, Mr. Teyiwa, Mr. Beta. Their wives played a pivotal role in Ruiyano UBC City, the likes of Mrs. Piteri, Mrs. Matanga, Mrs. Charlie, Mrs. Bonnie, Mrs. Matyanga, Mrs. Kombo, Mrs. Machekano, Mrs. Masango, Mrs. Teyiwa, Mrs. Chisoro and others. The active youths were Faith Kombo, Thandiwe Matyanga, Aletta Matanga, Joe Matyanga, Alick Matanga, Florence Beta, Faith Beta, Patricia Beta, Charles Kombo, Janice Masango, Shamiso Beta, Sanford Ndongwe, Caroline Piteri, Surprise Piteri. UBC City had a preaching point in Imbeza and Teyiwa was the chairman of the church. I used to go and preach at least once a month and conducted the evangelism outreach in the community. It did not grow because it was in a forest farm however, Mr. Teyiwa led the church very well for a long time and it was a promising church. In the UBC City, we needed a church stand and approached the Mutare City Council to apply for the stand. They told me to find a place where we wanted to build the church. I scouted the place and identified a suitable place near where we were renting a school building and submitted the application with the location and the street. The church stand was granted where it is today, years later in the place I identified but my predecessor, Rev. E. Pambuka, pursued to secure the stand with the elders of the church years later.

I was Pastoring the second church, Chikanga UBC and it was still a preaching point but it was growing momentarily. The early leaders of the church were Mr. Dube, Mr. Kurwaisimba, Mr. Kuyendepi and another Dube who died who was married to Mrs. Mhlanga, who I called my sister, and others who were living in Chikanga and Chikanga UBC was a preaching point of Sakubva UBC. As a Pastor, the Pastor, I was responsible to visit, encourage, organize prayers, and the meetings. However, Chikanga's umbilical cord was connected to Sakubva UBC as the mother church. Every activity, event and tithes were moderated by Sakubva UBC leadership and the church was not autonomous during my time. As UBC Mutare district, we continued to plan for Chikanga UBC to have its own stand. I approached the City Council for a church stand application and they told me the same thing as I was applying for the UBC City stand. They told me to identify a location where we would like to build the church. The best position I identified was where the Chikanga UBC stand is located today. The reason why I chose the location was that it is more accessible to the roads and it is central to Westlea suburb and Yeoville suburb. It was a strategic place where residents of Chikanga, Westlea and Yeoville UBC members could gather at a central place. After edifying the location, I submitted my findings and the church stand application near the clinic and the primary school. My processor, Rev. E. Pambuka with the leadership of church followed up years later and they were granted the stand at the very spot I had identified.

I was also a Pastor for Sakubva UBC, the oldest church in Mutare City to be built. It was Sakubva UBC that gave birth to all the churches in Mutare. The notable leaders and elders of the church were Mr. E. Myambo, Mr. Manase, Mr. Kuyendepi, Mr. Dube, Mr. Khanda senior, Mr. Kurwaisimba, Mr. Masingita, Alex Chitaka, Mr. Mutisi and others. Ruiyano UBC was strategically positioned in Sakubva to even lead the Ruyano UBC district. The notable Ruyano were Mrs. Myambo, Mrs. Manase, Mrs. Kurwaisimba, Mrs. Kuyendepi, Mrs. Chitaka, Mrs. Dube, Mrs. Khanda sir, Mrs. Khanda junior, Mrs. Masingita, Mrs. Mutisi, Mrs. Khanda junior, Mrs. Kombo, Mbuya Myambo and others. The active youths were David Dozwa, Embedzai Moyo,

Rudo Mukwambo, Rachel Myambo, Dalend Chikukwa, Margaret Kurwaisimba, Ashie Dozwa, Eddie Kurwaisimba, cliff Siyekhaya Mutisi, Teramai Makumbe, Ruth, Teressa Makumbe, Norma Mujati, Silindiwe Mutisi, Silindiwe Mabvisa, Shorai Mabviza, Karen, Vickie Masingita, Stella, Carol Hogo, Christine Mathende, Todlana, Priscilla Hogo and many others. These youths were my powerful engines in my ministry in Mutare on evangelism outreach and other programs and we took Mutare District by storm. The preaching point of Sakubva UBC was Burma Valley in the eastern part of Mutare about 40-50 km away. The youth choir was spectacular and the envy of many.

I was also Pastoring Dangamvura UBC, south west of Mutare City. The church was vibrant and full of youths and young adults. Notable leaders and elders of the church were Mr. Cephas Ngarivhume, Mr. Shumba, Mr. Mubare, Mr. Rusinga, Mr. Funani, Mr. Mutakura, Mr. Manzou, Mr. Tiengani, Mr. Masibera, Alick Murombo, Rev. G. Myambo, Mr. Saurombe, Mr. Gwasira, Mr. Mushanguri, Mr. Chikavhanga, Chaplain Njobo, Mr. Matenga and many others. Ruiyano at Dangamvura UBC who were actively involved were Mrs. Ngarivhume, Mrs. Saurombe, Mrs. Chikavanga, Mrs. Shumba, Mrs. Njobo, Mrs. Murombo, Mrs. Mutakura, Mrs. Mubare, Mrs. Rusinga, Mrs. Masibera, Mrs. Tiengani, Mrs. Gwasira, Mrs. Gwasira, Mrs. Rusinga, Mrs. G. Myambo, Mr. Matenga and others.

Dangamvura UBC youths were great singers such as the Sakubva UBC youths' choirs. They were always competing in the annual Youth Conference Contests. They used to alternate annually in winning the contests and the rewards at Youth Conferences at Biriri Mission. The youths that were active were people like Miriam Manzou, Nyasha Manzou, Ms. Chakavanga the Choir Master, Linda Gwasira, Abigail Tiengane, Patience Myambo, Tariro Myambo, Vision Myambo, Phillip Myambo, Blessing Njobo, Sanangurai Madenga, and others.

In 1993-1994, it was the climax of my ministry in Mutare UBC district. We started Odzi UBC and it was later organized into an organized church. I organized thirty couples' mass weddings for those who were married but had not officially wedded in the church in the holy matrimony. The counseling took some months to complete.

It became the biggest occasion in Mutare. I had to call Dr. Bishop J. Dhube from Harare to officiate the weddings. The ZBC media requested to come and cover the event but the UBC district committee denied, fearing that the mass wedding would be politicized and bring disrepute to the church. The massive wedding was conducted very well without incidents. I was single by that time. I was assisted by Rev. Guest Myambo to counsel the couples and he was in the Film Ministry but had been a resident in Mutare for some years and he had been a Pastor of the Mutare UBC district some years back. He knew the homes and the members of the church. He was a great help in my ministry in Mutare. We became a very close friend of mine and we worked together. He introduced me to many homes and to the members of the church and he interpreted for me as I did not know the local language. Rev. Guest Myambo was a very humble, loving and caring Pastor. God placed Rev. Guest Myambo as an assert in my ministry in Mutare. I was the District Pastor yet Rev. G. Myambo was always with me to show me the way and how the ministry was done. He had a loving wife, Mrs. G. Myambo with their five loving and humble children, Patience, Faith, Tariro, Phillip and Vision. I owe him everything! I would organize evangelism outreach and he would go with me and the youth district which was a vibrant force. He would supply me the films and projectors to show during evangelism outreach and most of the time he would go with me to show the films during evangelism outreach.

I had to train and coach some of the youth members to shoot the films. One notable young man who showed the passion for evangelism and pastoral gifts was David Dozwa. He is now a Pastor in the UK with his wife, Rudo Mukwambo Dozwa. We travelled to several preaching points for evangelism outreaches, especially with Sakubva UBC youths and Dangamvura UBC youths. We would plan and give the local people 3 months' notice that we would come and share the gospel with the local people. I would go first and talk to the local leadership ahead of time to seek permission. If the community leaders agreed, there were very few instances where they denied our requests, I would tell them the dates we would come. Our strategy was that we would go to the place where we would identify in our feasibility research to the unreached areas and we would arrive on a Saturday afternoon and spend the afternoon evangelizing the area and inviting all the people including the new converts for a Christian film show in the evening. Film shows were very appealing to the local communal areas. Many people would come and we would show the Christian films and then at the end of the film show, I would make some final remarks, explaining who Jesus Christ is, why he was incarnated and the reason why he rose from the dead on the third day and citing some evangelistic scriptures. The emphasis would be sin, what sin is and why we need a Savior (John 3:16, NIV), Grace, that grace unmerited favor and that it is the gift of God (Eph. 2:8, NIV). I would explain to them what justification means i.e., it is God declaring someone righteous as if he/she had not sinned (I John 1:8-9, NIV), and what salvation means to those who would have confessed with their mouths and believed in their hearts that Jesus is Lord who died and rose from the dead on the third day, (Rom. 10:9, NIV). It was soothing and thrilling to see multitude of people responding to the gospel and the outer call to give their lives to Jesus.

The places we used to have evangelism outreach were Imbeza, Odzi and Burma Valley. One incident caught the eyes of many youths about the belief and reality that we are not fighting against the flesh and blood but against principalities, against dark forces in the heavenly places, as Apostle Paul alludes in (Eph. 6:12, NIV). During the outer call, many people came forward with their charms, talisman, ritual cloths and ornaments as they wanted to trust in Jesus alone and surrender what they used to believe in. It was a scary service as many local people went home to collect their secret ornaments, charms dedicated to the devil. They threw their items in the front and the heap grew up slowly until it was huge. One woman came to me to hand over something in her hand, a charm. She said that the charm was for her luck and protecting her life and she had depended on it for many years but she wanted to depend on Christ alone. I took it in my hand and I remember, it was dark with some few lambs around. When I stretched my hand toward her to receive the charm, the charm was breathing. It was wrapped in cloth, black and greasy cloth and breathing as if it had a heart-beat. I held it in my hands while I was leading people to dedicate their lives to Jesus. After praying with the people, and ending the service, I took some of the few youths outside the building to a youth advisor Mr. E. Myambo, who was also one of the prominent elders of Sakubva UBC. We made some fire to burn the charms, the ornaments, the clothes dedicated to ancestral spirits and also the charm that the woman had given me and placed on the hand.

As I was about to throw the charm from my hand into the fire, Mr. E. Myambo advised me that I should not burn it, instead we should dig a hole and bury it. He told me about an incident that was experienced by another Pastor who burnt such kinds of stuff, the ornaments and the charms in which the flames of fire lept on his body and burnt him entirely. So, he feared for me and he wanted to protect me from any dangers. He was genuine however, I believed God would protect me from such kinds of incidents. I threw the breathing charm into the fire too and everything was burnt to ashes. After discipling the woman with others, I baptized her in Sakubva UBC together with others who had confessed Jesus as Lord and Savior. Christ's name was exalted in Burma Valley UBC preaching point. We used to organize many evangelistic outreaches in Burma Valley. We would play soccer with the local teams with our aim of witnessing them during the games and inviting them to the evening programs in their places of gathering. The Lord was with us and He gave us the passion to witness for Him. The youths were the vehicle in which my ministry in Mutare district flourished. I connected well with the youth because I was a youth too although I was a Pastor. I also connected well with all the members of the four churches as I was Pastoring regardless of age.

The ministry was becoming overwhelming and I was also facing challenges of transportation. I would preach once a month in the local churches, but during the week, I would dedicate one week in one area, one week in UBC City, another week in Chikanga UBC, another week in Sakubva UBC and another week in Dangamvura UBC. The main work during the week was the visits to members of the churches in their homes. The church members valued house visitation to their homes as the best. I would visit them in their homes, to pray with them, to encourage them and also, I visited those who were sick or bereaved. Rev. Guest Myambo used to go with me during visits to the church members' homes. He played an incredible role as I was still single. The income was not enough even though I was Pastoring four churches with three preaching points. I discovered that my shoes were developing holes under the shoe soles because of walking up and down in home visitations. I would put some small cardboard boxes in my shoes to prevent the dust from coming in my feet but when it rained, the cardboard boxes in my shoes would get wet and all my socks. I did not ask my members to help in any way because the members of the church did not call me but I decided to go back to God, who called me in the ministry. I had another blind prayer and blind faith to my God, my Father and I told Him about my plight. I took my shoes with the holes and laid them on the floor, facing the heavens. I prayed to God and asked Him why He was allowing such things to happen to me when I was serving Him earnestly. I asked God to intervene in my situation and to do something. I did not ask any specific request but I asked Him to provide something for me to serve Him with a happy smile.

Within a week, the Head Office called me to come and get a motorbike that was assigned to me from the Mine Ministry. Rev. Beckett had sourced the motorbike because I was also ministering in mines sponsored by the International Mine Ministry (IMM). When I received the call from Rev. Beckett, my heart warmed and I knelt right away to thank God for His faithfulness and the answered prayer. My gratitude to God was unending. I boarded a bus to Harare the following day to get my brand-new motorbike with plastic. I appreciated and thanked God on the way to Harare for what He had done for me. I also thanked Rev. Beckett for proving the motorbike for me. I had already got my driver's license. I had a joyful ride on my motorbike back to Mutare. My transportation was resolved by God after an earnest prayer. My home visitations to the church members were made easier now that I was using the motorbike. Rev. G. Myambo had a motorbike too which was for the Film Ministry. We used to ride our motorbikes together going to the mines as far as Nyanga, Odzi, Imbeza, Burma

Valley and other various places to visit our members and to witness for Christ and to expand UBC to all the corners of Mutare and outside Mutare.

There was something else which was itching in my heart, that was about my future family. I thought of getting married but I needed a suitable partner who would complement my ministry and as a life partner. Although many friends, my family and church members urged me to marry. Although many people advised me to find a lady to marry, the final decision rested entirely upon me to take action. I also felt a need to find a life partner. There were so many beautiful ladies in my four churches but I had to pray and seek God's guidance and His will in this new adventure which I was about to take. There were so many voices in the air, advising, recommending and of course, praying for their single Pastor. It was one morning during my devotions as I was reading the book of (John 15:7, NIV) that I came across that it caught my attention, verse 7. It read, "If you remain in me and my words remain you, ask whatever you wish, and it will be given to you," (John 15:7, NIV). I jumped out of my bed and wondered what it meant. I took it literally and the words sank into my core. God is our Father and my real Father. I take God's words literally, sometimes, I don't usually interpret verses by my own thinking or my own understanding but I take them as if God speaks to me audibly. What I have discovered in my Christian walk is that every Christian's relationship with God differs in some degrees and levels. No one should judge how one should speak with or to God, the Father and Christ. The way one relates to God is different from one another. How close one is to God has nothing to do with anyone's relationship with God. My upcoming book entitled, "The Heathen Church" discusses and attempts to answer that plethora of conceptions. I am saying this to demystify such thinking as I narrate what and how it happened with me. When I read (John 15:7, NIV), I said to God that I was going to write all the qualities, the character, the type of a wife I wish to marry. I wrote ten qualities of the wife I would desire to marry. I wrote down first, the tribe, the stature, the height, the complexion, the character, good health, a committed Christian, her past experience, a good cook and the mother of my children. I wrote as specific as I wished and I stuck it on my bedroom wall. Daily, I would pray for my wife stuck on the wall I had desired to have.

One day, I told my friends whom I was with that I had found a wife whom I was going to marry. They were David Dozwa, Archie Dozwa, Musa, and Ngwena. My friends couldn't believe it, and they enquired what I meant in astonishment and perplexed. I called them to my bedroom and when they entered my bedroom, they were very alert, thinking that they would find a girl but I showed them the ten qualities of a wife I desired and she was stuck on the wall. They all exclaimed that she was very beautiful after reading the ten points. I continued to pray faithfully and hoped that one day, God would provide me with my life partner at the proper time.

At Mutare Pastors' Fraternal, we organized a crusade for the whole city to evangelize the city and we invited a guest speaker, Christopher Alams, from the Middle East. The crusade was for a week, from Monday to Saturday. We put together the teams from various churches and trained them to counsel and how we would allocate the new converts to various churches that were Bible believing churches. We decided to distribute the new converts, equally according to where they lived for easy access to local churches. The counseling team was responsible for registration of new converts, allocation and to pray with them. Mutare Pastor's Fraternal was composed of various Pastors and Pastor Victor Manhanga was the chairman of the Pastors' Fraternal. The Scripture Union was also very involved with the Scripture Union Director Pastor Napoleon Gomo and Pastor Ronny. The Pastors were responsible to pray for the new converts, leading them to the new churches, and counseling them. They were also responsible for leading worship, putting things in order. The members of the churches were actively involved and my youths from the four United Baptist Churches were actively involved. The crusade was held at Sakubva Stadium, from 5:00 pm to 9:00 pm from Monday to Saturday.

It was on a Thursday in the middle of putting things together for the crusade when one of my youths came with her cousin-sister who had visited them. Her name was Margarete Kurwaisimba, a very devoted and active youth at Sakubva UBC. She introduced me to her cousin-sister, Judith Kurwaisimba. She was a beautiful girl, innocent and kind. I was very impressed by her looks, smile, kindness and her positive attitude towards me. I asked myself, could she be single, without a boyfriend, such a beautiful lady? But I quickly came to my own conclusion that she can't be single because she was too beautiful to be single, I thought. Well, she was still very young, about 20 years old and not ready for marriage, I concluded. I never compared her with the one stuck on the wall of my bedroom which I have been praying for. As time progressed, some who were similar to the one on the paper stuck in the bedroom came in and out and I eliminated them one by one because they wanted to confuse me. They were not matching with the ten points I stuck on the wall. An advice, don't be trapped with what you don't desire. This is the most crucial time for a young man or a young woman who wants to get married to the right person. Don't rush to get someone who comes on the way but be prayerful, be patient and stick to your principles and God's standard. Remember, you are choosing a life partner and if you miss the target, you regret for the rest of your life. Some people got married because of a mistake, or by sympathy, or by coercion, or by manipulation. These types of marriages usually end in separations or divorces. You have to marry someone whom you love dearly, knowing that you will spend the rest of your lives together and in eternity together.

Margaret Kurwaisimba used to live in Sakubva near one of the churches I was Pastoring. Whenever I met her, I would ask Judith how she was doing. Judith had completed her school but still she was living at home in Chimanimani and doing her temporary teaching at Mutambara Mission School. Margaret realized that I might have been interested in Judith and she told her also that I was always asking her. The United Baptist Church used to have Youth Conferences and continues the tradition even today in April of every year. All Pastors are required to attend those Youth Conferences annually, to support and to teach and to preach to the youths. I was in the Youth Conference in April 1993, and the Chimanimani United Baptist Church Youth was their turn to serve Pastor's lunch. Judith came to serve my table and brought the plate to me. I was happy to see her and her smile melted me. I saw her again between the services and different sessions.

The Guest Speaker for the Youth Conference was Rev. Chigumira, a United Methodist Minister, who was preaching about living in purity, with holiness, and righteousness in honor of God. He told the youths that no matter how beautiful you may be, one had to guard herself/ himself from being loose and getting involved in bad behaviors. He looked into the crowd for someone who was beautiful to give illustration. He moved around in the crowd of hundreds of the youth packed in a hall. He picked Judith in the crowd and brought her on the platform, presenting her as a good example of a beautiful girl who should refrain from doing bad things because she was beautiful. He said that to be beautiful does not give that person a license to be loose but that the girls should be proud of themselves and pray always to please God, not to please people. That was really a confirmation to me that Judith was really beautiful. When the Youth Conference ended, we all parted ways going to our respective areas. Within two weeks, I received a letter from Judith although at first it got lost to our neighbor, a church member. Our friendship began slowly and I asked her to pray for me for my life partner. She agreed and we continued to pray for each other for some time. As I continued to pray and seek God's will and guidance, one morning I went back to the paper which was stuck on the wall with the ten points for a life partner I had desired and I had been praying for. When I read it closely, I realized that Judith was tallying with the ten points that I had written and it dawned to me that, "Yes" Judith was befitting the qualities I was looking for. However, she had become my prayer partner and a friend and to disclose to her that I wanted to propose to her, it was very difficult. However, with a push in my heart, I finally replied to her a letter which she had written to me and it was just a general letter saying that it was good to have met and chatted with each other at the Youth Conference. I had to tell her that I was in love with her and that she was the one I had been praying for. Her response was "no" and she told me that we were just friends and prayer partners. She also told me that she did not want to be married to a Pastor because the work of a Pastor's wife had a lot of demands. Those were not justifiable reasons to give me. She was testing my seriousness about my proposal as our culture demands for such tests from girls to boys. Those excuses did not deter me from the pursuit of my proposal.

After such a long proposal, she finally told me that she was willing to come to Mutare, where I was, to respond to my proposal, whether positively or negatively. I got excited! She asked me where we could meet. I waited for her at Meikles Park and we walked together to Mutare Museum, the place I knew which was very beautiful with a botanical garden, beautiful flowers, shrubs, with indigenous and exotic birds which were flying freely in the open cage that was a wide and long canopy. It was just a beautiful place to be and I had pre-planned it. We walked to the museum, my heart pumping and in great anticipation of good news. We sat at the back of the museum where there were flowers and birds, flying above us, swooping in from different angles as if we were on plane show, with different planes zooming in the sky. But the sound of the birds' wings flipping and whistling was sensational, punctuated by the smell of the beautiful flowers around us. For a moment, I thought I was in paradise and in eternity, with human imagination but only to be reminded that I was still on earth, in juxtapose with the ones I can spend my life with and eternity. After about thirty minutes of a general talk, there was silence between us, no talking but both of our minds were wrestling to ponder on whether that was the moment to tie our hearts together forever or it was the breaking of the hearts. With a deep sigh and a sincere look, I turned to Judith, face to face, eyeball to eyeball and asked her what she thought about my proposal to marry me.

Slowly, Judith stood up, walked away from me, clutched her hands and arms like in a motherly fear, looked up in the sky, stood still, and looked at the birds racing above her head. I did not move, I remained seated, breathless and knowing that it was a breaking point. I was sweating, my heart pouncing and praying that it was the time. My eyes never left her, I was still looking at her with admiration and in awe of God's creation. Slowly, Judith turned around and came slowly towards me, still her hands and arms clutch like in a motherly fear, stood before me and shot her eyes directly into my eyes and said, "Sam, I have been praying and thinking about your proposal. I am now convinced that God has spoken. You will be the father of my children!" I jumped and embraced her in my arms and we stood there for a moment in silence and our hearts were uniting and making a covenant. That was the best moment of my life to have a life partner, a soulmate, the mother of my children and a friend. I was so glad that Judith had accepted me as her husband to be, the father of her children. When you find what you need and what you want, you don't wait but you move to the next stage.

In August of 1994, we got engaged and it was administered by Rev. Guest Myambo, my friend. In August of 1994, I paid dowry (lobolo) and her parents allowed us to go ahead and prepare for the wedding. We scheduled our wedding on December 10, 1994. The preparation of the wedding was crazy but all the four United Baptist Churches in Mutare district were actively involved in the wedding preparations. The Mutare UBC District organized and tasked each church to play its part, including Men's Fellowship, Women's Fellowship and the Youth Groups. It was so pleasant to see the four churches working together for their Pastor. Mr. Jose Masango bought the three-layer cake and soft drinks, Michael Myambo bought 50 kg bag of rice, Mr. Mubare was a camera-man, Mrs. Eve Piteri prepared the high table, Mrs. Hannah Charlie provided the gown, my father-in-law and mother-in-law Noel and Noriah Kurwaisimba supplied a beast and a bus to ferry the relatives from Rusitu and Chimanimani. All the members of the four churches contributed immensely and everything was coming together very well. The Dangamvura Youth Choir sang and Sakubva Youths organized all the logistics with the elders. It was so exciting to see everyone participating in our wedding.

One week before the wedding, men and the youth organized a Bachelor's party at my house. They organized it on a Sunday knowing that I would not be home. That very Sunday, I was preaching at Dangamvura United Baptist Church as I used to rotate to preach on the four churches. After service, Mr. and Mrs. Ngarivhume invited me to their home for lunch. They served me a good lunch and entertained me that Sunday afternoon. Meanwhile, Mr. Ngarivhume was communicating with the elders and the youths at home who were grilling and preparing food. I did not have any idea what was happening or to think that they were preparing for a surprise Bachelor's party. I tried to tell Mr. Ngarivhume that I was about to depart. He had advised me to leave my motor-bike at his home and that he would drive me home that day. I was amazed by the kind gesture that he was offering me and I felt so special that day. They kept me in their home until around 6:00 pm and then Mr. Ngarivhume took me home with his car. He had communicated with the men to check if they were ready for me. When we arrived, there were no cars parked outside my house and around to eliminate suspicion. All the lights were switched off and when we entered, they suddenly switched on the lights and shouted at once, "Bachelor's Party Brother Sam!" I was shocked and mesmerized to see men who filled my house in that manner without my knowledge. The party began. They were all laughing and lifted me up in the air, tossing me around. That was the most fun day of my life, ever. We all celebrated, speech after speech, food was plenty and we all enjoyed it to the full. It was an awesome experience and the best Bachelor's party I have ever been to.

When the day of the wedding came, it was as if the whole of Mutare had converged at our wedding. We rented the Mutare Anglican Church in Mutare City, on December 10, 1994, from 9:00 am to 5:00 pm. The ceremony and reception were conducted at the same venue with the Anglican church on one side and the church hall on the other side. My relatives and friends came from Bulawayo. The bridesmaids were six and six males. My best-man was Letters Mukoyi, a great friend from Theological College of Zimbabwe whom we had agreed that the first one to wed, the other one would be the best-man. Judith's best-lady was her cousin-sister, Margaret who had introduced me to her. Our Marriage Officer was Dr. Bishop Joshua Dhube who was the Church Chairman of United Baptist Church. My mother, Josephine and my brothers, Alexander, Zenzo, and my sisters, Gladys, Mavis, Senzeni, Sithabile, Daisy, Lilian, aunt Agnes, the nieces, Cynthia Hlongwane and Petronella Ndlovu, nephews Manndlenkosi Maseko and Nqobile

Phumuzile Dube, uncles, Jonas Dzonzi, extended families, friends, classmates from Theological of College of Zimbabwe and some of me of Professors Jenny Smith and Joan Sanderson a Theological College of Zimbabwe Librarian, came to witness our wedding. The church was packed with people from Judith's relatives from Chimanimani, Rusitu, Nyanyadzi. Mutare United Baptist Church District and local churches filled the beautiful Anglican Church. The district chairman was Mr. Mutisi. Mr. Cephas Ngarivhume was the Master of ceremony for our wedding.

After the ceremony, we went to Mutare Park, adjacent to Meikles Park to take wedding photos. The wedding went very well and the food was well served and people ate to the full and people had a good time. After the wedding, people went back to their various places. We went home and Judith's aunts had to fulfill their traditional and customary rites. We stayed two more days before we went for our honeymoon at LaRochelle hotel. After two days of making sure that people had left their homes and that all was cleared, everything clean and in order, my neighbor and my friend, Machina, drove us to LaRochelle hotel, about 25 km away. On our honeymoon, that's when we talked and planned our lives, the number of children we wanted to have, where we wanted to live and many future plans, including furthering our education and carriers. We spent a week on our honeymoon and it was really rewarding, indeed. We rested, bonded, had intimacy, prayed together, cried together, and comforted each other. At the end of the honeymoon, we were ready to adventure and to implement what we had planned.

In January, 1995, my wife, Judith, was admitted at Mutare Teachers College to train as a teacher. She commuted from home every day while we lived at Greenside. I used to go in the morning to drop her on my motorbike and to pick her up after her school in the afternoon. I continued to Pastor the four churches, Mutare City UBC, Chikanga UBC, Sakubva UBC, and Dangamvura UBC and the Preaching Points, small churches, which were Imbeza UBC, Burma Valley UBC, and Odzi UBC. I had also been admitted to Africa University to study Bachelor of Theology (M. Div. USA) and Education, specializing in History and

Music. I started in August 1995 and it was a four-year program. Both of us were to go to school. After two months of marriage, I gave Mutare District UBC a six months' notice of my study leave as I was going for further studies. The news did not go well with many people because they loved me and I loved them. We had a good bond with the Mutare local churches and the district. Although I enjoyed it and I was living comfortably, I had decided to further my education because I knew that if I was not educated, there was no security to remain in the same position forever. Pastors used to be moved to different churches and places and no one was immune for those transfers and the transfers were not exceptional. One could be transferred to another city, peri-urban or in the rural or country-side of which I was no longer prepared to Pastor in a rural or country setting any more. I had calculated United Baptist Church's policies and I saw how easily one could end up being transferred far away from towns and cities where there is no running water, transportation which would be a nightmare.

Judith and I were on track on our first plan, i.e., to start the journey of education together. I had already attained a three-year Diploma in Theology from Theological College of Zimbabwe and a Certificate in Business Studies from the Commercial College of Zimbabwe and part of Mutare Poly-Technical College. However, it was a new start, a new beginning with my wife. I had applied to two places to further my studies, at Africa University and Beria College in the USA where they had promised me some scholarships. While going through tests of English as a second language, the application fees, F-1 visa application and many requirements, I got so frustrated with the requirements and abandoned the application all together and concentrated on going to Africa University. I loved Africa University so much that I wanted to be part of the University community. My wife had already started her studies at Mutare Teachers' College. She was commuting from home and I was dropping her in the morning and picking her after school, Monday to Friday on my Motorbike. I was still Pastoring, waiting to resume my studies in August, 1995. We had to relocate and find a new house because the five-bedroomed house we were living in was to house the new Pastor who was going to take over from me, Rev. E.

Pambuka and his family. We got a house to rent in Yeoville, from one of our Mutare City UBC members who were now living in Harare, Mr. and Mrs. Chisoro. It was a good transition and by July, 1995, we had moved to a new house.

I started my studies on August 4, 1995, and I was going for boarding because the University gave me a full scholarship for my tuition and boarding and the stipend for living expenses. My wife also got an accommodation at Mutare Teachers' College and she had a government student loan, for her tuition and for her boarding and everything was covered. We were now both living on campuses, meeting home on weekends. We had to find someone to share the house with because we were only home on Fridays to Sundays. This was not cost effective because we were barely at home. It was also becoming more expensive for us to rent a full house. We decided to find two rooms to rent for our furniture in Chikanga and we kept some of our furniture at our friend's house, Napoleon Gomo who was the Director of Scripture Union in Mutare. They were a wonderful couple, indeed. We would meet in Chikanga on weekends and at least, it was cheaper and affordable with the utilities.

I was enjoying my school and the fellowship with students from different African countries and from Europe and America. Africa University was very diverse and rich with various cultures across. We had renowned Professors from around the globe and the Chancellor for the University was Bishop Decavalor from Angola and the Vice Chancellor was Professor John K. Z. Kurewa from Zimbabwe, succeeded by Professor Rukudzo Joseph Murapa from Zimbabwe. The Dean of Theology was Professor David Kekumba Yemba from Democratic Republic of Congo who is now the current African University Chancellor. Some of my Professors were Professor David K. Yemba, Dr. Nhiwatiwa, Dr. Kunonga, Dr. Chikafu, Rev. Kajesi, and others, including Mr. Matsikenyire, the Professor for Music. My classmates included Gift Masengwe, Bridget from Sierra Leone, Atmos Gaye from Liberia, Yolanda, Barnardo, Vivian from Liberia, Sapalo from Angola, Gomez from Mozambique, Michael from Germany, Sandra from USA, Alice, Mafandizo, Sam Dzobo, Munguri, Annie

Grace Chingonzo, Moses Mlato from Mozambique and many others from both Theology and Education Faculties. I was enjoying the good relationship between the university student body and the university faculty, both the Professors, faculty staff and the administration staff, and all other university staff.

I joined the Africa University Choir which was formed by Dr. Matsikenyire and it was mostly composed of those who were doing Music as Major. I was also doing History and Music in the faculty of Education. To join the choir was not easy but it was not difficult either. Many students joined the choir including my friend, Gift Masengwe. The practice was intense and timely. That made a lot of people who were not serious about singing and music fall away as time progressed. Dr. Patrick Matsikenyire informed us that we were going to the USA to sing in the Annual Conference in Colorado, Denver in April 1996. He began to intensify the practice more. Many students tried to join the University Choir when they heard that we were going to the USA in April and we had six months to work and practice harder. Dr. Patrick Matsikenyeri started to scale down to remain the choir members with those he kept those with good voices and who were singing well. He started to test the voices of each choir member by listening and evaluating how one could modulate his/her voice to the required level and to assimilate with other voices of the choir members, eloquently. I was one of the choir members who passed the tests and I was excited to be part of the University Choir going to the USA. One of my best friends, Gift Masengwe did not make it to the selected list.

In April 1996, we headed to Harare Airport with a rented bus and it was as if we were going to paradise with all the excitement. There were about twenty-five University Choir members and Dr. Patrick Matsikenyeri, the Conductor. We boarded Air Zimbabwe to Johannesburg in South Africa. Then from South Africa, we flew to Dakar, Senegal but we did not disembark. It was to refuel and to take a long journey across the ocean to Washington DC and connected to Detroit, Michigan. We were welcomed by the United Methodist members who hosted us and had assigned us to their various homes. Four of us, males only, were hosted by a lovely couple, Michael and

Sarah and they had grown up children who were already having their own families. The choir members were allocated to various families too. It was a marathon tour to churches and to the universities. We were also taken to resort places and the historical museums such as that of the car plant in Detroit and that of the "wire telegraph" with Guglielmo Marconi, an Italian inventor in 1895. We toured six states and ended in Washington D.C. It was an awesome tour and we visited the USA and we made some friends and some connections for our life-time. Most of us, it was our first time to see and test snow and to see a lot of food, clothes and more stuff than in our respective countries. We were overwhelmed by many new things in the USA that we saw and experienced. It was a good experience and we thanked God and Dr. Patrick Matsingenyire and everyone who supported us.

We flew back home with new things such as new clothes, electric gadgets, chocolates, candies for our families and our loved ones. It was an eye opener and a great exposure to see the other parts of the world. It was good to be back home, sweet home in Zimbabwe and to be back at Africa University, a boiling pot, full of vitality and life from the backdrops of African cultures and traditions that clashed many times because of their differences. The university politics, the policies, the programs, the affairs both of the students and the administration gripped me. A number of students became more concerned about the way the university was run and the Vice Chancellor Dr. John Kurewa and his administration. The faculties were also complaining about how things were run. At the same time, they introduced high tuition and boarding fees. All along, we were given full scholarships to cover our tuition, boarding and living expenses. Honey-moon ride of full scholarship was over. They had initially given students full scholarships at the beginning and in the inception of the university when it was opened in the early 1990s, to attract students. When it started, it was free education for all but now the university had started to transition and let the students pay from their own pockets or from their churches. The Zimbabwe government was providing the Vocation Student Loan to students in government Colleges, Polytechnical Colleges and Universities. However, they did not give to students in private Universities. It became very difficult for students to pay for their tuition and the boarding fees, especially the Zimbabweans. The students from other countries did not have any financial constraints compared to their counterparts, the Zimbabweans. The Africa University administration introduced tuition and boarding abruptly without a gradual planning and informing the students. The students were caught by surprise to hear that the tuition and the boarding fees had been hiked.

It was in 1997 and a number of students approached and begged me to run for Student Represent Council (SRC) President. They asked me to contest the position. At first, I was reluctant because I had many fish to fry. After so many calls and persistence to represent the students, I finally agreed. They were four candidates running for the position of SRC Presidents. There was only a week before the elections that I submitted my candidacy. I presented my manifesto to the students and how I would represent them in any way necessary. When other candidates learned that I had submitted my candidacy for SRC President and I was in the race for elections, all except one dropped from running for the position, saying that I was the right candidate and knowing that no one could beat me in the ballots. During the election day, the students had already convinced the other candidates to drop from running. I won the election overwhelmingly and I became the SRC President in 1996 to 1998. I had good rapport and bilateral relationships with the Student Union and the University administration. I was already known by the administration and I enjoyed good respect, including from the University Chancellor, Professor John Kurewa. I had to put together my Student Representative Council. The SRC had an executive committee that was voted in by the Student Union and other various positions. My Vice President was Atmos Gaye from Liberia, the Secretary General was George Okeyo from Kenya, the Financial Controller was Lemi from Zimbabwe, Gift Masengwe was for entertainment and transport from Zimbabwe and we also had many positions filled.

As the Africa University Student Representative Council Executive Committee, we had a lot of tasks to implement during our term to benefit the student union. The first thing we proposed to the Africa University administration was to have a satellite dish for the student body for entertainment. Within a few weeks, we were granted that request and the student body was excited to have a satellite dish for entertainment. The administration met most of our demands for improvements including the cafeteria and the quality of food, clean and improved dormitories and the rules and the regulations in the residences. The biggest challenge was the abrupt introduction and increase of tuition and boarding fees without informing and consulting with the students. They sparked grievances and led to two weeks of student demonstrations against the increase of the fees. We approached the government, Ministry of Education if they could consider granting vocational students' loans to students in private universities. The Minister of Education that time was Dr. Ignatius Chombo and the negotiation resulted in the private universities students being allowed to apply for vocational student loans just like the government Universities. It was a milestone achievement that we achieved. African University was the first private University to be granted that permission followed by Solusi University in the Matabeleland North, southwest of Bulawayo.

Even if the government granted the private universities vocational student loans, to ease financial constraints, the loans were not enough to cover most of the educational costs because the private universities tuition and boarding fees were very high compared to public/government universities. The student union asked the Africa University to lower the increase of the tuition and boarding fees but the AU administration rejected that request which caused the student body to demonstrate so that they could be heard of their plight. As the Student Representative Council President, I organized the student body and told them how we were going to demonstrate and how we were going to conduct ourselves during the demonstrations. We did not anticipate that it would take very long. My Vice President, Atmos Gaye abdicated his position and left for the USA for his studies. It was another blow and he said that he could not continue at Africa University. He was from Liberia and the students from other countries were not affected by the fees increments. Zimbabwe students were the only ones affected hence we demonstrated, demanding that the Africa University administration consider reversing the increment but the administration did not to budge. However, my Secretary General, George Okeyo who was from Kenya, participated fully although he was not affected directly as he had his full scholarship just like his other colleagues from other countries.

I gathered the students at the Student Union Hall and told them the strategies we were going to use which we had planned with my executive on how we were going to conduct the demonstration. However, I warned all students that we were not going to tolerate any violence, the destruction of the university property, harm anyone or say any vulgar words or inappropriate language or behavior to anyone both the students or the staff. I made it very clear that our demonstration was to send a message about our grievances, fees that were beyond our reach. I told the student body that if anyone commits the offenses stipulated above, it would be upon his/her personal responsibility and he/she would meet her own peril on his/her own. Moreover, the Africa University Student Representative Council would not represent any member of the student union who is involved in any form of misconduct and misbehavior of any kind. I had to make all those guidelines to protect the university property, the administration staff and any student who did not want to get involved because of some certain reasons. The demonstration started well at the university campus and to get more attention and sympathizers, we marched to Mutare City and camped at Meikles Park. The whole Mutare community brought lots of food to feed the students at the Meikles Park. I had to talk to the Pastors around the city that I knew and they donated their buildings to accommodate the students. Pastor Ronny, had a church nearby at Meikles Park, the Scripture Union Director, Pastor Napoleon Gomo provided accommodation, food and some space.

The private universities joined our demonstration, demanding that the private universities should be allowed to apply for Vocational Students Loans just like those students who were in government universities. Solusi University in Bulawayo was one of the private universities that joined us. National University of Science and Technology in Bulawayo also joined to support us although it was a government sponsored university. The University of Zimbabwe also joined us in support of our plight. The Student Representative Council President of the University of Zimbabwe, Learnmore Jongwe invited me to come to the university to address the student body in support of our grievances. We became close friends with Learnmore Jongwe and he called the student body to the student union building so that I could address the students and to inform them of the reasons for our demonstrations. I addressed the students and they supported us even financially. I slept in the room of Learnmore Jongwe and he went to sleep with one of his friends, leaving me in his room. He was a warm-hearted young man full of grace and kindness and very smart and intelligent. One of his Secretary General, Fortunate Mnguni and also Job Sakala who were in the Student Representative Council were very supportive and the whole student council. In fact, Job Sakala was sent by Learnmore Jongwe to go to Africa University to address the Africa University Student Body, in solidarity with the University of Zimbabwe student's body.

During that time, the Africa University Board of Directors was having a three days meeting at the Holiday Inn in Mutare City and the Board of Directors were composed of various countries, USA, Africa, and Europe who were Bishops from other conferences, the Chancellor and Vice Chancellors and other administrators. The membership of the Africa University Board of Directors was big, almost one hundred members. I was a member also because of my position as Student Representative Council President. We held the meeting at the Holiday Inn in Mutare City. I told the students that we had an AU Board of Directors meeting and the students marched to Holiday Inn to express their grievances to the Board of Directors at the meeting. I had presented the grievances of the students to the Board and they accepted them and asked Dr. John Kurewa to address the plights of the students. The Board really appreciated my presentation and the fact that the students came to show how desperate they were to be given an audience by the Board. I remember one of the bishops loved my speech so much that he promised me a full scholarship to study in the USA after completing my studies at Africa University. The Board never condemned us as they said our grievances were genuine and legitimate. The Theology Faculty in which I was a student in, never castigated our demonstrations. They were very supportive because they saw and understood what the students were going through. They entered our world with empathy. The administration was obligated to address the issues that we were raising as the university was growing. The Faculty of Theology, Dean, Dr. Yemba was very gracious and a source of encouragement as he constantly said that it was part of leadership skills, I was gaining which I was going to face in the future. He was one of my favorite professors on the campus. After the Africa University Board of Directors ended, the members returned to their respective countries and we had to continue with requesting to meet with the administration to resolve the grievances but the administration was not willing to meet with us and to address our grievances.

We had to find a lawyer/attorney, Brian Kagoro, to represent us and file our case to the High Court in Harare. Four of us, George Okeyo, Lemi, Gift Masengwe and I had to go to Harare to meet with Brian Kagoro to compile and to submit our case to the High Court. We spent the whole night writing, compiling, signing and we submitted the Africa University Student Body case against Africa University in the morning to restate all of us because the University had dismissed all of us as African University students. We won the case and the High Court granted us permission to go back to the university and it ordered the university to consider our grievances. We all celebrated the victory. However, Africa University lawyers/attorneys, Bere Brothers challenged the verdict of our case. They filed against the High Court verdict and they challenged the results, appealing to the Supreme Court. The Supreme Court granted the Africa University Lawyers/ Attorneys, the Bere Brothers, win of the case. The students had already returned to the campus while we were fighting our case in Harare. After the appeal by the Bere Brothers to the Supreme Court and winning the case against us, our Lawyer, Brian Kagoro, advised us to go back to the university because the Supreme Court was the highest Court in the country and we cannot challenge or appeal against their judgement. We had to go back to the university to resume our studies. The media flooded Africa University and I was all in the news as the RSC President. Zimbabwe Broadcast Corporation (ZBC TV), the Herald News Paper, the Chronicle News Paper, the Manica Post, came to interview students and me. I was always on the news, on TV, and in papers. I was like a celebrity for those two weeks on the TV interviews and media papers.

Those who knew me were calling me to check how I was doing from all over, from Bulawayo, Harare, Gweru, Victoria Falls, Mutare and my former classmates. It was a good time to connect with many friends and relatives whom I had not seen for a long time. After some few months, when I was walking in the streets of Bulawayo, I met my Metalwork teacher who used to scold me in the class, discrediting Christians that they were not smart and intelligent. When he met me in the street, he was very shy and embarrassed for what he did to me those days at my High School. He said he was wrong and had learned a lesson that one should not despise anyone in life. He apologized to me, sincerely. He told me that he saw me on TV, read in the Herald News Paper, the Chronicle News Papers and heard my interviews on the radio and he was very surprised to see me being the Student Union President at Africa University. My former teacher learned a big lesson, not to undermine, look down or despise anyone, you never know what he may become. Only God knows. I am glad he acknowledged his mistake and learned from it. He regretted having said those harsh words to me because I was a Christian and he should not have hated me because I was a Christian. It was a persecution that I faced in my Metalwork class.

We went back to the universities and we were all readmitted again one by one and Jim Sally from the USA and he was part of the administration administered the readmission of all the students and there was no one who was dismissed from the University. However, new rules and policies kicked in and the administration started a new era of giving the students partial scholarships and in part, the students had to find their own funds for their education. The three Faculties during that time were Theology, Education and Agriculture. Those in the faculty of Education and Agriculture, were now allowed to apply for Vocational Student Loans from the government just like other students in the government universities. Those who were in Theology, their churches had to pay for them. My church, United Baptist Church could not pay for my fees because it did not have funds. It actually meant that I had to source my own funds if I had to continue with education at Africa University. I applied to all the departmental stores in Mutare. I had to look for a job. It was now 1998 and I was out of school. I had my first son born in 1998 and my wife had graduated from Mutare Teachers' College. I was having a small family now and I had to support them and at the same time, to try to raise funds to finish my degree at Africa University. I had at least one more year to complete my studies. Although my wife graduated in 1998 and she was deployed in Mutsvangwa Secondary School in Chimanimani more than 200 km away, out in the bush, next to the border between Zimbabwe and Mozambique. I was given tuition by Africa University but not the boarding fees and the food in the cafeteria that I had enjoyed for the past three years. Things had changed and money talks.

Now I was living alone and with my wife having been deployed far away from me and she would only come on month-end to collect her paychecks. She would come on Fridays at the end of each month and she would go back to her school on Sundays. It was the policy of the Ministry of Education to deploy new graduated teachers far in the villages because in towns and cities, the positions were reserved for senior teachers who have been in the Education Ministry longer. It was rare for a newly graduated teacher to get a teaching position in towns or cities except through corruption or by luck. It was a big challenge to live separately while married. It was common and not unusual for families to be separated because of jobs. At least my wife had a job and we could pay the rent and I would also pay overheads. We had to find a better accommodation at Hospital Hill, a three-roomed cottage that had a spacious sitting room near the Highway to Africa University for easy access to transportation. When I was in the USA in 1996 when we visited with the Africa University Choir, I had befriended Ernest and his wife who sent me some money. Ernest really helped me because with that money and with the help of my sister, Senzeni Gasela, I managed to buy a small car, a Ford Escort that I used to give rides to some students and some of my Professors to the Africa University and back. I was able to buy petrol/gas and to buy food and pay for electricity and water and other things necessary.

Things were not as rosy as you may think, it was hard to reconcile my finances because the tuition from Africa University dried off. I had to suspend my studies to find money for my school fees. I had to apply to many stores and places in Mutare. I finally got a job in Meikles Store, as a salesman, selling furniture and electrical gadgets. I could not do part-time pastoring because all the four churches were having Pastors. I sold a refrigerator to one of our Pastors and a friend, Rev. Guest Myambo at Meikles Stores. Pastor Trevor Manhanga came in to buy some furniture. He was surprised to see me selling and he scolded me, telling me that I was supposed to be out there preaching the Word in steading selling the store stuff. I told him that I was tent making. Surprisingly, I worked at Meikles Stores for six month and the gross profits that the store earned was 3 million more and the Manager credited that to me because they had never had such sales profits. The Manager was not a Christian but he highlighted to others that the man of God was within us that's why they did well. After I left the Meikles Store, I was offered to be a C10 and I was promised a house, the fees and a car if I accepted the offer. The bait came during those difficult times I was going through financially. The agents had seen how I led the Africa University students without engaging to violence. They loved my leadership skills and they wanted me to join them. But I denied the offer because of my ethics, beliefs and moral values as a Pastor and my Christian values. The bait which was extended to me, God gave me the strength not to fall into it, the temptation like that of Jesus Christ in (Luke 4:1-13, NKJV). He also says, "No temptation has overtaken you except what is common to mankind. And God is faithful; he will not let you be tempted beyond what you can bear. But when you are tempted, he will also provide a way out so that you can endure it," (I Cor. 10:13, NKJV). God is faithful, caring and loving.

I left the Meikles Store and volunteered to work with the Scripture Union. I worked in the Scripture Union office with Napoleon Gomo and Ronny and others, visiting both primary/elementary schools, secondary/high schools in peri-urban and rural schools and Mutare Teachers College to teach religious education. We travelled to most of the schools in Mutare, Marange, Mutasa, Honde Valley, Makoni and various district schools. Scripture Union was not paying me because they had their own budget. I was fulfilling the passion to teach children and students the Word of God. One morning while I was having my breakfast alone, God spoke to me in a powerful way. It was as if He was saying to me that I was not trusting Him, but running around looking for help from other places and people or sources. I put my cup of tea back on the table, put back the bread on the plate and started crying alone, saying sorry to the Lord for not trusting Him. I cried for a long time alone begging God to forgive me. After asking for forgiveness, I felt the peace in my heart that transcended all my frustration and hopelessness. My hope in the Lord to restore me again and give me whatever He had in store for me. It was God who answered my prayer and the peace that I would go back to school.

While I was busy at Scripture Union with school programs, a position had arisen of an Administrator at Facts Caring Trust (FCT). I was informed by Landelani Ndlovu, one of my youths from the United Baptist Church, Mutare City who was working there as a Financial Controller. He wanted me to take the position and encouraged me to apply. I applied for the position and the Director of the Family Aids Caring Trust (FACT), Dr. Foster, invited me for an interview. I knew him personally, from other platforms. I was positioned to be employed in a decent place that was paying good money. While I was waiting for the interview which was already scheduled for the following week, one of my friends from Africa University came to my house with the news that Mr. Forbes, the Student Welfare Director, sent him to tell me to come to the university to continue with my studies again because the funds had been sourced for me to continue with my studies. Mrs. Pfukani was the University Registrar that time. One of my Professors, Dr. Pond and the other Professor from the USA had appealed to a Baptist Church in the USA to support my studies, knowing that I was a Baptist not a Methodist. This Baptist Church in the USA had donated some money for me one time to complete my studies. They did not want me to know them but it was a unanimous gift. I was overwhelmed with the news and excited the way God had answered my prayers. Now I had one tough decision to make, go back to complete my studies or to go for the interview for the position of Administrator at Family Aids Caring Trust (FACT) as I was assured, I would get the job and it was going to be a permanent and full-time position.

With prayer and advice from my friends, especially Napoleon Gomo, I decided to go back to complete my degree at Africa University. I had to cancel the interview at Family Aids Caring Trust (FACT). God was in it and I was ready to go back to the University to complete my degree that I had started. I had lost the whole year out of school because of financial constraints. Now the Lord had once more opened the door for me to complete my degree. When I went back to school, the faculty of Theology was so happy to see me back and the students were thrilled to see me back too. They called me a legend and their hero. That's why I named my first son, Qhawelenkosi, meaning the hero of God. I had fought for the students in my term as the Africa University SRC President and we achieved a lot for the student body and for those who were to come after us. I thank God for the lessons I learned. The students loved me and I loved them too. The Africa University administration really appreciated me for leading students peacefully. There was no vandalism or building damages or anyone hurt or harmed both the students and the administration stuff.

When I returned to the university, I worked hard to complete my degree. I was still communing from home using my small Ford Escort car. I completed all the requirements of my degree and the year went very fast. I graduated on July 1, 2000 with a four-year Bachelor of Divinity/MDiv/Education as a minor. BD/MDIV, as my major and Education as a minor. I enjoyed my time at Africa University, made friends, and had wonderful classmates from all Africa, Germany and the USA. Those years were fruitful at Africa University and I will always cherish them and be grateful to the Theology Faculty, Faculty of Education and the Africa University administration.

After graduation, what was next? I had already decided that I would go for teaching for a while before I return to Pastoring because Pastoring was my calling while teaching was my profession. We decided with my wife, Judith to relocate to Bulawayo, my home city. We had lived in Mutare for almost ten years and it was time for us to go and live in my home city in Bulawayo. I graduated on July 1, 2000, and I went to Bulawayo to look for a teaching position. My wife was still teaching at Mutsvangwa High School and our hope was that after securing the teaching position, my wife Judith would get a transfer letter and we would teach at the same school, God willing, in Bulawayo. We prayed about God's guidance. The schools were to open in early September 2000. I wanted to beat that time so that by the beginning of the term, September to December, I would have secured a teaching position. Our plan was that we would move to Bulawayo after I got a teaching position in Bulawayo. I went to Bulawayo and the following day; I went to the Ministry of Education Recruiting Head Office which was located at the Main Post Office by then. I got into their office and met with the education recruiting officer who told me that I could not get any teaching position in Bulawayo district or peri-urban, it was impossible because they were a list of senior teachers who were waiting to transfer to come to Bulawayo City and for me as a new teacher, I should first be deployed to the rural schools before applying for a teaching position in Bulawayo City. They told me that that was the procedure.

There were two officers in the office and when they looked at my certificates, they were very impressed with my Bachelor's degree certificate from African University. They looked at my transcript and saw that my major was Divinity and my minor was Education in History. One of them took me to the other office to check on the openings. They started talking to each other and one of them said that there was an opening at Pumula East Secondary School. They started arguing that as a new teacher, according to the policy, I could not start teaching in the City when there were thousands of teachers who have been waiting to transfer to come to teach in Bulawayo City and they could not violate that policy. It would be detrimental to their responsibility and the breach of the Ministry of Education policy. They went to another office to check and they left me in their office. After thirty minutes, they came back and told me that they were going to give me a letter to the Headmaster/Principal of Pumula East Secondary School to take the opened History teaching position. I could see the favor of God upon me, no doubt about that, because just the fact that they agreed to let me go with the letter to the Headmaster/Principal of Pumula East Secondary School, was not something unheard of.

I took the letter to the Headmaster/Principal of Pumula East Secondary School and when I got there, I got into the Headmaster/Principal's office. The Recruiting Education Officers from the Ministry of Education had called the Headmaster/Principal and told him that I was on the way to fill the teaching position of History. He was pleased to offer me that History teaching position at the school. I was amazed as to how God directed the whole process so easily and without any delays. It was as if the position was kept for me with great favor. The Headmaster/Principal was so friendly and he took me to the classes I would be teaching when the school opened in a few weeks. He showed me my own class and the office. I was so excited to start my teaching career in my home city, Bulawayo. I thanked God and praised Him for His mercy and His intervention at an appropriate time. I went back to Mutare and told my wife what had happened and the way God had opened the doors for me to teach in the City of Kings and Queens, Bulawayo. It was school break that time and we started packing to move to Bulawayo.

While I had gone to Bulawayo, my wife told me that one of the members of the National Committee, Mr. Cephas Ngarinvhume had come while I was away who was sent by the Head Office of United Baptist Church to ask me to go and teach at Rusitu Bible College as a lecturer. What a surprise and the turn of the events! He had told my wife, Judith that he would come again to see and talk to me about asking me to be a lecturer at Rusitu Bible College. I thought to myself that God is not God of confusion. He could not open two doors at the same time. Mr. Cephas Ngarivhume and the Principal of Rusitu Bible College, Rev. Timothy Barrow, eventually, came and told me that they had been sent by the National Committee from the Head Office and Dr. Bishop Joshua Dhube to ask me to go and be a lecturer at the Bible College. They presented to me a crisis that Rev. Tim Barrow, the Principal of Rusitu Bible School, was taking another position full time at Serving in Missions, (SIM) and they needed me to bridge the gap while waiting for the incoming new Principal, Rev. Onias Tapera to take over from Rev. Tim. Barrow. Rev. O. Tapera was to come some few months to come but he was still in Denver, Colorado. He had just completed his Masters in Divinity from the Seminary. So, my task was to go to be a lecturer at Rusitu Bible College and to be an interim person between outgoing, Rev. Tim Barrow who was leaving for a new position in Serving in Missions (SIM), and incoming Principal, Rev. Onias Tapera from the USA.

It was the shock of my life how to handle the two dilemmas in front of me, to be honest. Whom do I pledge my allegiance to, the Ministry of Education or the Church, to serve as a lecturer? To put it simply, to be a Lecturer at a College or to be a Teacher at High School? Which one would you choose if it were you? Well, it was a dilemma for me for a while. Teaching was a good job offer with a reliable salary every month. I had secured a teaching position in the city of Bulawayo, my own home in which so many teachers had waited for five or ten years to get a teaching position in the city of Bulawayo. I had just got a teaching position without any struggle at all. The Lecturers were the same as the Pastors who were struggling to get decent pay or salary every month. Now I was left with two choices, to bend to a secular job or to stretch to God's work. I asked them to give us a few days to ponder and pray about the request. We discussed and prayed about the right decision to make with my wife, Judith. Finally, God helped us to choose His work rather than the secular job although there were some greener pastures in the secular job, I decided to suffer with the people of God than to enjoy the pleasures of this world for a season. It was painful to call the Pumula East Secondary School Headmaster/ Principal to tell him what had transpired and that I was no longer coming to join his teaching staff in September 2000. The headmaster was very disappointed about my decision because he was looking forward to working with me and he said that he was thrilled preparing to introduce me to his teaching staff and to the students when schools opened and also to restart again in looking for a history teacher.

I finally accepted the position to be a lecturer at Rusitu Bible College and to act as an interim person between Rev. Tim. Barrow and Rev. Onias Tapera who was anticipated to resume Principalship at Rusitu Bible College. One of the requests that I made to the Head Office was for my wife to be transferred and be given a teaching position at Rusitu High School of which they agreed, liaising with the Headmaster, Mr. Thabani Siwela. We packed our furniture and belongings to move to Rusitu Bible College. After the interviews and all the procedures necessary, we moved to Rusitu Bible College. "In their hearts humans plan their course, but the Lord establishes their steps," (Proverbs 16:9, NIV). Rev. Tim Barrow moved our furniture to Rusitu with his truck. My wife was still a teacher at Mutsvangwa Secondary School as I moved to Rusitu Bible College. It did not take long before my wife was given a teaching position at Rusitu High School, per our request. It was a great benefit for the first time to live together with my wife under one roof. It was in August, 2000 that we arrived at Rusitu Bible College. Our second child, a daughter was born in September, 2000 after we had settled at Rusitu.

Rusitu Mission is a United Baptist Church owned. The Mission has four pillars of institution, the Bible College, the High School, the Hospital and the Church. They core-exist and complement each other. The mission was founded by the missionaries in 1897 as they came from South Africa, under South Africa General Mission (S.A.G.M.), evangelizing the local communities. These missionaries were Dudley Kidd, Huskisson Ranney and John Copeland. The whole area was called Gaza land by then. It is a densely populated area with indigenous people living around the mission station. There is a beautiful climate and fertile landscape. The place is known for vast banana plantations, sweet potatoes, avocado pies, pineapples, yam plantations and of course, corn, and subsistence farming for family consumption is normal. The people are friendly and religious. The place is known for the descent of the Holy Spirit on October 10, 1915 when the missionaries, led by Rees Howells fasted and prayed and asked God to intervene as they had evangelized to the local people for ten years without a single convert. However, one day, while they were praying and fasting in the church, the Holy Spirit came down just as in the days of the Pentecost and people were baptized in the Holy Spirit and there was massive conversion, according the records by the same missionaries who were eye-witnesses including the local people. People gave their lives to Jesus Christ and some committed themselves to be the messengers of good news even across the border to Mozambique. There is a fascinating narrative of history in this area about the movement of God in the area. There was great revival in the area.

It is also narrated that there were cases of epidemic such as influenza that struck the area but the mission station was not affected and infected. As a result, the local people who were sick flocked and flooded the mission station and anyone who sought refuge at the station was healed. The massive conversion continued as God manifested Himself in miraculous ways. When we arrived at Rusitu Mission, we were welcomed by the Station Head Rev. Denny Sithole local church, and the villagers. It is a superb community of believers who love and look after one another. It was really good to be in the environment of belonging and taking care of one another. It was as if it was a holy ground that we had come into. Although we knew the place, because we used to come and stay for a few days for conferences or meetings but to live there, it was another experience. In fact, my wife Judith did part of her high school in the same Mission School. We were now happy and raising a new and young family. Almost everything was there, the preschool, the elementary school, high school, hospital, Bible College, the Church, all were there to cater for the needs of the community.

I found Rodney Kastner and Rev. Masango Matimura who were the lecturers and I took over some of the necessary positions to put things in order as Rev. Tim Barrow exited and he showed me what to do before Rev. Onias Tapera came. I was given the mandate to be an interim person, while waiting for Rev. Onias Tapera to come from the USA. Judith Khumbula was the College Secretary. Rusitu Bible College started in 1963 with only one student but it has grown steadily now. The College gets its sponsorship from the churches and well-wishers for the running of the College and for paying the lecturers although their salaries come directly from the United Baptist Church Head Office. I was now in charge of the College, awaiting the coming of Rev. Onias Tapera and it did not take long before he arrived with his family. I showed him what Rev. Tim Barrow had shown me to show the new Principal. I was the lecturer and the Dean of Students.

We had great students from different churches who sent their students for theological training and to be equipped for ministry, with United Baptist Church students being the majority always. We became so close with Rev. Tapera, Rev. Masango Matimura and Rev. Timothy Myambo who later joined us as a lecturer and Rev. Onias Tapera became the College Principal. We had a good community of friends. Rev. Timothy Myambo became a part-time Pastor for our Mission Station, Rusitu United Baptist Church. He organized family fellowships in the mission in which we would gather every Saturday and brought potluck for each family to share. It was a good time to be close to families within the Mission Station in the community. Notable families that we became so close to where, Rev. Tapera family, Rev. Matimura family, Rev. Myambo family, John Simoyi who was the Hospital Administrator with his lovely wife, Silindiwe Simoyi, Mr. Thabani Siwela family who was the Headmaster at Rusitu High School, Tsopo family, Pukutai Wonzemoyo with his wife, Mr. Mukondomi, the Headmaster of Hode Primary School, Mr. Matende the Deputy at Rusitu High School, and some of the married students such as Mrs. Mkuze, Mr. Mupara with his wife and many more. It was a group of families focused on improving our families and living in harmony with each other. I officiated several weddings during my stay at Rusitu, for Innocent Dube, John and Silindiwe Simoyi, Gwinyai and Nyasha Myambo, Mr. and Mrs. Zunga, the mother and father of Rev. Gladman Zunga, Kana Khanda, and Peter and Phoebe Chibinjana.

We were four lecturers with less than forty students. We assigned each other classes to teach, preparing the lectures and working with the students. It included the practical application of the practical courses. I taught Systematic Theology courses, Hermeneutics, Pastoral Epistles, Homiletics, Evangelism, Pastoral Counseling, Paul's Epistles, Church Administration, Church History etc. For the practical application on evangelism, I used to organize evangelism outreach in the local villages. The notable students were Irvin Moyo, Nevhar Femayi, Joshua, Fanadzo, Jane Moyo, Farai Mukama, Roma, Thomas, Sikhululekile Mutenyemvure, Collette Manjengwa, Divason, Beauty, Thinkmore Chivumba, Mambewu, Chaka Mhlanga, Mukoma James, Cliff Siyekhaya, Esther, Sande, Panganai Sithole, Hambirepi, Inzwirashe Mutingwende, Lucia Kufandirori, Christopher Manzanga, brother Kufandirori, and others. Antony Dandato and Tawanda Masango were not at Rusitu Bible College, but they were great and spiritual young men who had the zeal for the Lord although they were still at Rusitu High School, studying. We would organize revival meetings at Vimba village. The students would walk more than fifty kilometers to the village of Vimba and invite people to come for the revival meetings, starting on Fridays, Saturdays and we would conclude on Sundays with a Sunday service and many people gave their lives to Jesus, we would welcome them. Those who gave their lives to Jesus Christ would bring their charms, talisman, ritual artifacts, sacred clothes and so on. The students were on fire for the Lord. The same strategy I used for evangelism outreach when I was a Pastor in Mutare District, is the same strategy I used with the students at RBC. I used to preach at Rusitu High School Church and Ndakopa UBC and I baptized new converts at Rusitu River with other Pastors. It was an active life at Rusitu Bible College, with the churches around and in the community.

Rev. Onias Tapera, the Principal left Rusitu Bible College to start his own organization in Mutare. The Head Office appointed Rev. Timothy Myambo to be the next Principal at Rusitu Bible College. In 2002, the country suffered economic slump and high inflation because of the land reform that was done haphazardly without good planning. In fact, the war veterans invaded the white farms without compassion.

They based their actions on the ten-year agreement with the British and America at Lancaster House Conference in which they had agreed that within ten years, the white farmers would sell some of the farms so that the government could relocate and settle indigenous people who were crowded in the arid land and were without each land for decades. They had agreed on a policy of willing seller and willing buyer, without excessive force to take the land back. The President of Zimbabwe by then, Robert G. Mugabe, did not badge after those ten years elapsed. He let the war veterans to forcefully repossess the land reforms without compassion. As a result, about 3,500 to 400 white commercial farmers were evicted from their land in 2000. Some of them were killed, others were injured and yet others fled the country to the neighboring countries to start new farming opportunities in Zambia, Mozambique, South African, and Botswana. There was chaos across the country. By 20002, the country was reeling itself to economic collapse and food shortages and commodities were scarce and people began to experience difficult life and nearly impossible to put food on the table for their families. We had our third child, who was born in Bulawayo, Thandolwenkosi, in 2002.

At Rusitu Bible College, both the students and the staff had not enough food. Maize/corn would be delivered to the local schools and we would run after the truck with Rev. Timothy Myambo, to try and buy food for the students and our families. Things became worse for the next seven years with shortages of food, petrol/gas, after the farms were forcefully taken from the white commercial farmers and given to the local people who did not have resources and knowledge to do commercial farming. As a result, the economy collapsed, the farming production dwindled drastically and the country experienced economic depression from 2000 to 2009. We survived the economic tsunami but it was the survival of the fittest. We continued doing what we were doing and life went on. One time, our son Qhawelenkosi was playing outside the house alone and he ate a poisonous flower. We rushed him to the Rusitu Mission Hospital which was some a kilometer away but his temperature remained high regardless of antibiotics he was given. We had our car, a Ford Escort and we rushed him to the

Chimanimani clinic where my in-laws lived, my wife's father Noel P. and her mother, Noriah Kurwaisimba. Actually, my wife's mother, Noriah Kurwaisimba was a nurse in a Chimanimani clinic. In the clinic, they tried to monitor and to give him all kinds of drugs to keep his temperature low but all did not work. We had to proceed to Mutare Medical Center and they managed to cool his body. We don't know what kind of infection he had but thank God, he recovered and we went back the following day to Rusitu Bible College.

It was in December 2002 when we went to Biriri High School, one of our Mission Schools about 70 km from the National Assembly. All Pastors, Station Heads, Headmasters, Heads of all Departments and United Baptist Church District Representatives would gather every December to decide on church policies, appoint people to various positions, to institutions, transfers of Pastors, assign new Pastors to churches, institution personnel transfers, appointments such as Station Heads, College Principals, and approval of new lecturers. It was a long and tiresome procedure that demanded aptitude, patience, staying focused and prayerful for every activity taking place. Some of us who were just lecturers had no part to play except contributing to the debates of issues, policies or anything that needed our contributions. Our College Principal was the one giving reports just like the Headmasters, Hospital Administrators, Hospital Doctors, District Superintendents, Station Heads, Church Vice Chairman, Church Chairman, Board of Trustees Chairman, and other departments.

The final day would be for voting candidates for various positions in the church. For the institutions, the National Committee was responsible to appoint the Church Chairman and Dr. Joshua N. Dhube remained in the position as the Church Chairman for decades. For someone to be voted at the National Assembly, he should first be nominated by the local churches, then the districts would approve his name to be sent to the National Assembly to be considered. That was the process and it is still the process. Then if the district approves the nominations, then the candidates' names are sent to the National Committee for final approval before the names are sent to the National Assembly for the final votes. Then the candidates are voted on the final day of the National Assembly and fill the positions after the final winners who got the most votes. So, in 2002, we went to attend the National Assembly as we were required to be there, all the Pastors including the College lecturers. All the procedures are strictly followed and adhered to as the church constitution is a road map for the church to move forward. The membership of United Baptist Church was 13, 000 + in 2007. The following is the structure of the organization, United Baptist Church.

United Baptist Church: Organizational Structure

National Assembly
(The Highest Body Which Makes Decisions)

↕

National Assembly
(Deliberates on Issues and Recommends to National Assembly)

↑

Church Chairman
(Chairs the National Committee)

↑

Vice Church Chairman
(Assist the Church Chairman and Chairs all the Boards, except Board of Trustees)

The National Assembly, at the end of its deliberations and it was ready to vote for the nominated candidates, learned that one of the candidates who was supposed to be voted in the position of the Vice Church Chairman had withdrawn his name not to be voted. It was Rev. Onias Tapera, the former Rusitu Bible College. They were three nominees who were contesting the elections. There was Rev. E. Pambuka, Rev. Onias Tapera and Rev. D. Musona. Rev. Tapera had withdrawn his name and the Executive National Committee convened an emergency meeting to decide what to do with the absence of Rev. Onias Tapera. The Executive National Committee decided to let the National Assembly nominate someone among the Pastors present to join other candidates. The National Assembly decided to nominate Rev. Sabelo Sam Mhlanga to join those who were contesting. I was not even there in the conference room when they nominated me. I was in my room with Rev. Austin Mabhena as we were tired and the National Assembly conference was on its final deliberations. I was just laying on my bed when we heard a knock on the door. It was Rev. Munjuwanjuwa who was sent to call me to come and contest for the election for the position of the Vice Church Chairman.

Rev. Munjuwanjuwa told me that I was being called to a conference and he told me that the National Assembly had nominated me to contest for the position of the Vice Church Chairman. I was really shocked to hear that. First, I thought he was joking with me but he was serious about the message. Everything changed suddenly. He went back and my name was already on the ballot and the members of the National Assembly were already voting for the candidates and my name was there. I sought advice from Rev. Austin Mabhena on what his thoughts were. I had no time to consult my wife as those days landlines and cell phones were not easily accessible. I was baffled and confused about what to do and what was happening. We knelt and prayed with Rev. Austin Mabhena, seeking the will of God. After a prayer, I sensed that God was calling me to a high calling to serve the church and Rev. Austin Mabhena indicated that if it was the will of God, I should take the position. I went to the conference room and people had already started voting. The results were that the two candidates who got the most votes would be selected to be voted again, but now facing each other. I came at the top of the votes followed by Rev. E. Pambuka. In a matter of a few minutes, the final round of votes indicated that I was the winner and I was declared the Vice Church Chairman of United Baptist Church for a term of two years. I was happy to win the elections and appreciated the National Committee and the National Assembly for trusting me to serve the church with Bishop Joshua Dhube and myself as the Vice Church Chairman. People were congratulating me and calling me the Vice Bishop. God is awesome and amazing!

When the National Assembly was over and people departed, I headed to Rusitu Bible College, wondering if my wife would accept the call because we were settled and happy with what we were doing and the people we were around with. When I arrived at home and I told my wife what had transpired at the National Assembly and that I was elected as the Vice Church Chairman of United Baptist Church, my wife could not accept the news. She told me that she would not leave the Rusitu community. In fact, she told me that to teach in Harare in the Capital City, it was impossible. She said that we were now settled at Rusitu and to relocate and live separate lives again as a family was not prudent. To find a teaching position at Rusitu High School was a hard struggle and to start another fight in Harare was a huddle. She was very correct for sure with all her justifiable reasons. However, the decision had been made and I was now the Vice Church Chairman and we were to relocate to Harare, by December 31, 2002. As we prayed together, I convinced her that it was the will of God to submit to His authority and the church's appointment.

Finally, she agreed that it was the will of God and that if God willed it to happen, He would provide the way and pave the path for her to get a place in Harare to teach. However, it needed prayerfulness, perseverance, patience and above all, hope in Christ to make a way. We had three weeks to prepare to move but it meant that my wife would remain teaching for a while. I went ahead of the family to Harare to start my new job on December 30, 2003. Rev. Jealous Manyumbu was the Church Administrator and he was responsible for arranging the housing and transportation for the transfer of the Vice Church Chairman. My students were very disappointed to hear that I would be leaving them to go to Harare to be the Vice Church Chairman. It was a bittersweet for them and the whole church community at Rusitu Mission. I also felt the sadness to leave Rusitu Mission but I had to leave and explore what God had in store for us in Harare. On December 30, a truck came to take our furniture and I left my wife with the children as she was still teaching at Rusitu Mission School. We took almost every piece of furniture but I left only a few pieces of furniture for my wife and the children to use while she was winding up her work.

On January 6, I started my new job, having been oriented, handed over and being shown around and being introduced to the United Baptist Church Head Office Staff. It was the Church Chairman Dr. Joshua Ngoweni Dhube, the Church Administrator, Rev. Jealous Manyumbu, the Book Keeper, Tafadzwa Shumba, Head Office Secretary, Rhoda Mazemo who took over from Mai Mwanaka, who was a relative of my wife Judith and Assistant Secretary, Angela Gororo. The Church Administrator showed me my office and I did not like the desk that was used by my predecessor. The National Treasurer, Tafadzwa Shumba and the Church Administrator gave me a choice to choose and buy a desk I wanted with a new chair and I made sure that my working environment and conditions were in line with my work ethics. It took almost two weeks for me to settle down and to start assimilating into the new system of the United Baptist Church. I read my job description and I made sure I was in an alignment and conversant with my job description. The first disappointing thing I observed was that I walked to work daily for about a mile and a half. When I got to work, I would be tired and sweaty. We had about three fleets of cars in the Head Office which were used only for work. I asked the Church Administrator why I was walking to work and back while the Head Offices Vehicles were there and could not be used by the workers. The Church Chairman said that there were some risks of car thefts if the workers went with the cars to their homes. I suggested that the two drivers at the Head Office could come in the morning to pick us up and drop us off at our homes after work. It was actually two of us, Rev. J. Manyumbu and I needed transport assistance. The Church Chairman, Dr. Joshua Dhube was having his own car. The Church Chairman agreed to the idea to be picked up in the morning and dropped off after work. It was a big relief to us. Mr. Albert Makacha and Wendyson Matyanga were the Head Office drivers who took that responsibility. They had their job at the Head Office too. Although Mr.

Wendyson Matyanga was the Conference Manager, who took over from Mai Moyo who was a relative of my wife, Judith, driving us was an added responsibility which was extra money for him. Mr. Albert Makacha was also working within United Baptist Church projects. Mr. Chikati was the Director of UBC National Projects and he worked at the Head Office. Mr. Kenneth Muzanya was the bookkeeper of the Conference Center. The cooks were Nessley Manase, Mrs. Muchini, Mr. Dliwayo, the maintenance man, Mr. Konde, the security guard, and Mereta, also a relative of my wife Judith. Mai Pambuka joined the Head Office Staff as Sunday School Coordinator but she was living with her husband, Rev. E. Pambuka who was still Pastoring United Baptist Church Mutare City.

I started my new position as the Vice Church and the Vice Bishop. I had a huge responsibility in terms of job description. **Vice Church Chairman** – United Baptist Church, 2003-2007: Responsibility- Chairing the National Financial Committee, overseeing the welfare of Pastors, chairing all Boards, (except the Board of Trustees), managing the office personnel, organizing Pastors' Conferences, evangelism outreach, directing the Mine Ministry and Planning for Church growth and chairing the National Assembly. **Board of Education Chairman** (Rusitu and Biriiri High Schools) 2003-2007: Responsibility- Interviewing and recruiting the headmasters of the two Schools. **Board of Governors Chairman** (Rusitu Bible College) 2003- 2007: Responsibility – Recruiting, interviewing new staff and overseeing College and working with the principal and chairing the Board of Governors meetings. **Hospital Board Chairman** (Rusitu Hospital) 2003-2007: Responsibility - Recruiting staff, Doctors, nurses and medical staff. Working with the Hospital Administrator and the Medical Doctor/Physician.

It was a new community of workers and that I had to develop relationships and trust with them because they were working under me. I was living in Wenlock, in a Mission/Church house and I allowed Rev. James Mafake's family to live with us at the cottage as he Pastored United Baptist Church Harare City Church. We became close friends with Rev. James Mafake and the family while I waited for my wife

Judith and children to come and join me in Harare. We prayed for my wife to get a position of teaching in Harare. I joined the United Baptist Church Conference Center as a member. Rev. Gladman Zunga was the Pastor and he had a lovely family, Mai Zunga and two children, Deliverance and his sibling, a girl. The members of Conference Center United Baptist Church were Rev. Alfred Simango with his wife, Evangelist Edward Mutema and his wife, Teremai, and two daughters, Bongai and Kudzi and their son, Gareth, Mr. and Mrs. Mhute, Mwanaka family, Moyo family, Gororo family, Matyanga family, Dube family, Mr. Dliwayo and his children, Rev. Andrew Muchechetere family, a close friend of mine, Sisi Rhoda Mazemo, Sisi Tafadzwa Shumba, Nessley Manase, Mai Mutisi, Makacha family, Muzanya family, Matyanga family, and other families. This new family had a great impact on our lives as a Gasela Mhlanga family.

During the school break, my wife and children came to join me in Harare but my wife had not yet found a teaching position. She applied to the Ministry of Education Harare School District. When the schools opened in April, 2003, my wife got a teaching position at Mufakose High School. It was like a miracle to get the teaching position in Harare so quickly. God answered our prayers and He was, indeed, guiding our steps. What my wife was worried about ever getting a teaching position in Harare became a reality. She was happy to start her job in Harare, unbelievably. We were now living in Harare with our three children, Qhawelenkosi Blessing, Sinqobile Shalom and Thandolwenkosi Prosper and Thandolwenkosi Prosper. I enrolled with Zimbabwe Open University, studying Masters in Educational Administration, Policy Studies and Planning. My wife Judith also enrolled at the University of Zimbabwe studying Bachelor of Education. We all got busy with life in Harare, the Capital City. I was studying, attending to family welfare and the Church duties as the Vice Bishop. Everything was going smoothly in 2003 and life was flowing smoothly. In 2003, all things seemed to indicate that we belonged to Harare, the Capital City of Zimbabwe and one would think, what on earth were we doing at Rusitu valley where it seemed nothing was happening compared to life in Harare. In 2003, I consolidated my position, my relationships with the Head Office staff, the church and applied my skills and experience in administration and the church policies in the new job I loved. I had great exposure to many people, got many opportunities and I was watching my family growing well right on my watch. At the Church Head Office, I worked very well with Dr. Joshua N. Dhube, the Church Chairman and also with Rev. Jealousy Manyumbu as the Church Administrator. We knew our job descriptions and we worked as a strong team. Some of the good highlights of our 2003 were when I officiated the wedding of Ronnia Mwanaka and Saul Muchenje. The wedding was spacious with high quality wedding features, food and activities. The couple rod on horses and a chariot. The entertainment was superb.

The wedding of Ronnia and Saul Muchenje was followed by the wedding of John Mugandira with his fiancé, the daughter (niece) of Zimbabwe's President, Emmerson Mnangagwa who was by then the Speaker of the Parliament of Zimbabwe. The wedding was in Borrowdale and many government Ministers and the relatives attended the wedding, including Minister July Moyo. After the wedding, we went for a reception and when I sat at the high table with Minister Emmerson Mnangagwa and Minister July Moyo and others. The Minister, Emmerson Mnangagwa took me aside and thanked me and appreciated the service I had conducted. He urged me to continue with the work of the church that I was doing and he told me that the government was depending on the Church because of the Church's moral values and ethics which are Christ-centered. These two weddings capped the best of 2003 of our relocation to Harare from Rusitu Bible College.

When Rev. Jealous Manyumbu was transferred from Head Office as the Church Administrator to a local church in Glenora B. United Baptist as a Pastor in 2004, the National Committee appointed me as the Acting Church Administrator. I had two positions at the Head Office now and the whole load of the two positions was on me. It was as if I was running the whole Church except the Church Chairman, Dr. Joshua Dhube who was responsible for appointments, transfers and steering and chairing the National Committee. However, the Vice

Church Chairman and the position of Acting Church Administrator gave me all the authority to run the institutions, personnel and all the arms of the Church. I was very loyal to the Church Chairman, Dr. Bishop Joshua Dhube implemented his orders but also suggested some changes that were legitimate. I also had the authority to hire or to fire the personnel who were not complying with the Church constitutions and policies. **Church Administrator** – United Baptist Church, 2004-2007: Responsibility- Planning, implementing National Committee resolutions, and overseeing all the interviews and the personnel for the Association, representative of the United Baptist Church for all internal and external public relations.

In 2004, our son, Qhawelenkosi was attending a pre-school when one day, he came from school saying he had seen something that scary at school and he could not exactly tell us what it was. He was behaving strangely. We tried to investigate and trace his illness but there was no concrete narrative from the teacher. Qhawe was five years old and his health deteriorated gradually from that time. We took him to private hospitals to be tested with all forms of technology equipment. After a few weeks, Qhawe developed pneumonia-like symptoms and high fever. We really got baffled with his sickness. I was out at Rutendo United Baptist Church on evangelism outreach with Rev. Pardon Chingovo when my wife called me and told me that our son, Qhawe was not feeling well and had a high body temperature. It was in the middle of the night when she called. I got up and drove at night back home, to Harare.

When I arrived, he was very sick and we took him to the hospital and they tested his blood to determine any infection in his blood and body. They tested him for malaria, HIV/AIDS, flue, and many tests but all the tests came negative. They transferred him to another hospital that was smaller but his temperature was always him and they did not know what kind of infection he had. The hospital where he transferred to was having children who were dying in great numbers and we decided to transfer him to another nearby hospital. When he got to the new hospital, they decided to take him more tests and even a brain scan. When the tests did not indicate any results of any infection, they decided to take spinal fluid samples, lumbar puncture, which is needed to test the fluid around the brain and spinal cord. The test was to find out if Qhawe had meningitis which is a serious infection around the brain. Meningitis may be suspected in babies but it is usually conducted in babies less than one month old. However, they made the test procedure on Qhawe. The symptoms of meningitis include vomiting, headache, tiredness, fever and Qhawe exhibited those symptoms. After going through lumbar puncture procedures, Qhawe's situation became worse. He could not walk, speak, and his limbs stifled. He was five years old, and he became like a two-year-old boy. He could not produce any sound, he could not crawl, and do anything. He just became a baby again. He was diagnosed with pneumonia, called encephalitis pneumonia (inflammation of the brain) due to infection. The infection is due to infection caused by bacteria or viruses. They confessed that they had made a mistake during the procedure of taking the lumbar puncture tests that caused severe damage to his spine. We stayed in the hospital with him for more than three weeks.

Our son actually got paralyzed the whole body. During that time all of our three children got the fever, Qhawe, Sinqobile, and Thando. However, the other two recovered, and Qhawe continued to be sick without any signs of recovery. My wife spent the nights at home with children and I spent the nights with Qhawe at the hospital. Our other children were still young and they needed much care. We had a maid called Chenai who was a great help during the day, taking care of children to help my wife. The sickness of my son affected me grossly and I was refusing even to eat. I was not fasting but I was not having any appetite to eat anything. My son was only able to eat liquids like yogurt, porridge, etc. He became so skinny that you could see the ribs on his side. During the nights, I would lift him up to go to the toilet/bathroom and he was not able to stand on his own or to walk. The Doctors actually gave up on him and said he will never recover because his brains had inflamed because of the infection. One of the American visiting Doctors told us that Qhawe will never walk, talk, or do anything because his brain had reversed to be that of a two-year-old boy. She said that he will never recover and that we had to take him home because there was no hope in any kind of medication that was available. She recommended that we take him to a therapist to help his limbs to stretch. One night, as I saw my son's health deteriorating and his strength gradually and slowly dissipating, I cried to the Lord bitterly beside Qhawe's bed in the midnight in the Hospital and asked God because He had allowed me to be the Vice Church Chairman and the Church Administrator and to bring us to Harare only to lose our son in His presence. I cried the whole night and begged God to heal my son. After that deep and fervent prayer that night, I felt God had heard me and I felt at peace and from that time on, I knew that God would heal my son gradually, because He heard my cry and plea. I had a conviction that whatever would take place from now on then, God was in it.

We had a powerhouse of prayer worries who came to pray for Qhawe, encouraged us and comforted us just like Job's three friends who came to cry with him, to comfort him and to give him some advice although some of his friends did not give him prudent advice, especially his closest friend, his wife. Men's fellowship (Vakweyi) was led by Dorobha, the Pastors, the women's group, Dr. Bishop Joshua Dhube and many others came to comfort and to pray with us. Dr. Joshua Dhube encouraged me to eat as I had refused to eat for several days, seeing my son dying in my presence. As the Vice Church Chairman, one of my duties was to organize and chair the Annual Revival Meetings. I had drafted the programs and planned and got prepared to go to Annual Revival Meetings at Biriri Mission School. As the Vice Church Chairman, it was my job description and mandate to chair the Annual Revival Meeting of more two to three thousand attendees. I had organized and arranged all the necessary things with the National Committee and we were ready to kick off. When the sickness struck my son, Qhawe, it was impossible to go, leaving my son dying with this sickness. However, I respect and honor my wife Judith, who encouraged me to go to the meeting saying that God would take care of the situation. Dr. Bishop Joshua Dhube had accepted that I should not go so that I could attend to my sick son and family. Dr. Bishop J. Dhube was very supportive with his lovely wife, Mrs. Bishop Dhube. I was so grateful to be surrounded by such a loving and caring community of believers. Against all odds, I listened to my wife, Judith and braced to go to the Annual Revival Meeting in August, 2004. By faith I headed to Biriri, leaving my wife with an ailing son and three children with the help of the house maid, Chennai who was very helpful by all standards.

The Annual Revival Meeting started very well as I chaired the whole meeting and announced that my son was very sick to the point of death but that I had to come to fulfil my duty as the chairman of the event, for God's sake. The members of the church prayed for my son The Revival Meetings started on a Tuesday to Sunday. On Thursday, the whole assembly prayed and some of the people fasted for Qhawe, our son to be healed. On Friday, the following day, I called my wife to check how Qhawe was doing, and she was happy to tell me that Qhawe had started to try to speak and he was able to say "mama." I reported to the conference and there was a thunderous praise to God from the congregants. There was a progression of his recovery. On Saturday when I called to check his condition again, my wife told me that Qhawe was able to crawl and to stand on his own and sometimes holding on to something. We serve a miracle working God, indeed! On Sunday, when I went back home, I found Qhawe looking live and recovering well. Within a week, he was able to eat solid food, able to walk and to say some meaningful words. A five-year-old boy who was able to do everything like any five-year-old would do but he had taken three years steps backway and now he was recovering in our very eyes while we saw him being struck by paralysis. God is faithful and dependable God!

Qhawe, spasmodically, recovered slowly but sure. They were certain things that if one was not aware, one would be surprised how a five-year-old could behave in a certain way. Some of the teachers at schools, even though they were informed how Qhawe was affected by the encephalitis pneumonia, they could not understand his situation. His capabilities and abilities were affected and he needed more time to recover slowly and a lot of support and love. Some of his decisions were, of course, not accurate. Within a year of his recovery, he was playing with other children at the Conference Center because we had moved to a missionary house adjacent to the Head Office, closer to the Conference Center. Qhawe climbed a tree and without calculating accurately his steps on top of the tree, he fell headlong and his arm broke in half. He came home running, holding his broken arm. We should have closely monitored his play but it was too late. My wife was at work as a teacher and I called her and told her what had happened. I drove him to the hospital and they had to put a cast on his arm which took a long time to heal. From that time onwards, we were monitoring his playing because he was not careful when playing. He was too adventurous and careless in many ways. However, he was a genius and good planner. He would plan things for the following day and asked us what was the plan for the following day and the day after. We used to plan things in advance just for the sake of Qhawe. If we did not plan for the following day and the day after, he would not stop asking what we had planned. He would ask what we would be eating the following day. He would be able to plan and help to accomplish the plan with us. He was such a great help in the house. He would clean, put things in order and made sure the house was locked and secure always. He took care of his siblings so well. He made sure they were safe, fed and happy. He was such a blessing to us. His mother named him "Blessing" because he was a blessing to us all and to the neighbors.

God consoled us with our third son, and fourth child, Nkosilathi. We were so glad that God smiled on us again. We were so grateful for such a wonderful gift. My mother Josephine Nyathi Gasela visited us to see her grandchildren. We had four families that we prayed together on Fridays. Mr. and Mrs. Mwanaka, Evangelist and Mrs. Mutema, Rev. and Mrs. Zunga, our local Pastor and Rev. and Mrs. Mhlanga. We used to gather to pray for each other at our home and sometimes we would rotate on these four homes. We became close friends and to each other as families. In 2003 to 2007, we had a school that was run by United Baptist Church, in Mozambique and a farm which was a church project led by Mr. Chikati, Project Manager. We were always busy monitoring those projects and at Rushinga and as the Acting Church Administrator. I was always in the office and out of the office.

In December 2004, we had the National Assembly at Rusitu Mission to conduct church policies, for the reports and for the new appointments as usual, which was a yearly routine and procedure in December. However, we also had crucial elections in the church to elect the United Baptist Church Chairman and the Vice Church Chairman. Bishop Joshua Dhube had been the Church Chairman for more than thirty to forty years since he took over from the missionaries. He had reached the retirement age and a new Church Chairman had to be elected at the end of the National Assembly from 2004 onwards. In honor and insurmountable contribution of Dr. Bishop Joshua Dhube to the United Baptist Church, the National Committee drafted an amendment clause of the Church Constitution in order to add the position of Church Advisor which was to be filled by Dr. Bishop Joshua N. Dhube. This position was not an administrative position but a position to cater for Dr. Bishop Joshua N. Dhube as an appreciation for his role he had played to consolidate and lead United Baptist for many for more than four decades. While the elections of the Church and Vice Church took place and Rev. Alfred Simango was duly elected by the members of National Assembly as he was nominated prior to the National Assembly with the Vice Church Chairman having the same procedures of nomination before the National Assembly. I was also duly elected as the Vice Church Chairman by the National Assembly in 2004 to serve four years in the office.

The United Baptist Church Executive, starting in January 2005 for another four year term and had the new leadership hierarchy as the following: Dr. Bishop Joshua Dhube as the Church Advisor, (not an administrative position), Church Chairman, Rev. Alfred Simango, Vice Church Chairman and Acting Church Administrator, Rev. Sabelo Sam Gasela Mhlanga, National Secretary, Vice Secretary National Treasurer, Board of Trustees Chairman etc. I was in the Board of Evangelical fellowship of Zimbabwe (EFZ) and we had a task of bringing peace between the two political parties, ZANU-PF and Movement of Democratic Party. We had several meetings led by Evangelical

Fellowship of Zimbabwe and the President of the organization was Trevor Manhanga and another organization was Zimbabwe Council of Churches. When the Vice President of Zimbabwe, Joyce Mujuru was elected, we were invited to pray for her at Celebration Church International, Borrowdale, Harare. We also met with the President of Zimbabwe, President Robert Mugabe to try to broker peace deal with the opposition parties as the opposition parties were persecuted, adapted and murdered because of their political affiliations. The peace deal was not successful.

In 2007, Rev. Andrew Muchechetere, the Secretary General, asked me to translate the Constitution of Zimbabwe Amendment No. 18 Act, 2007 from English to Ndebele. I did the section I was assigned. I was also in the Board of Directors to start Gazaland University in Chipinge when United Church of Christ and United Baptist Church agreed to build the university together. The two churches have worked together in many areas including Hymnal Books for both churches. I continued to represent United Baptist Church in national and International forums, as the Church Administrator and the Vice Church Chairman and most of the time going with the Church Chairman in some of the meetings.

In 2005, there was a Baptist World Alliance Conference in Birmingham in the UK. As the Church Administrator, I organized for those who were planning to go to the conference. I processed their UK visas and connected them with the Baptist Churches in the UK. I never thought I would go there also because of the financial constraint at the Head Office. As I was busy organizing for others, I met Rev. Timothy Barrow who was now the Director of Serving in Missions (SIM) and his office was at the Head Office. Rev. Tim Barrow was my friend and he asked me if I wanted to go to the conference because there was a church of his wife in the UK that was willing to sponsor me and Rev. Alfred Simango to attend the conference. God had intervened in our dire situation. When Rev. Tim Barrow mentioned that there was a Baptist Church in the UK that had indicated that they wanted to pay for me and Rev. Alfred Simango for our air tickets, and other expenses, I accepted the offer with open arms. Rev. Alfred Simango and I were covered with everything for the conference. We also organized that the Church would pay for the tickets and other expenses for the Church Advisor, Dr. Bishop Joshua Dhube so that he would be one of the delegates to represent the United Baptist Church together with us. I sent the passports for the Head Office officials, for Dr. Bishop Joshua Dhube, Rev. Alfred Simango, for me and the National Treasurer, Danny Gwenzi, who paid for himself. Many other United Baptist Church members who wanted to go, sent their passports for visa application processes through the Head Office and I facilitated all the processes as the Church Administrator.

Rev. Tim Barrow previously had organized for me to go to a week-long conference in Ethiopia, in the Eastern part of Addis Ababa. Serving in Mission, (SIM), paid for my air ticket and all the hotel expenses at the conference and food in 2004. I had enjoyed the hospitality of the Ethiopians who were kind and served us with spicy food, served with Injera. It was a good experience and cultural shock to be fed by the women as a sign of showing kindness if you were a visitor. They also serve each other on some occasions. I bought my family the Ethiopian attire and bought my wife a bag with a sign of 13 months of sunshine and it was very colorful. Rev. Tim Barrow had also organized a ticket for me to go to Ghana in 2005 to represent the United Baptist Church at Serving in Mission (SIM) conference in partnership with local churches but the dates clashed with the Baptist World Alliance conference in the UK. The Baptist World Alliance was an international conference for all Baptists in the world who were to converge in Birmingham, in the UK.

When the time came, we boarded air Zimbabwe to Birmingham airport. When we arrived, they were shuttles organized by the Baptist World Alliance organized and we were whisked to the hosts. The hosts allocated us to various homes and some of the attendees were located in schools, gyms, halls and hotels. The following day, we went to meet with all of us at Birmingham Amphitheater that housed thousands of people at once. It was pleasant to see the sea of people from all over the world from different races, tribes, languages, and nations. I remember one of the speakers was from South Korea, Seoul and his church sang and danced for the conference beautifully. It was as if it was a foretaste of Heaven. Everyone looked beautiful and we had only one focus on Christ Jesus, our Lord. I will never forget that experience of the body of Christ in one union and one accord just like in the early church, "All believers were one in heart and mind. No one claimed that any of their possessions was their own, but they shared everything they had," (Acts 4:32, NIV). We were indeed, one in heart and mind. Christians in Birmingham opened their homes, businesses, community schools and universities for believers to feel welcomed and comfortable.

We slept from one house to another and from one college to another, from one university to another for the duration of the conference, for the whole week. One of the universities we slept at was Charles Spurgeon University. I got interested at the university and in the morning, I went to the admissions office and asked how I should apply for admission. They gave me the university forms and I filled them and submitted them. I had come with my documents, resume, and photocopies of my certificates. When I went for the conference, I had the intention to apply to many universities to do a Masters in Theology. I did a Bachelor of Divinity/Education, both Theology and Education at Africa University. I had done Masters of Educational Administration, Policy Studies and Planning at Zimbabwe Open University. I wanted to do a Masters of Theology in the UK. I always wanted to study both the Secular degrees and Theology degrees. I achieved and graduated with a Bachelor's degree of Divinity/Education from Africa University. I did the secular Master's in Educational Administration, Policy Studies and Planning but I had not done Masters in Theology at Zimbabwe Open University. When I submitted my application to study Masters of Theology at Charles Spurgeon University in Birmingham, I was very excited that if I was admitted, I would go back home and get a study visa.

On Thursday, in the middle of the Baptist World Alliance conference, I was on the line for lunch which was served at one of the buildings within the conference building. When I got to the table where they were serving food, I found out that the cost for the lunch was 20 pounds. I did not want to spend 20 pounds for lunch because it could have offsite my budget. I left the line hoping to go outside and get a cheaper lunch but the man behind me in the line asked me why I was leaving the line. I told him that the cost for the lunch was too expensive for me and I was opting to go outside to get a cheaper lunch. He offered to pay for my lunch. I thanked him and appreciated his kindness. After getting my lunch, he invited me to sit together at the same table to eat our lunch. We introduced each other and where we came from. His name was Roy Livesey and he had a publishing press, called Bury House Books. I told him my name and where I was coming from. He got interested when he heard that I was from Zimbabwe. During that time, Zimbabwe was always on the world news because of the repossession of the white commercial farmers without compassion. Most of the countries in Europe and USA condemned the repossession of the white commercial farmers without compassion. Roy was interested to hear more about Zimbabwe's political and economic crisis as he owned a publishing press. I updated him about the situation in Zimbabwe.

Roy Livesey got interested in what I was doing in Zimbabwe as a Pastor and he was excited to have met with me and he wanted us to connect as friends. He asked me when I would be going back to Zimbabwe after the conference. I told him that I had applied to Charles Spurgeon University in Birmingham for admission. When Roy Livesey heard me mentioning Charles Spurgeon University, he was shaken with shock. He told me that Charles Spurgeon University had become so liberal that he could not recommend me to study there. When we finished our lunch, it was time to go to other sessions. He asked me if I could spend two weeks at his home after the conference. He actually called his wife asking her if they could invite me for two weeks at his home when the conference was over. The wife, Rae agreed and told him that it would be wonderful to have me a guest at their home from Zimbabwe. The conference was ending on a Saturday and it was Thursday. Roy told me that on Friday he was not coming but that he would come on a Saturday and that after the conference had ended, he would take me to his home. He also promised to take me to one of the renowned Pastors in his city and a Theologian so that he could recommend to me the best universities or colleges to further my studies. I really felt that the Lord was guiding my steps and I was so grateful to Roy who took me to his home. However, I had my sister (niece), Sithembile Gasela in East London, in Ilford, waiting for me after the conference. I told her that I would come to her house after two weeks because I had a friend who had invited me to his house with his wife.

On Saturday, Roy Livesey called me and told me to bring my bags so that when the conference ended, we would drive to his home. I was so excited to go and see Roy's home and his wife. They had adult children. I was with my team and we woke up in the morning and I made sure I had all my language. Bishop Joshua Dhube was staying with different families too. We met at regular intervals because there were so many people and we could just call each if we wanted to meet. Rev. Alfred Simango, I never saw each other at the conference. When we arrived at the airport from Zimbabwe, his son, Thomas Simango picked him up and that's where he was staying with his son all the duration of the conference. We had return tickets which had different dates to return to Zimbabwe. We were now on our own and each one had scheduled his return ticket with Air-Zimbabwe. I came with my bags and we called each other with Roy and sat together at the conference until the conference ended at 12:00 pm. We then drove to his home, a Glasco UK on the Southwest of Birmingham which was about 4 hours and 49 minutes. When we arrived at Roy's home, we found Roy's wife waiting for us.

I was shocked by the mansion Roy and his wife, Rae, had. Roy was, indeed, a businessman. It was a beautifully decorated white mansion on a large farm. He had some horses and other animals in his farm. The mansion had two floors, the ground floor and the second and floor, a two-story mansion. They gave me the whole of the first floor, with many bedrooms, sitting rooms, library, gym, and some of the rooms were built with glasses. It was a beautiful mansion. I had never stayed in such a house ever in my life and I was so grateful to Roy. Roy liked visiting places. We did not stay much at home but he used to drive me to various places to tour and to many of his friends. They took me to their church on Sundays. The congregation was so welcoming and friendly. You could hardly see any black people around that area. They are some towns that he took me to where you could not see any race except the whites only. Roy did not mind, he took me to those such towns, to museums, resort places, rivers, valleys, castles and more. Roy was the lover of natural resort places, historical places, where they were monuments.

The following Monday, he took me to Swansea, in South Wales. Swansea is a city and county on the south coast of Wales. He had his friends there and we spent the whole day, visiting his friends and introducing me to his friends. We went to the sea-shows and beaches. Within two weeks, we had visited so many places I could not number. Each day, he had scheduled visits to some places, shops, and restaurants. He was a kind and a generous man. He gave me some money to buy some clothes for myself, my wife and children. There are over 4,000 castles in England but we visited two Castles, Windsor Castle and Buckingham Castles. It was at Windsor Castle, when visited where we saw Queen Elizabeth 11 in her chariot and horses crossing from one place to another. I took some photos in the background when the Queen was passing by. On Thursday, he took me to a city which was bombard by the Nazi army of Germany during the World War II, in 1945. One could tell that Adolf Hitler wanted to conquer the British and he wanted to take over the country, the whole of Europe, for that matter, and the whole world. Some of the buildings were destroyed by the bombs and were never repaired to this very day for remembrance of the atrocities of Adolf Hitler who wanted to annihilate part of humanity. Roy Livesey took me to every place unimaginable and spent his money on me, liberally, to make sure I was happy and cared for. He was a devoted and committed Christian. He loved the Lord, dearly.

On Friday, I spent the whole day resting and helping him in his farm with the horses and gardening. On Saturday, we went to another town with his wife, Rae and we spent the whole day shopping and visiting places. His wife, Rae, was not fond of walking or visiting places unlike Roy. I was surprised that in the town we visited, I did not see any black or any Asian persons, or any race except the white people. I just felt out of place and everyone in the streets was looking at me but not bothered at all by presence. I felt scared but they were no show of any racial discrimination. People were doing their own businesses without bothering themselves about anything. I later discovered that people in Britain live according to the homogenous unit principle, "the kind of people." They live according to their races, especially in the small towns. That was my observation. I never experienced any racism at all, whatsoever.

On Sunday, the Pastor asked me to preach at their church. It was a local, small and friendly church. I was given the pulpit to preach. They appreciated my preaching. In the afternoon, we had an appointment with a Pastor, Thomas Williamson whom he had told me that he would recommend me to a good university or college to do my Masters in Theology. We joined them in the afternoon service. They have actually three services on Sundays, the morning service, the afternoon services and the evening services. I discovered that they were not Baptists but that it was a Reformed Church. The women dressed in long dresses and covered their heads in the church. After the service, we had lunch with the Pastor's family. When we had finished lunch, he took us to his office where he explained to me their church doctrine and their beliefs. There were not many differences with the Baptist Churches except that some few doctrines especially, their emphasis on predestination and head dress for women. He advised me that Charles Spurgeon University was a liberal university and that it was sad that a university which was one of the best evangelical, conservative and Bible centered University had turned to be worldly university, in contrast to what it stood for and with the name it was named after one of the greatest preachers great in England and beyond, who loved the Lord and preached experiential sermons in the same categories with John Calvin, John Bunyan, John Wesley, St. Augustin, Martin Luther etc.

I was surprised to hear Pastor Thomas Williamson recommending a seminary in the USA. I had never thought of studying in the USA. I wanted to study in the UK but he said the best seminary was in the USA, the Puritan Reformed Theological Seminary, founded by Dr. Joel Beeke of the Netherland Reformed Church, in Grand Rapids,

Michigan. He highly recommended it and advised me to apply there instead of the Charles Spurgeon University. While we were talking, he decided to call Dr. Joel Beek to speak with him about me. Dr. Beeke was very excited to hear that the Pastor had recommended me to go and join his seminary. Dr. Joel Beeke asked to speak to me and he said that he was excited to speak to me and that he would like me to come over and join the Puritan Theological Seminary in the USA. He promised me that the Seminary would give me a full scholarship with the living expenses and that they would prepare the house well-furnished, with clothes, a car and that all our children would go to a private school paid for by the seminary. That was unbelievable news to hear. I was too good to be true and to believe. He actually connected the call to the Seminary Registrar, Henk Klyen, to send me the application forms so that I could start to start the application process to be approved. They wanted me to go directly from Britain to the USA. Henk Kleyn, the Registrar of the Puritan Reformed Theological Seminary spoke with me and sent the forms to Pastor Thomson Williamson through the fax for me to fill. I spent half of the afternoon filling the forms and sending them back through the fax. When Roy and I went back home, I was already admitted and they wanted to send me the air ticket but the immigration office requires that the student apply for the study visa from his/her home country.

I was excited but I could not phantom what was really happening. I tried to comprehend what had happened and prayed to God if it was real. Roy congratulated me and the following Monday up to Friday, I was now busy with the paperwork to go to America. It was incredible but also confusing. Beware what you are praying for, God's answer to your prayer may overwhelm you if you were not prepared to handle them. I never thought that God could answer a prayer and while you are on a different agenda, God can add another agenda that can shock you. The time for me came to depart and head to my sister, Sithembile Gasela in Ilford, East London. Roy Livesey bought me a surface train ticket to London Central and then from there, to board a tube train to Ilford, East London. The trains are so fast in Britain. I had some friends from the Baptist Church of Roy and his wife, Rae accompanied me to the train station. They came to bid me farewell and gave me some gifts and money. There were two friends, Tessa Mitchell and Kate MacArthur who became so close to me and they were thrilled to know about my family. I got into the train and the train departed around 9:00 am to London Central. It was a joyful ride and, in my heart, I was overwhelmed by joy and thanked God for all the opportunities and the connections I had in the UK and also in the USA. What achievement and opportunities that I had struck with so many people within two weeks in Britain? I imagined that I had come for the conference but the conference birthed many opportunities and connections with so many people. Only God could do that as he guided my steps even to meet and connect with Roy Livesey. It was such a blessing!

I arrived at the house of my niece, Sithembile Gasela but she had gone to school as she was studying to be a nurse at a local University. She had left the keys hidden under a stone that she told me where it was. Sithembile Gasela is a lovely sister (niece) as I usually call her. She has a very kind heart and is very helpful to everything possible. We grew up together and we used to play together and became so close to each other. She had left the family back home and her husband, Mr. Pfukani Ndebele, pursued her nursing career. They had met while they were both working in the Ministry of Education in Zimbabwe. She was staying with Christopher Mathema, one of our cousin brothers. Christopher was also a kind and compassionate brother. We soon synchronized to a powerful team. They both welcomed me and we lived together, peacefully. They used to go to work in the morning and I remained home but I would visit places, board buses to visit, especially Central London where there were some activities taking place. Central London was a hive of all human beings from all over the world. I had plenty of time and I was having a visitor's visa and I was not allowed to work. I spent the whole day out, visiting alone except on weekends where I would visit places with Thembie and Chris. There was one time I applied to study Dental where my sister was studying at Gifford University but the scholarship was impossible for foreigners.

In our neighborhood, there was a Little Ilford Baptist Church in East London. Whenever I passed by that area of the church, I prayed to God that I could start a new church around that area, United Baptist Church/UK. I would pray and ask God to open the doors but I never thought about what I was praying for, and God was listening. My time to go back to Zimbabwe had come and I was needed back for work. There was a lot of work demand at the Head Office and I held two very important positions, the Vice Church Chairman and the Church Administrator. Rev. Alfred Simango could not cope alone with such demand. I had to go and carry on with the work. Although my sister Sithembile and brother Chris did not want me to go, I was compelled to take responsibility to go back. However, I had strong conviction to start a church in Britain and I promised that I would be back to plant a church in the UK. The flight took 10 hours and 30 minutes. Rev. Simango sent a driver, Mr. Wendy Matyanga, who was also the Manager of the Conference Center to pick me up at the airport. We were very close and good friends too with Wendyson Matyanga. He picked me in the morning. I tried to rest that day but the Head Office brought work in my house, to sign checks, respond to emergencies and many other stuffs. I was glad to reunite with my family, my wife and children. They had missed me so much and I had missed them too.

I had a strong conviction to go back and start a church in the UK but with my responsibility to the church and family, I tried to suppress that conviction and passion. My visa was still open and I decided to take my annual leave instead, so that I could go back and start a UBC/UK church. Some of the members of the church who had gone for the conference did not return home. I looked for work in Britain and brought their families later. I shared my vision to start a UBC church in the UK with Rev. Alfred Simango and Dr. Bishop Joshua Dhube and the National Committee. All said, it was not necessary. The Church did not have money to send me back to the UK. I decided to ask some of my close friends to raise money to buy my air ticket. First, I approached Rev. Onias Tapera and shared my vision with him and he gave me part of the money. I approached Steven Gwasira and shared my vision with him and I asked him if he could help with some money to buy the air ticket. He agreed and I still remember when we knelt at Steven Gwasira's office when he was still an Executive Director at Zimbabwe

Bank and he prayed a fervent prayer, asking God to open the way. He gave me the money. I also approached Joel Matyanga, a close friend of mine who was one of my youths in Mutare when I was still a Pastor at UBC City Church and he gave me the money. The three friends gave me the money I had needed to help me to buy the air ticket to go back to the UK with the mission of planting a church there.

I flew to London, UK London, Heathrow airport and I took a bus to my sister's house. I told Sithembile Gasela and Christopher Mathema that I had come to plant a church. They convinced me that after planting the church, I should stay in the UK as a Pastor and bring my family. People who went to the UK don't usually go back home because of the political and economic situation. They encouraged me to look for a job or apply for asylum because of the political and economic upheavals, with the killings of the opposition party members in Zimbabwe. Well, I did not belong to any political party but I remained neutral and condemned each side if they were perpetuating violence and violating human rights, especially those human rights that were in contradiction to the word of God. You know when you are living with people who have a different perspective than you have, they easily drill their opinions on you until you see as if it was true and logical. My sister Sithembile and Christopher said how could I go back to a torn apart country like Zimbabwe when God had allowed me to come to the land of Canaan in the UK, flowing with honey and milk. They said that if I would bring my family to the UK, it would be the best option than to go back to Zimbabwe. Sithembile called my wife to convince her that she has to come over with the children.

Those voices seemed to diminish the zeal and passion for the word of God to spread in the UK. The question was which voices do you listen to? Their voices made sense and were very genuine considering the situation in Zimbabwe. The question was posed to me intuitively, as to who do you listen to? Do you listen to your relatives and consanguinity with all the good intentions for your personal comfort and development or do you listen to God to fulfill His purpose? On Sunday, I went to Ilford Baptist Church near my sister's house in the area and I was always passing by the Church and I would pray for God to open the opportunities to plant a church. I would always do a prayer walk around that area. I entered the church and sat down and the service was wonderful. The Pastor, Michael Tuttiett was preaching on Jonah, who ran away from God's assignment. This message was directed to me, not anyone else, I thought. Pastor Mike explained why when a person who is sent by God to accomplish a task, should never run away from God. He explained how easy it is to go where you want and to accomplish your ambitions but not the will of God. It was an incredible sermon but piercing in the heart. My vision and passion were resurrected and when I told Sithembile and Christopher, they agreed that the sermon was true but that I had to consider my family's welfare too. When I was home, with the voices around me I would ponder again as to what to do. The second Sunday, Pastor Michael Tuttiutt was still on Jonah again. He was preaching the series on Jonah. God was talking to me through Pastor Michael to listen to His voice not anyone's voice.

To pacify myself and justify my action to exactly what Jonah did, I applied to study Masters in Theology at Oxford University in the department of Divinity/Theology. I was called to come for an interview. My sister paid for my bus ticket and off I went. I was interviewed by the Dean of Divinity/Theology. He was impressed about my background and what I had achieved and my position I had held. When he asked about the funding of the studies, I had nothing to offer and the British could not give me grants for my studies because I was a foreigner. The Faculty Dean said that there were no scholarships for foreigners and that life would be very hard to maintain at the University as a foreign student if I didn't have strong financial support. It actually seemed God was closing doors in the UK. I went back disappointed but still hopeful. On the third Sunday, I went to Little Ilford Baptist Church again for Sunday Service and now I was getting used to Pastor Michael and I never told him that he was speaking to me directly with his preaching series on Jonah. That day he introduced me to the congregation and I did not want to tell him that I was a Pastor in case he might want to trace where I was from and what I was doing in East London. When he heard that I was from Zimbabwe, he told the whole congregation that there was a Zimbabwean who had been a member for some time.

When he introduced me to Shepherd Ziko, I told Shepherd that I knew someone called Mr. Ziko of Cashel Valley. He told me that it was his father. I was shocked. I told him that I was a Pastor in the United Baptist Church in Zimbabwe. He was so excited to know that I knew his father. I told him the whole truth that I was the Vice Church Chairman and the Church Administrator of United Baptist Church, currently. He was flabbergasted. He said he heard about me through his father and the church at large but never knew that I was in the UK. I knew his father very well, a committed Christian who loved the Lord dearly and he was a humble man who was one of the leaders in the Men's fellowship, (VaKweyi), a National Committee member at United Baptist Church. Then Shepherd asked me what I was doing here in the UK instead of leading the church back home. I told him that I had come to plant a church, United Baptist Church in the UK. He looked right in my eyes, and said that it was a good idea and that he always wondered how it could be done to have UBC/UK. God had led me to meet Shepherd Ziko and to go to attend the church at Little Ilford Baptist Church. It was a great boost of my vision and passion. He actually agreed if we could start a United Baptist Church in the UK. He took me to his house which is not far from my sister's house just around the block, very close. Now I found the voice that echoed the same sound of planting a church in the UK.

I called Francis Ndongwe and told him that we wanted to plant a church in the UK. Francis Ndogwe was very committed and I knew him before he got married. He was a close friend of mine and his friend Hlakaniphani Myambo. They used to come to my house when I was still a Pastor in Mutare and they used to study at Mary Mount Teachers' College in Greenside, Mutare. When he heard that I wanted to plant a church and that I found Shepherd Ziko who was fully committed to start with us. I had to go and meet Francis at McDonald's to plan organizing people. We organized and called the people whom Francis Dongwe, Shepherd Ziko knew. Francis Ndongwe and Shepherd Ziko knew people who were scattered around the vicinity and invited them for our first meeting and service on Sunday. Many people were excited and they came with their families. We scheduled the meeting to be held on November 21, 2005 and we met at Mr. and Mrs. Makufa's house. Many people came and we started with the service and ended with the meeting and election of a UBC/UK committee. The elections were held and Francis Ndongwe became the Chairman, Shepherd Ziko became the Secretary and Mrs. Makufa became the Treasurer. We chose some people to be committee members and the United Baptist Church/UK became official and established on November 21, 2005. God had done it through us! Praise be to God!

Sithembile and Christopher were excited to hear that a church has been planted in the UK. However, they did not give up on discouraging me to go back to Zimbabwe. Instead, they encouraged me to be the Pastor of the newly formed church. I spoke with the members of the new church to be their Pastor. I applied for a Religious Visa to Britain Homeland Security. They told me to send the passport with supporting documents of financial support for them to grant me the Religious Visa. They were very friendly at British Homeland Security but the church was still young and had no financial statements and it was just starting. I saw that God did not allow me to be in the UK. It seemed God was blocking anything to do with living or serving in the UK. I listened to God's voice to plant the church and now who was going to tender and shepherd the new church. God did not allow me to be the Pastor of the United Baptist Church/UK. God had someone else in mind to shepherd the flock. Something twigged my heart to remind me about the American pathway. My mind was in the USA but my heart was in the UK. God wanted me to be in the USA but I wanted to be in the UK. Let's see who would win in the tag of war.

At last, I was convinced to go back home and my work home was piling. I got prepared to go back. At least, I had accomplished what God had sent me to do, to plant the church, UBC/UK. For my personal gain, God did not allow me to accomplish it. The day to depart to the airport was messed up. Sithembile had organized one of our friends to come and pick me up to go to the Heathrow airport. I was supposed to check in at 5:00 pm and Air Zimbabwe was to depart at 7:00 pm.

The person who came to pick me up was delayed. When we left the house, it was 4:05 pm and it took about 50 minutes to Heathrow airport average, about 34 miles. There was heavy traffic and congestion that delayed my arrival at the Heathrow airport. I was late. I tried to run as fast as my legs could carry me but when I tried to check, it was closed. My heart sank and I knew I was in trouble in many ways. We drove back very disappointed because if you miss the plane, there is no refund. I had to rebook again but I was not having enough money for the return ticket. I had to call my friends at Glasco, Tessa and Kate. They sent someone who was bringing the money. I went to rebook an agent for Air Zimbabwe. I had to wait for four days before the plane was available. I made sure that I boarded the bus to the Heathrow airport and I arrived 5 hours before the check-in. I had learned a lesson.

We landed at 7:15 am and Wendy Matyanga came to pick up. It was great to reunite with my family and the Head Office staff. There was a lot of back-log of work on my desk and the preparation of the National Assembly at Biriri Mission School. I managed to compile my reports as the Vice Church Chairman and as the Church Administrator to report at the National Assembly in December, 2005. I reported how we managed to plant a new church, UBC/UK. The UBC/UK was geared to support the UBC Head Office with a large budget in British Pounds. With the economic slump and the highest inflation, the world had ever known, UBC/UK came as a big blessing to the whole church. Although some of the members in the National Assembly did not receive the news with joy, for other reasons best known to themselves. We kept moving on even if I faced unjustifiable antagonisms. However, many of the members of the National Assembly including Pastors appreciated the job I had done, especially, Rev. Timothy Myambo, my friend, who supported the worthy cause I had initiated. After the National Assembly Meeting, the highest governing board, with representatives from all the provinces, we went back to our respective homes.

We made an appointment for the interview with my wife Judith with an American Embassy for a study visa application, the F-1 visa and the F-2 visa, respectively. The appointment for the interview for the F-1 visa was on January 11, 2006. When the day of our interview arrived, we took all the necessary documents required for the interview, my original education certificates, birth certificates, marriage certificate, ordination certificate, marriage officer certificate and other certificates. We got into American Embassy to meet with the consular at 9:00 am. There were a number of people in the line for visa applications. We had confidence that they would grant us the visas because we had everything we needed, educational certificates, professional certificates, full scholarship, and money for living expenses. When my turn came, we went to the window of the consular. The interview took almost 15 minutes. We were denied and we were not granted the F-1 and F-2 visas, despite having shown the consular evidence of financial support from the Puritan Reformed Theological Seminary, educational certificates and supporting letters from the Church Chairman, Rev. Alfred Simango. The main reason the consular refused to grant us the F-1 and F-2 visas was that there was no evidence that we would come back if we went together to the United States as a family. She said that at least if my wife and children remained, it would be evident that I would come back to rejoin the family. We were disappointed and the Puritan Reformed Theological Seminary were also disappointed to learn that we had been denied the visa as they were fervently praying for our interview. We went back home and anticipated going back again.

Meanwhile, I continued to work, drawing the strategic plan for the United Baptist Church and all our institutions. I mapped the vision 2020 for the United Baptist Church, to plant new United Baptist Churches in all cities in Zimbabwe by 2020. The UBC Youth Director was also under my supervision and we had to organize a strategic plan for the youth leadership in one of the hotels of Mutare. We had invited Rev. Onias Tapera to be the Guest Speaker. Ngonidzashe Chindondondo was one of the National Youth Executive Committees and he attended the meeting. I had met and saw the passion and the zeal of this young man for the Lord in Glenview United Baptist. They were about four boys, including Tawanda Ndarera in Glenview United Church who sang melodious music, acapella and clap and danced. I just connected with Ngonidzashe Chindondondo. Harare South and North United

Baptist Church Youth District organized an evangelism event in Rushinga and they invited me to be a guest speaker for the weekend. I got interested in Ngoni's preaching, singing and the passion he had for the Lord. When we met again in Mutare for the National Youth National Committee, I had known him for a while and recognized for his gift of preaching and the talent of singing. At lunch time, we sat at the same table and I inquired from him what he was doing at that time and he told me that he was not doing anything because he had got laid off from his job about six months prior. I asked him if he had ever considered to serve the Lord as a Pastor. The answer was no, he had his own plans to be accomplished. I asked if he would accomplish his stipulated plans while serving the Lord but he refuted that idea. I had seen his passion, the zeal and to serve the Lord as a Pastor, was very fitting according to my observations and the discernment. I was not surprised about his answer because most young people think serving the Lord is after they accomplish their own plans. I had a conviction that he would one day respond to the call but I prayed that God would direct his path. I shared with the leadership at the Head Office, Rev. Alfred Simango, Rev. Jealousy Manyumbu and we prayed for Ngoni and to also talk to him. I loved him dearly and I saw how the church would be blessed if he joined the ministry. Patiently, we waited for the Lord to speak to him, directly but it seemed it took more time than anticipated. Praise the Lord that later, after some years, he responded to the call. We are so grateful to God to have such young people, like Ngoni, serving the Lord with passion and conviction.

On March 14, I went to the American Embassy for the second time for a F-1 visa now alone without my wife or children. When the Consular called me to her window, the second time and she asked me why I had come again within a short period of time. She asked if anything had changed to be granted the F-1 visa and I told her that I was leaving my wife and children. But the Consular denied me the F-1 visa application once again. She gave me a reason that I did not have enough property to compel me to come back. She also gave a surprising reason which really shocked me because I was not ready for it. She told me that she has never interviewed anyone with the full scholarship, tuition covered, housing cover, and everything covered. She also asked me what my intention was as I was already having obtained my Bachelor's degree, Masters in Educational Administration, Planning and Policy Studies, holding two positions of the Vice Bishop and the Church Administration, asking why I was going to a tiny Seminary in Grand Rapids, Michigan, which is not even in the world map. Those were challenging questions. I told her how unique the Seminary was with deeper and incredible theological training for international leaders to usher new dispensation of intellectual and vibrant scholars of the 21st century. Regardless of my articulated answers to her, she still denied me the F-1 visa application. I was really disappointed to be denied the F-1 visa application.

I started to question God if it was His will to pursue going to study in the USA. It seemed the doors were closing everywhere. I had tried in the UK and I did not succeed, I was trying to apply to go to America but the doors were closing. The Puritan Theological Seminary in Grand Rapids, Michigan, prayed for me and wrote an appeal letter to the American Embassy to grant me a F-1 visa, but the consular denied. Evangelical Fellowship of Zimbabwe (EFZ) General Secretary, Rev. Andrew Muchechetere, and Evangelical Fellowship of Zimbabwe (EFZ), Rev. Trevor Manhanga, all wrote appeal letters and recommendations to the American Embassy for me to be granted the study F-1 visa. Even the United Baptist Church Chairman, Rev. Alfred Simango wrote a recommendation to the Consular, to grant me the study visa, but all the appeal letters were denied. After successive disappointments of being denied an F-1 visa application to go to the United States for further studies, I nearly gave up. I kept doing my work as the Vice Church Chairman and the Church Administrator. The doors of going to further my studies overseas seemed to have closed but I kept the faith. I did not go to the American Embassy again until July 20, 2006 to try once more. I decided in my heart that if I was denied again, I would not go back again to apply for the F-1 visa and I would forget about going to America any more. I made an appointment again and Henk Kleyn from the Puritan Reformed Theological Seminary (PRTS), the Registrar paid all these appointment fees as who sent me all the time from my full scholarship that I was granted by the PRT Seminary.

On July 20, 2006, I went to the American Embassy for my appointment for the third time to apply again for the study visa. The interview did not take long because the young male Consular asked me what had changed in my situation to be granted the visa. He honestly told me that he could not grant me the visa because his boss had denied me the visa and if he granted me, that would contradict the reasons she had denied me in the first place. I went for the fourth time on September 5, 2006. I was like I was just pushing the doors to open but God did not allow that to happen. I was finally denied and he told me not to come again until at least a year. The male Consular gave me advice to come after a year or else if I could come back soon, they might put me in another list. That was the end of my desire to go to America to further my studies. It was a clear sign that God did not approve to go to America either. To study in the UK was a nightmare with lack of scholarship. To study in America, with the full scholarship but I had been denied four times. I asked God why. I concluded that the door to study in the United States was closed too. I was pretty sure that God had closed the doors in the UK and now he had also closed the doors to study in the United States. I vowed that I would never pursue studying in the USA. However, studying a Masters in Theology was still in my heart. I had to push another door to open but now it was South Africa, my motherland.

In 2006 Annually Revival Meeting, I suggested to the National Committee meeting to hold the Annual Revival Meeting in Harare for the first time. The National Committee agreed to give it a trial with the support of young National Committee members, the likes of baba Mapaike, baba Gwenzi, Chikavanga, Gwasira and many others. However, it had never happened ever to have Annual Revival Meeting in Harare. I was both the Vice Church Chairman and the Church Administrator. I was running around, organizing everything with the help of Wendyson Matyanga and Albert Makacha. I looked for several possible venues to hold this big meeting. I finally secured it at Belvedere Teachers' College. We paid the fees for Wednesday,

Thursday, Friday, Saturday and Sunday. We rented the whole College for five days as the students were on vacation. This included the Main Hall, the dormitories, the kitchen, two dinning-rooms and some other stuff.

The buses ferried the members of the church as far as Rusitu, Chimanimani, Chipinge, Rushinga, Bulawayo, Masvingo, Mutare, Gweru, Kwekwe, Kariba and many areas where United Baptist was present although others did not make it. People were thrilled to be in Harare, some of them for their first time ever. The plan was to introduce United Baptist Church in Harare City in a massive way. Of course, we had United Baptist Churches in Harare but we wanted to mark its presence in Harare, the Capital City of Zimbabwe. We organized to march on Saturday from the Reserve Bank of Zimbabwe in downtown to Belvedere Teachers' College, singing and praising the Lord our God in the streets and many people joined us as we proceeded with the Police Escort in the front, on the sides and at the back. I went to Pocket Hill TV Studios to place United Baptist Church advert for the Annual Revival Meeting for the first time ever. That's when I discovered how expensive the TV adverts could be for just 30 seconds which was aired twice. I had to organize for the Police escort also, to start from the Reserve Bank of Zimbabwe to Belvedere Teachers' Collage. They told me that they did not have petrol/gas and I promised to provide the petrol/gas for them which I did. The Saturday's march from Reserve Bank of Zimbabwe to Belvedere Teachers' Collage was spectacular with women (Ruiyano) and Men (Vakweyi) in their respective unions, black color, representing sin, red color representing the blood of Jesus Christ that washed our sins away and the white color representing the righteousness that was imputed to us through our faith in Christ Jesus as we were cleaned to be as white as snow. Women (Ruiyano) uniform is added with a white apron, signifying the Christian Service. I was chosen to be the Guest Speaker that year in 2007, Annual Revival Meeting and I was preaching from the book of Amos. It was a successful Annual Revival Meeting held in Harare for the first time. Many church members of the Church appreciated so much to have come from come from very far away and be in Harare.

Over 3,000 people attended the Annual Revival Meeting, according to the statistics conducted by the Head Office. Mr. Headman Mukondomi extended his gratitude to us for affording his people from Rusitu to come to Harare to attend the Annual Revival Meeting for their first time.

Meanwhile, after being refused four times the USA F-1 study visa, I decided to apply to George Whitefield College in Cape Town, South Africa to study Masters in Theology. I was admitted to George Whitefield College and the College gave me a partial scholarship for tuition and boarding but it was not adequate to move with the family. I had to raise funds for the whole family. I applied for the study visa in the South Africa Embassy and I was granted a South Africa study visa on December 12, 2006 that would expire on December 31, 2009. I was excited that at least South Africa opened the doors for me but I was now trying to raise the funds to be able to go with the whole family to South Africa. Meanwhile, Puritan Theological Seminary had given up praying for me because it was like three years praying for me to come over but they also concluded that God had closed the door. Henk Kleyn, the Seminary Registrar, organized for me to take my classes online. He connected me with the professors and they sent me course outlines, syllabus, books and sent me some money for my scholarship to buy a computer and a printer. I knew how difficult it would be to do Distance Learning but I started the school online. Meanwhile, I was preparing to go to George Whitefield College in South Africa.

When I informed the church, United Baptist Church National Committee, through the Church Chairman, Rev. Alfred Simango that I would be going for a study leave to further my studies at George Whitefield in Cape Town, South Africa in January 15, 2007, the National Committee and National Assembly in December 2006, appealed and persuaded me to postpone my studies to 2008. The reason they filed that request was that as I was the Vice Church Chairman and still the Acting Church Administrator, there were many activities happening in the church they need my attention and monitoring, such as I had initiated the auditing of the two schools, the Conference Center, Rusitu Hospital, Rusitu Bible College and also wrapping up the closer of the school and the farm in Mozambique. The auditing of all these institutions required my attention and to see their logical conclusion. The work was massive and they asked me if I could postpone my studies to 2008, instead of 2007. I was the one in the control of all these institutions and as the Board Chairman of the institutions. I agreed as I felt the weight and the need for me to conclude all the auditing of the institutions, the winding of the school and the farm in Mozambique. I accepted the request and I told the Principal of George Whitefield College that the church had asked me to postpone my studies to January 2008. He agreed and accepted a postponement to start on January 17, 2008.

2007 was a year of working flat out to make sure that I completed all the tasks and to bring them to a logical conclusion with smooth transition too. On February 2, 2007, Rev. Alfred Simango and I went to Mozambique to have a meeting with the teachers and the missionaries in Mozambique and the Pastors who were responsible for the farm to conclude the mission work there. The mission work in Chimoio, Mozambique was concluded. We wanted to start new mission work in the Southwest of Mozambique after being given a farm in Mutsongi area. On May 23, 2007, we went to Mutsongi United Baptist Church in Mozambique on the Southwest of Mozambique, a different area than the one which had the school and the farm in Chimoio. We drove to Vimba village and parked the car at the Vimba shopping center and we crossed the Rusitu River in a small boat in which we paid the fee to cross to the other side. Chief Mutsongi gave the United Baptist Church a farm to develop it into a massive agricultural farm and to build a school. We were invited to visit and see the farmland and to organize a church there. The Rusitu River was full and scary to cross in a small boat, fitting only two people and with the boat peddler, who was always standing, who was able to control the small boat. After we crossed the river, we walked about 5 km to Mutsongi Village on the path because there was no road at all or a bridge for cars. When we arrived, they were waiting for us anxiously and with excitement. They received us with open arms, ululating and singing as if we were missionaries from another country and of course we were. They were excited to have the United Baptist Church Head Office officials. There was a glimpse of hope of starting a farm and a school in Mutsongi Village. The chief was excited to see us and he took us for a tour of the farm that he had given to United Baptist Church. The villagers were so excited to be part of the occasion. We had all night prayer, singing and preaching and many people repented and accepted Christ as their Lord and Savior. I was the guest speaker with a Portuguese interpreter because they speak Portuguese in Mozambique, not English.

The following morning, we had a meeting with the Chief and the elders of the local church that was drafted as a working committee. We discussed how they would be working with the Chief Mutsongi and how the Head Office would be conducting the meetings and the official registration of United Baptist Church with the Mozambican government for the memorandum of understanding and the lease agreement. It was a fruitful meeting and worth of the sacrifice. Rusitu District was responsible for liaising with the Mutsongi UBC in Mozambique as the local authority with Chief Mutsongi. After the meeting in the morning, we left around 11:30 am and we headed to the Rusitu River to cross with a small boat again to Zimbabwe. After crossing over to Zimbabwe in a dangling small boat, we were soon safe on the Zimbabwe side. We drove to Rusitu Mission to sleep there before we drove the following day to the Head Office in Harare. I continued with my work in 2007.

One day, when I was out of the office attending to one of the trucks, the Hilux, that we used for travelling with at Farai Matyanga's garage who was a mechanic, my wife called me and told me that the American Embassy Education Department at East Gate downtown in Harare called and they wanted to speak to me. I was really shocked to hear that the American Embassy called me. For what and why? I did not want to hear about the American Embassy any more. I had concluded that I would never have anything to do with American Embassy again. My focus was now to go to South Africa where they had granted me the study visa. It was August 2007 and I had about four months to go before I left for my studies in South Africa in January, 2008.

When my wife, Judith, told me that they wanted to speak to me, I refused to call back. I was done with them and I was no longer interested in dealing with them. They had denied me an F-1 visa application four times and I had concluded that God had closed the door. With the insistence of my wife to call them back because the lady who called had emphasized that I had to call her back because it was very, very important. I then returned the call, reluctantly, on the phone number that she had left with my wife Judith to give it to me. When I called her, the lady sounded lively on the line. She was happy and excited to hear that it was me. She asked if I was Sabelo Sam Mhlanga. I told her that I was. She told me that she was calling to inform me that I should come on August 17, at American Embassy Educational Department at East Gate at 9:00 am for American educational orientation because I was one of those with a study F-1 visa. She told me that I was one of those who had been enlisted to come to American Education Department for orientation. I was shocked to hear that. However, I told her that I did not have a study F-1 visa. I told her I was denied the F-1 visa application on September 4, 2006. She was surprised to hear that I did not have a F-1 visa. She told me that maybe I did not know what the US visa was and she was very confident that I had an F-1 visa because my name was on the list with those who were granted a visa. Something in my heart said, "God directs your steps and He holds your future." I insisted that I did not have an F-1 visa. She told me to come the following morning to show me the F-1 visa on my passport and that I should come with all my educational and professional documents.

I told my wife Judith all what had transpired and she said that maybe God is in control of this situation now. The following morning, I took my passport and my educational and professional documents, all the scholarships that I was granted by the Puritan Reformed Theological Seminary, an admission letter, a letter signed by Ernest Bradley as a financial guarantor for all my financial needs. I went to her office and she welcomed me and she took a look at my passport page by page looking at the F-1 visa in my passport. She was shocked to see that for sure, there was no F-1 visa in my passport. She wondered how my name was in the list of those who had been granted the F-1 visa. She said that it was a mistake that my name was in the list of those who were granted the F-1 visa but how it was included, no one knew how. She looked at my educational and professional documents, the financial support, the scholarship, and I found out that everything was in perfect order and she tried to enquire why I was denied the F-1 visa when everything was in order. He called the American Embassy and checked everything and found that I deserved to have had a F-1 visa. She told me to go and apply for an appointment at the American Embassy. She gave me her phone number and told me that during my interview, if they deny or ask for additional evidence, that I should give the Consular her phone number so that they can call her for any verification. I left her office with a glimpse of hope that maybe God was now paving the way for me to go to America. I could not imagine how my name got in the list of those who had been granted the F-1 study visa. This God we worship, He is a miracle working God. See what He has done. When He says He will fight for us, He means it. When He shuts the door, no one can open it and when He opens the door, no one can close it. Wow, this is an awesome God. Glory be to God! I will exalt the Name of God forever and ever!

In the morning on November 30, 2007, a month before I was prepared to go to study in Cape Town, South Africa, I went for the interview appointment at 9:00 am, I was interviewed and the Consular did not even ask many questions. I was also ready that if she asked for more proof, I would give her the number of the Manager at the American Embassy Department of the Education to call her for any clarifications or verifications. She simply granted me the F-1 visa and stamped it, just like there without any problem. I called my wife and I told her that I was granted the F-1 visa and she was so excited and she could not believe it. I wrote an email to Henk Kleyn and told him that I was granted the F-1 visa. The whole Seminary, bursted into cheers and they could not believe it. The three years that they had been praying had resulted in answered prayers. They had given up to pray for me because they thought God had closed the door for me to go and join them. When you allow God to take over after you have exhausted all you might and wisdom and it comes to nothing, and then you let the Lord Jesus Christ take over, the results amaze you. Peter and his friends tried all night to catch fish but they caught nothing until Jesus Christ came and he said, "Throw your nest on the right side of the boat and you find some." When they did, they were unable to haul the net in because of the number of fish," (John 21:6, NIV). That was my experience too. I was trying with my own effort to push the doors open but Christ was not in it. God is awesome and His name will be praised and exalted in my life forever because of His goodness to me.

I told the National Committee and Rev. Alfred Simango that I got the F-1 visa. They were happy for me. The United Baptist Church National Committee and the National Assembly in December 2006, played an important part because they had asked me to postpone my studies to 2008. If they had not asked me to postpone to 2008, I would have gone to South Africa at George Whitefield, Cape Town in 2007 and I could have missed going to the United States. God's timing, patience and obedience is vital in every believer's life. God's timing (kairos), Greek, is always perfect. To wait upon the Lord is always fulfilling. Abraham and Sarah were promised to have a son but they were not patient enough, as a result, they schemed a plan to have the son, Ishmael through an Egyptian slave girl, Hagar. The promised son, Isaac was born later in their advanced age, (Gen. 16:1-1-16, NIV). It is important to wait upon the will of God not our own will. What a lesson! "But those who wait on the Lord Shall renew their strength; They shall mount up with wings like eagles, they shall run and be weary, they shall walk and not faint, (Isaiah 40:31, NKJV). This verse became reality in my life. I have every reason to believe that God wanted me to be in America, no doubt about it. My presence in the United States is God approved and I am so grateful to Him and all those who have played pivotal roles, God's steps on purpose for a purpose. To God be the glory!

CHAPTER NINE

The American Dream

I had to leave my family back but it was necessary for me to depart so that they would follow. The Head Office staff and my relatives accompanied me to the airport. My aunt, Agnes Ndlovu and my niece, Madawu, my wife, Judith, the four kids, Wendy Matyanga, Rev. Jealous Manyumbu and his wife and other Head Office staff escorted me to the airport to see me taking off. To part with my wife, Judith and the kids was the most painful thing I had ever experienced. I had left them in the hands of Rev. Alfred Simango, my aunt, Agnes and other Head Office staff. The family was in good hands. I had faith and conviction that they would join me in a short period of time. I knew that God would open the door for them as He had opened the door for me. I flew from Zimbabwe on January 16, via Johannesburg, South Africa and Dakar, Senegal and I arrived in Grand Rapids, on January 18, 2008 in the evening. Henk Kleyn paid the Sevis for my immigration and paid for my air ticket from Zimbabwe to South African to Dakar, Senegal and then to Washington D.C. and then to Grand Rapids, Michigan. I was excited to land on the USA soil once again since 1996. I was happy to have landed safely and seeing all the beauty around me. I started thinking back home about my wife and the children back home. It was a big mountain to climb and the challenge was for my wife and the children to get their visas and to follow me but I was supposed to go first before they could apply for their F-2 visas. The plane was delayed and Henk Klyen and his lovely wife, Margaret had come earlier to welcome me but the plane had been delayed. I asked at the information desk to call Henk Kleyn. The lady who was there was so kind and so gentle with me. She was willing to call Henk and Margaret Kleyn to come pick me up at Grand Rapids Airport. I did not think that the same lady would be a supporter of my family for the whole duration of my studies at the Seminary. She supported my family anonymously, sending gifts during all the holidays, including Thanksgiving, July 4th, Christmas, Easter, and St. Columbus Day. She supplied some books for the children, gift cards etc., through Henk Kleyn. She revealed herself when she came for my graduation as a surprise to me after two and half years.

Henk Kleyn and his lovely wife, Margaret picked me up and took me to their lovely house where I stayed with them for two weeks. What a lovely couple they were. They did everything for me, buying me new clothes, jackets, shoes and many things. The following day, Henk took me to the Seminary and introduced me to the faculty and students. The faculty was so excited to see me as they had prayed for me for more than three years. I was introduced to Dr. Joel Beeke, the founder and the President of the Seminary, in Grand Rapids, Michigan. Dr. Joel was so excited to meet with me and offered a prayer of thanksgiving for my arrival after a long time of waiting. Henk took me for a tour of the Seminary and introduced me to staff, students, and all the lecture rooms. It was not a big Seminary but it was spacious and had a great community of believers who loved the Lord and each other. Henk introduced me to Dr. Bilkes, one of the Professors and to Professor David Murray, originally from Scotland with his wife, Shona, a physician. It was like I was dreaming, to realize that I was in the United States after some many years I had anticipated to come. God's timing is always the best. Henk oriented me with the schedules of the Seminary, classes, classrooms, the library, the food pantry and every necessary thing that I needed to know. Henk was the Seminary Registrar and was conversant with everything in the

Seminary. The classes had already started and I joined in and became busy like others.

The Seminary students were from different countries in the world with diverse students from South Korea, China, Philippines, Brazil, Malawi, Zimbabwe, South Africa, Ghana, Nigeria, Myanmar, Ethiopia, Europe, Syria, Canada, and other countries. I lived with Henk and Margaret Klyen for about two weeks and then he told me that after two weeks, I would be living with Marty Singled and Dereck Bars, while waiting for my wife Judith and the children to come from Zimbabwe. They were from Canada with the brotherly love that was true Christian love in action.

Meanwhile, they were furnishing the house I and my family would be living in. After two weeks living with Henk and Margaret Klyen, I then moved to stay with Marty and Dereck. They were students from Canada and were very fine young men who loved the Lord dearly and they were very kind. They used to cook for our dinner or they would take me out to eat out and they would pay for my meals. They did not let me buy food, toiletry, gas, electricity or pay rent. I really enjoyed living with Marty and Dereck and we developed a bond and friendship with each other. Dereck Bars was blind and very smart in everything and more independent. It was really a blessing to stay with Marty and Dereck. They made me feel welcomed and taken care of with the love of the brethren. I am indebted to Marty Singled and Dereck Bars for their kind hearts, generosity and care for me in the first weeks in the USA. When I began my classes, I had an educational shock. The British English, English spellings, words, the meanings of words, most of them were different. Zimbabwe is a former British colony and the country used British English and all the examinations were from Cambridge University examinations. Zimbabwe was dependent on the University of Cambridge Examinations Board for almost twenty to thirty years after independence. The shock was frustrating and confusing. I did my elementary, high school, college and university education in the British English with the British standard. Now to change and make adjustments was a great challenge. The educational shock was to learn that I had to type my own assignments using the laptop or the library computers. The Seminary bought every student a laptop to write assignments. All assignments were to be submitted, typed and formatted with Turabian style and formatted. I had to flow with the crowd and to adjust to the Turabian style formatting all the scholarly documents. I had done my Bachelors and Masters in Zimbabwe using the APA style formatting for academic and scholarly documents and now I had to change to use Turabian style formatting.

The grading of the papers, examinations and dissertations or thesis was different. I had to adjust to meet the American standard of education. I was not the only one going through the adjustments, almost all foreign students had to go through the initiation. With the laptops and computers, it became easier because the American English was in the Microsoft Windows 7, 10 and 365 and would automatically correct the words, spellings and grammar. The Microsoft Windows were the changers because whatever was documented, the Microsoft Windows would format accordingly.

My wife Judith and the children went for the interviews at American embassy to get the F-2 visas to join me in the USA in February, 2008. The interviews did not take very long. My wife went with the children to apply for the F-2 visas. She had instructed the children to kneel and pray when she was asked to come for the interview at the Consular window. When she was being interviewed, the children knelt and prayed. When the Consular asked her where the children were, my wife told the Consular that they were praying because they wanted to go to be with their father in America. The Consular's heart melted and she was moved by the children who were innocent and longing to join their father. My wife and the children were granted the F-2 visas and then Henk bought the air tickets for them. On February 25, 2008 they flew from Zimbabwe to Johannesburg, South Africa. In Johannesburg, they transitioned from Air Zimbabwe to South Africa Airways. They boarded South Africa Airways, to Dakar, Senegal then to Washington D.C. After fifteen minutes taking off from Johannesburg, South Africa airport, the plane developed electrical faults in the mid-air and there was smoke that engulfed the whole plane and the pilots announced that they were turning back to Johannesburg airport for emergency landing.

Blessing, our first-born son, who was ten years old, encouraged his mom who had panicked and knelt and prayed for their survival, together with other passengers in the plane, fearing that the plane would crash. Prayer changes things. The plane returned and they had a rough emergency landing. Thank God, the plane did not crash, "He will not allow your foot to be moved; He who keeps you will not slumber," (Psalm 121:3, NKJV). I was waiting for them in Grand Rapids Airport in Michigan when I heard that their plane had been delayed because of technical faults. My heart sank and I prayed for their safe arrival. The plane was fixed and they boarded the same plane the following morning. They finally arrived on February 26, 2008 and I was with Henk and Margaret when we welcomed them at Grand Rapids Airport. They were all exhausted because of the long flights and the trauma they had in the plane the previous day. It was truly a joy to see them arrive and they got the shock of their lives because Grand Rapids was carpeted with snow all over and they could not see even the houses when they landed. It was so cold -15 degrees that day. Henk and Margaret took all of us to McDonalds for lunch. I had moved to our new house a week before they arrived. Henk and Margaret drove us to our new house which was well-furnished, closed, filled the clothes and the kitchen with all kinds of food. It was like we had arrived in a new strange world where there was plenty of everything. It was a three bedroomed house, a beautiful house near the Plymouth School, owned by the Netherland Reformed Church and supported by the Free Reformed Church and the Seminary.

The house was strategically positioned so that the children would walk to and from school. Henk and the Seminary had organized and arranged our house so perfectly for our arrival and for the private school for our children who were 10, 7, 5 and 3. The Seminary community, the church community was so friendly, loving and caring that we were thrilled with the Christian environment. My wife and the children were welcomed in both churches, the Free Reformed Church and the Netherlands Reformed Church in which Dr. Joel Beeke was the

Pastor with Rev. Vanderzwag was the associate Pastor. In the Free Reformed Church in which Henk and Margaret Kleyn were members and the Pastor being Rev. Bilkes, Sr. We were so much welcomed that we felt at home and we were so appreciative to God and the Christian community to be among them. My wife and I were shocked when we visited stores that were packed with a variety of food on the shelves compared to Zimbabwe where we left the shelves empty because they were food at all because of the economic slump and corruption, exacerbated by commercial farms which confiscated by the political system and regime of President Robert Mugabe and the productions of agricultural produce had ceased. We once joked to each that we might have been taken by rapture.

We consolidated and started our new life and new home in America in a different style and environment, with sincere gratitude to the entire Christian community of the church and the Seminary. The center of interest and daily routine were the Seminary, the church and our home. They bought us a van and I had to go for road tests even though I had a Zimbabwe Driver's License. Pete Van Kempen trained and taught me how to drive in American roads and Highways and he also took me for driving lessons to be familiar with the roads and the road regulations. I appreciate Pete Van Kempen's dedication and support to help me pass my driving license which he did voluntarily and to many students at the Seminary. We slowly got used to each other with the student body at the Seminary from various and diverse countries. We soon befriended Brian Kamwendo and Chimwemwe family from Malawi, George and Bridget Kalengo family from Malawi, Taboek Lee family from South Korea and David Kim family from South Korea, Koos and Elzar from South Africa, Antoine and Nicolene family from South Africa, Matalius Lukhoozi family from Malawi, Pastor Brian Najapfour from Philippines, Anteneh Taye Abarah family from Ethiopia, Marty Singled and Dereck Barrs from Canada, Thomas from Ghana, Mustafa from Syria, Tiago from Brazil and many families and brothers from the USA and other countries all over the world. That was the best time to meet such godly brothers from across the globe with the true love of Jesus Christ.

The Seminary and the church community, the Netherland Reformed Church and Free Reformed were like one big family. However, there were many cultural shocks in many ways. The first shock was the amount of snow Grand Rapids had accumulated and continued to accumulate during the winter. When our children saw the snow for the first time, they were so excited and they wanted to go outside to play in the snow. We dressed them with socks, jackets and hats to warm them and let them go to play in the snow. Within 5 minutes playing outside, they came back running into the house feeling very cold and they vowed that they would not go back again. My wife and I were laughing our lungs out when we heard them screaming and wanting to warm their hands, feet and ears. Well, within a few weeks, we all got used to snow and families used to take us out for sledding. We became used to it and we were able to go out on our own to sled and had fun. The snow kept on falling and I would wake up early every morning to shovel the snow for the kids to be able to walk to board the school bus at our gate. By the time they came back from school at 3:30 pm, the snow would have accumulated again and I would shovel again. I developed a back ache by shoveling the snow every day. It became a routine. We explored many things in the new land, America. We developed relationships and friendships with many families, and couples such as Pete and Mimi Van Kempen, Moedeck, Bruce, Tim DeVries, etc. Pete and Mini Van Kempen used to invite our family for tubbing in their lake with Brain and Chimwemwe Kamwendo, George and Bridget Kalengo and all our children. We used to have fun with all these families.

At the Seminary, I was made to sign an agreement form, stating that I would not talk about baptism at the Seminary to the students and the staff as I was a Baptist student. Most of the students were Presbyterians and Reformed Church members. Their belief on baptism is by sprinkling as their doctrine and for the Baptists, it is baptism by immersion. They did not want me to have any influence about baptism by immersion to any students and staff. There was another student who was a Baptist from the Philippines, Brian Najapfour and I don't know whether he was made to sign the agreement too. Another Baptist student was Johnny Serafin from Brazil. The Seminary treated students equally regardless of their race, nationality or creed although one could see the elements of prejudice in one area and another, especially in the church. Actually, I was made to be aware that I was black. Back in Zimbabwe, I never knew that I was distinct from other people. I never experienced prejudice in Zimbabwe, except tribalism which was the tribal differences between the Ndebeles and the Shonas. With much exposure in American culture, with prejudice and discrimination, I became aware that there is a big gulf between the blacks and the whites. I did not notice the prejudice between the whites and the Asians but between the blacks and whites. I felt the differences and I started to realize that I was a black man. Before that I thought people are all the same created in God's image, (*Imago Dei*), and equal but then I became conscious of who I was and that I was different from others around me who had different skin colors. I now understand fully that we are fallen beings, who need grace and mercy to treat each other equally and with dignity. It is even sad when it comes from the church that profess Christ who broke the barriers between the Jews and the Samaritans, showing them that they are all equal in the eyes of God. However, I continued to treat people in the same way with dignity and mutual respect but I was now aware of the gulf between the races. The fact that the Seminary was a Christian Institution and that it had a diverse student population, it was not visible and not announced as such but the skin was compared everywhere.

When I was in Britain in 2005, I never felt any kind of prejudices and there was no profiling of anyone I know. People lived in their diversity in harmony in Britain unlike in America. I started to feel uncomfortable with the gulf that was existing among all races. In Britain, prejudice, according to my observations and analysis, was deep under the skin and it was not as visible and obvious between the blacks and the whites as in the United States. The race issue was made more clearer to us in 2008 when we came because it was the time when Senator Barack Obama was the Presidential candidate for the Democratic Party against President George W. Bush. There was a gulf between the Blacks and the Whites because of the political divide. The divide escalated when President Barack Obama won the 2008 elections and became the first Black President in the American history. Through his Presidency, from 2008 to 2016, the color-bar, the racism, discrimination, and the divisions became more and more. As a family, we did not dwell much on politics and social media but we concentrated on what we had come for in the USA, that is education and mission work. My focus was my education and the mission work to spread the good news of Jesus Christ that He is alive and telling people about the hope in Him.

The good part of the Seminary was that those students who were ordained as Ministers were allowed to preach or invited to fill the pulpit supplies across the country in Reformed Churches. The Seminary would assess you and recommend you as a seasoned preacher and they would send the names of the ordained students to Reformed churches across the country. I was one of those who was invited to fill the pulpit supplies to many Reformed Churches across the United States. I became one of the popular preachers in Reformed churches as a pupil supplier. I went to preach in Harrison, Arkansas several times, more than seven times. I loved that church, the Grace Reformed Church. The three services were planned by the preacher, the Psalters, the Scripture, bulletins, and everything. The Sunday School, the first service, the afternoon service and the evening service. The Lord's Day was packed with teachings and preaching the whole day. I would teach the Sunday School, preach in the morning services and afternoon service. They used to come with cooked lunch and we would share the lunch together. During lunch time, we would discuss the sermon with very good questions from the members of the church. They loved the Word of God so dearly. Then we would have an evening service also. Three sermons and Sunday School in one day. They would buy me the air tickets, rent a car for me and book a hotel for me and they would bless me with almost a thousand dollars as a thank you gift. Many times, I was hosted by Joshua Selvy with his lovely family. Grace Reformed Church in Harrison, Arkansas was really a great church.

I also preached at the Reformed Church, in New Jersey. I was hosted by two lovely families on two different occasions as I was invited to preach two times in New Jersey. One family took me for a tour to New York City on a Saturday. We visited the twin towers which were bombed by the terrorists on 9/11/2021. I was shedding some tears standing on ground zero where almost three thousand innocent people perished and the two Twin Buildings collapsed when two planes were hijacked by terrorists. The twin towers were the symbols of the World Trade Center that were opened on April 4, 1973 and were destroyed in 2001 during the September 11 attack. The North Tower stood at 1,368 feet (417 m) and the South Tower stood at 1,362 feet (415.1 m). These two Towers were the tallest buildings in the world and symbolized the mighty New York. The Twin Towers rested directly on the rock. It was the worst tragedy in human history and it was the display of the gravity and the human depravity at its core. When I stood on ground zero in 2009 as they were constructing the foundations again from the bottom up, I shed tears in mourning the innocent souls that died painful deaths. I still remember when it happened on September 11, 2021, when I was a lecturer/ professor at Rusitu Bible College when my friend Rev. Onias Tapera was narrating to me how it happened. We cancelled the classes and called the students to pray for the American people in unison with the whole world.

After the ground zero Twin Towers tour, my hosts, a couple and one of their sons, we boarded a boat to cross the Hudson River, to the Statue of Liberty. This is the Hudson River where the US Airways plane, flight 1549 which made an emergency landing in January 2009. I was in New York in June 2009, six months after that flight had an emergency landing and all the 115 passengers survived and the Pilot, Captain Chesley "Sully" Sullenberger managed to maneuver the US Airways Flight 1549 to land on Hudson River and he became a hero overnight. He was hailed as the legendary hero for his heroic and bravery for the control of the plane. We crossed the Hudson River on a boat and we landed on the Statue of Liberty. When we got there, I marveled at the gigantic sculpt statue that stands tall, lifting a torch, which denotes, "The Statue of Liberty Enlightening the World" which was given as a gift of friendship from France to the United States, on July 4, 1881. It is actually a universal symbol of freedom and democracy.

The Statue of Liberty was dedicated on October 28, 1886, made from copper. It was amazing to visit three places in New York, the ground zero at the Twin Towers that collapsed when the two planes were directed into the buildings by the terrorists, the Hudson River, to see the spot where the US Airways Flight 1549 had an emergency landing and the Statue of Liberty on a Saturday before I had to preach the following Sunday. The Reformed Church in New Jersey really treated me like a king. I appreciate so much the love and care they showed me.

I also went to preach in the city of Pella, Iowa in Marion County. It is a small city with about ten thousand people. It was one of the cities in America that I visited and I did not see any blacks in the streets and it is populated by immigrants from the Netherlands. The congregants were very friendly and kind. The church assigned someone to come and pick me in from the airport and they booked me a hotel. I preached on Sunday morning and after the service, I presented about the situation in Zimbabwean politics, economy and religion through the slides. The congregation was so touched that they got interested in supporting the work in Zimbabwe. The church organized to send drums of clothes, books and other items to the needy people. It was a blessing to connect with the church and have concerns about your own people. Julie and Curt Hoyer, from Covenant Reformed Church, a lovely couple, organized to send clothes, shoes, books and other items to Zimbabwe through Cargo-Link International, to my church back in Zimbabwe, United Baptist Church. The drums of clothes were received by Rev. Peter Chibinjana, January 21, 2010 at the United Baptist Church Head Office, who had succeeded me when I left for the states. After lunch at one of the Dutch restaurants in Pella, we visited the John Deere Manufacturing Company, one of the largest companies that manufactures agriculture, construction, and forestry machinery, diesel engines, drivetrains and farm equipment and automotive for John Deere products all over the world. The founder of John Deere who invented the farming equipment, 1837-1886, developed the first commercially successful scouring steel plough. It was interesting to see how John Deere revolutionized the farming equipment in a massive way. I had a fruitful and blessed weekend in Pella, Iowa. I also preached

Southfield Reformed Presbyterian Church in Detroit, Michigan and Jon Hughes.

We lived in Grand Rapids, Michigan in the Seminary for two and half years. The American dream became a reality. Those two and half years were filled with joy, happiness, fellowship, with loving kindness, caring, devotions, studying the Word, preaching and traveling like the Seminary President Dr. Joel Beeke. We used to travel in the same planes most of the time from Grand Rapids Airport and then we would part ways when we would be transitioning to different planes to different directions. He used to joke that I was now just like him, traveling to preach all over America. One time, I boarded the plane with him from Grand Rapids to Detroit and the plane went through rough turbulence and it was shaking as if it was going to crash and the bags in the cabinets were flying across the seats. People were screaming in panic. I started to pray asking God to intervene. Dr. Joel Beeke was closing his eyes as if he was sleeping and at peace and did not panic. I was comforted whenever I looked at him. My seat was just opposite to his. The plane finally stabilized and he opened his eyes. He asked me if I was scared and I told him that yes, I was, of course. I asked him if he was scared and he said that he wasn't very much because he told me that he had more dangerous turbulence than that. Those were the best days of my life in America. The good picture of the American dream was real and sweet. I never knew that I would not experience such happiness in the Christian community like I did in Grand Rapids anywhere in America again. I will always cherish the love, the care, the fellowship, the support, prayers, the acceptance, and the spirit of oneness in Christ in Grand Rapids, Michigan.

One Monday morning, Henk Klyen told me that there was a church member of the Free Reformed Church who was in a nursing home and her roommate told her that she spent many years in Zimbabwe as a missionary. This member knew that I was from Zimbabwe while she was still fit to attend the church at Free Reformed Church and she told her roommate that there was a student at the Seminary from Zimbabwe. She was interested to know my name and also to pay her a visit. Henk arranged for me to go and meet with her at the nursing home. It was the shock of my life when I discovered that it was Florence Haadsma, the wife of Jerald Haadsma, the missionaries who shared the gospel with us in high school and led us to receive Christ as our Lord and Savior. What a small world we live in. This was the wife, Jeneral Haasdma who witnessed to us and baptized us with other school students from Jason Ziyapapa Moyo High School at West Nicholson in 1985. We both embraced each other with tears of joy streaming from our eyes. Out of their ministry at our J. Z. School, five more students became Pastor Austin Mabhena, Godfrey Ngwenya, Quickson Ndlovu and myself. I had no idea that twenty-five years later, I would meet Florence Haadsma who was always beside her husband. Unfortunately, Jerald Haadsma had died some years back and Florence had remained with their grown-up children and their own families. Their children I still remember are Jane, Paula, Jim and Sally. Florence was thrilled to see the fruits of their labor in Zimbabwe while they were missionaries. They planted the gospel seed in Zimbabwe and did not see it growing only to see the fruits twenty-five years later.

On September 19, 2009, we had Seminary Day in Toronto in Canada and most of the students attended and spoke at the conference and I was one of them. The Seminary asked me to drive Dereck Bars because he had graduated and he was going back to Canada, his home country. The Seminary rented a van and Henk Klyen asked me to drive the van with Dereck Bars and his luggage. It was Dereck and myself in the van when we drove to Canada from Grand Rapids, Michigan. At the border, the immigration officers could not believe that I was driving Dereck Bars from the USA and I was from Zimbabwe. They could not fathom how that puzzle could be solved. Dereck Bars was blind and the Seminary had asked me to drive Dereck to Canada while I was a Zimbabwean. After detailed explanations, they let us drive through. We drove for a while to drop Dereck Bars' language to one of his church members before we drove back to Toronto where the conference was. The conference was superb and we visited some Reformed churches to talk about how the Seminary had helped us with the scholarships and great teaching and our experience. We had a day off during the conference and we went to visit Niagara Falls, a spectacular fall with all its wonders and majestic features. It reminded me of Victoria Falls in Zimbabwe which is the widest and biggest in the world with natural features unlike the Niagara Falls which has been added with artificial features. We had a really good time visiting and meeting with the tourists from across the globe.

When the conference was over, I drove back with some of the students because the van was empty. We resumed our classes and we had a lot of fun at the Seminary. Our last winter in Grand Rapids, in 2009-2010 was brutal. Pete and Mimi Van Kempen invited us to walk and fish on the frozen lake where we used to do tubbing. It was scary but fun walking and fishing on the same frozen lake that we used to tub on the insipid liquid. It was my final year and I was now very busy writing my thesis and the graduation was approaching, on May 10, 2010. My supervisor was Dr. Joel Beeke, the Seminary President. We had really become such close friends and both theologians. I loved his classes and his teaching style. I also wanted to pursue my Doctorate after my Masters of Theology. In summer of 2009, in June to be specific, I had submitted my application for admission to about four universities/seminaries. We were invited by one of our friends, Dr. Quickson and Dr. Chipo Ndlovu in Pflugerville, Texas, who really influenced me a lot in my young life. They have a beautiful daughter, Linda Ndlovu.

We attended the same elementary, high school and also, we attended the same College, Theological College of Zimbabwe. I planned during the summer of June, 2009 to have campus visits to the universities/seminaries. We drove to Texas for about 21 hours, without sleeping on the way to rest. We had not studied accurately, the hours and miles from Grand Rapids, Michigan to Pflugerville, Texas. So, we drove from 10:00 pm and arrived at Pflugerville, Texas at 9:30 pm the following day. I was not used to driving long distances but I drove the whole night, morning, and the afternoon until I gave up and my wife, Judith took over although she was a new driver. She drove very well while I fell asleep. When we arrived, Dr. Quickson Ndlovu and Dr. Chipo and their daughter Linda were waiting for us and welcomed us. It was a good reunion and we chatted about the old school days and the Pastorate in the same denomination, United Baptist Church in the early 1990s before they left for the USA. We bid the Ndlovu family farewell, and thanked them for hosting us for a week. We spent a week visiting with them and on our way back, we drove to the Seminaries/Universities I had booked for campus visits starting in Austin City University. That was the first campus visit. The second campus visit was Southwestern Baptist Theological Seminary, in Fort Worth, Texas. We were allocated a beautiful guest house with my family and we bought some food to cook. We had four children by then. In the morning, we were led to a campus tour, being shown students housing, so many of the Seminary houses outside the campus, on campus housing, offices, lecture rooms, cafeteria, gyms, swimming pools, meeting with various faculty members and professors. It was a whole day tour. It is a huge campus and I was impressed by its massiveness and its beauty and architecture.

In the afternoon, we had a good time swimming with our children in the swimming pool and in the gym. We spent two days at the Southwestern Baptist Theological Seminary. It was interesting to know that the Dean of Theology spent several years visiting Zimbabwe, in hunting trophy expeditions. We struck up a friendship because of that connection. He really wanted me to be a student at Southwestern Baptist Theological Seminary and I was interviewed by a panel of professors. I thought that it would be my first choice, Southwestern Baptist Theological Seminary. However, Texas was extremely hot, averaging 102-105 degrees, which was unbearable. I developed a terrible headache. After two days at the Southwestern Baptist Theological Seminary campus, we drove to the next campus visit at Reformed Seminary, in Jacksonville, Mississippi. The Seminary was no longer offering Doctoral programs anymore but they gave us a nice guest house to spend two days with my family. It is not a big Seminary. We celebrated Emmanuel Nkosi, one of our sons, his 5th birthday in the guesthouse. We spent the two days swimming, and indoors because it was extremely hot, 105 and one could not walk outside. These were two states with extreme and different climates, compared to Michigan, which is very cold and snowy during winter. Mississippi is very hot and humid.

After two days, we proceeded to another campus visit to Covenant Theological Seminary in St. Louis, Missouri. We were welcomed and given a guest house for two days. The Covenant Reformed Seminary did not have a PhD program. However, the Seminary welcomed us and gave us a campus tour. We spent two days and we proceeded after two days to Southern Baptist Theological Seminary, in Louisville, Kentucky. While we were traveling, the admission office called and told me that they did not have the accommodation in the Legacy Hotel, the Seminary Hotel because the Seminary was celebrating its 150th centenary, in the fall of 2009. We couldn't go there because of the 150th centenary and we proceeded to go back home, in Louisville, Kentucky. By the spring of 2010, before my graduation, I had received admission offer letters from various universities/seminaries but Southern Baptist Theological Seminary was fast and efficient in dealing with students' affairs. Amanda Hays, was the Admission Secretary. My application and admission were being processed but as an international student, I was supposed to have a full scholarship that would cover the tuition, living expenses, books, and all the fees before the student is admitted and also to be issued with Sevis. One Sunday, I met with the Netherland Reformed Church Consistory and Dr. Joel Beeke told them that I was intending to go to Southern Baptist Theological Seminary to do my Doctorate and he told them but citing to them that I did not have money for my studies. He told them that I had told him that if it was the will of God to go to Southern Baptist Theological Seminary, God would provide. Dr. Joe Beeke said that they would wait and see what the Lord had in store for me.

I told my wife how steep the mountain to climb was to get the scholarship to keep us moving on to do my Doctorate. Money was a challenging factor because we had no clue where the money would come from. The Southern Baptist Theological Seminary was ready to admit me but they wanted me to prove that I have sufficient funds for my education as an international student. We decided to pray and fast for seven days, seeking the will of God. Most of my colleagues from other countries were graduating too and they were going back home. I was in a dilemma, between the devil and the deep blue sea, (an idiom), meaning to go back to Zimbabwe which had a political crisis and the economic hyperinflation rate, exceeding 1.25 million, representing 9.9 percent. Zimbabwe had one hundred trillion note dollars, the largest denomination ever issued in the world. Zimbabwe, once considered the breadbasket of Africa, was plunged into poverty and about 3 million emigrated to South Africa, Botswana, UK, News Zealand, Australia and to the USA, to seek greener pastures. It was a hard decision to make without any other choices except to pursue further studies. In the same vein, I had come with a Master's degree in Educational Administration, Planning and Policy Studies and now I was about to graduate with my second Master's degree in Theology. To go back with that level of education was not cost effective. According to economics, Cost Benefit Analysis stipulates that the costs should not exceed the benefits. If the cost exceeds the benefits, then it is an economic slump. The benefits should always exceed the costs.

We told our children that we would go for a week, praying and fasting for God to provide us with a scholarship so that I could pursue my Doctorate studies and we continue to stay in America. We started the prayer and fasting on a Monday and because the children were going to school, they did not eat breakfast in the morning but they would eat lunch with others at school. Judith and I would break our prayer and fasting at 6:00 pm. We started on Monday and continued Tuesday, Wednesday, and on Thursday, Henk Klyen called me to his office and I was wondering what had happened. When I got in his office, he had a smile on his face and told me not to be afraid because I was showing my facial expression that I was scared. What could have happened to me for him to call me in his office, I asked myself. Henk Klyen was the Seminary Registrar and it seemed everything was evolving around Henk Kleyn. He was the man in charge of almost everything. I sat on the chair with the chills on my body. Henk gently said that the reason he had called me to his office was because somebody came to his office enquiring about my plans after the graduation. He then told me that there was someone who wanted to sponsor and support me to pursue my Doctorate anywhere I wanted. He said that the person wanted to cover the tuition, the living expenses for the family. However, the person did not want to be known or disclose who she was but indicated that she was from Texas. She wanted to remain anonymous. The chills I previously had in fear had changed to be the chills of joy and excitement. I teared and became very emotional before Henk Klyen. I lifted my hands up to heaven in thanksgiving in the office of Henk. That was an incredible answered prayer before even the end of the week. We serve a living God, Jehovah Jireh, the provider who remains faithful as the Psalmist alluded, "The eyes of the Lord are on the righteous, and his ears are attentive to their cry," (Psalm 34:15, NIV).

The person told Henk Klyen that she did not want to get any tax returns from the gift she had given me and my family. So, she gave Henk Kleyn cash and Henk asked some of the Professors to put the cash into their bank accounts and send the lump sum of money to Southern Baptist Theological Seminary directly to my account. This was unbelievable to see the Professors participating in the blessings I had received. When I went home and told my wife and the children what God had done, there was excitement, happiness, joy and jubilation in the house. The children learned a good lesson that, "If you remain in me and my words remain in you, ask anything you wish, and it will be done for you," (John 15:7, NIV). It is imperative to show by example to your children what God can do for you if it is His will to be accomplished through you. Prayer and fasting works and Christians should not minimize it. If Jesus Christ fasted, it means we have to fast too because we are His followers. There are some Christians who minimize the power of fasting. Prayer and fasting works, especially for me and my family. We were all excited for what the Lord had done for us. We ended the fasting with the celebration of God's provision and His faithfulness.

I completed my thesis and Dr. Joel Beeke graded it and I was ready for graduation in May, 2010. We were busy preparing for graduation but also preparing to relocate to Southern Baptist Theological Seminary, in Louisville, Kentucky. We were excited for both the graduation and relocating to another state, a Southern state. We invited all those we knew, Florence Haadsma and Janke Banker, her daughter, to come for the graduation. We started with the Graduation Banquet in which Florence Haadsma and her daughter Jane Banker graced the occasion with their presence. I was a sweet surprise when Henk Klyen introduced us to a lady, I had first met at the Grand Rapids Airport, at the Information Center when I was stranded and she had called Henk Klyen to come and pick me. This was the very lady who continued to support us anonymously, sending the gift cards, cash, book supplies for our children and registering our annual membership at Meijer Gardens, which had roses, zoo, and natural forests. We did not know who was sponsoring us with all those beautiful things. Henk joked with me asking if I still remembered her. I said that I had no idea although her face looked familiar. I had seen her once at night at the airport and never saw her again. What a surprise to see the person who was supporting us all of the two and half years. We were all thrilled, especially myself. We appreciated her and with all the gratitude you can imagine. We sat on the same table for our Graduation Banquet, chatting. It was a sweet moment of our lives.

The graduation was superb and all the graduates were so excited and appreciative for completing our studies. We had developed the bond and great rapport with one another like brothers. We were all dressed in classic suits but without the gowns because the Seminary did not believe in wearing those glamorous gowns to pitch pride instead of referring that glory to Jesus Christ. We were all wearing suits for the graduation. We were with our families and friends and there was a jovial mood in the atmosphere. To be class valedictorian speaker, I was two votes shy, and one of my friends did the class of 2010 valedictory speech. The graduation was the whole day, starting with Graduation Banquet, Graduation Ceremony and Family and Friends' parties. I had a flash reflection of how God led me from Britain, Zimbabwe and then coming to the USA and graduation. It was more than a blessing and unbelievable what God could do with your life. While we were celebrating and enjoying the goodness of God and His provision ahead of us as we were preparing to transition from the Midwest, which is divided by the Census Bureau in the East North to the Southern state, in Louisville, Kentucky. We were very excited to transition to another state to see and experience another life in another state. Most of our friends that we graduated with were heading back to their respective countries for further ministries. We were preparing to go to Louisville, Kentucky.

I was in connection with Michael Withers, the Manager of International Student Services (PDSO), Amanda Hays in the Seminary Admission Office, and Haggai Habila for student housing. When I checked with Michael Withers about the Seminary accommodation, he referred me to Haggai Habila who was working as his assistant. I called Haggai Habila and he referred me to an apartment which was just a seven minutes' drive to the Seminary and that's where he was living with his family in the same apartment. When we arrived, we just clicked for the first time on the phone and we became close friends ever since. We called the Hospital Hill Apartments office to rent a townhouse starting June, 2010. After graduation on May 10, 2010, we hired a U-Haul truck after a week. We had hired a medium truck but they ended up giving us the full long truck because the medium truck was not returned on time. It was God's provision, indeed. We were so thankful to God for taking care of us in every situation. It was almost a six hours drive, 5 hours, 50 minutes to be specific. We bid them farewell to the Seminary staff, church family and friends and they blessed us with gifts. I wrote appreciation letters to the Netherlands Reformed Church where we were members of the church and the Free Reformed Church, the sister church. The Netherland Reformed Church was paying school fees for our children in Plymouth School for two and half years.

We left in the morning around 11:00 am in Grand Rapids and my wife drove our van and I drove the U-Haul truck. It was a 6-hour joy ride and everyone was excited to breathe the new breeze of a different environment. We arrived in Louisville, Kentucky around 6:30 pm and got into our new townhouse. It was interesting to see our children running up to the upstairs to choose their bedrooms. It took us a week to unload and arrange our new home. We accustomed ourselves with the schools, shops, libraries, highways, Louisville City, Kentucky and other places in the vicinity. The climate was humid and hotter than Grand Rapids, Kentucky. We went to Louisville during summer in

June and the weather was superb. We got connected with neighbors and the Habila family became our closest family and Moses and Bisi. The first Sunday, we went to our first church which was nearer to our home, a Baptist Church near us. We dressed classically, as we used to do in Grand Rapids, Michigan. We discovered that it was a white only church and we did not see even one black church member. The members were hesitating to come and greet us but the rest stood aloof as if they knew us without extending a hand of fellowship to the visitors. We were surprised to see that we were not welcomed in the church. The Pastor, tried to make us feel comfortable but the rest of the members were not interested at all. Actually, one of the elders came to us and told us that there were many good churches in the western part of the city of Louisville, saying that the blacks lived in the western parts of the city where we could fit very well with the black race.

It was sad feeling to witness prejudice in the church. The Baptist Church was so had so much prejudice that we could not go back again. They treated us like second class citizens in the church where love was supposed to be manifested. The Pastor advised us to go and check out another church which was nearby, St. Matthews Baptist Church and the interim Pastor was Terry Seelow. They were still searching for the Senior Pastor to fill the position. The Pastor told us that St. Matthews Church was a good church as if he was saying it was better than his church of which we discovered later that it was very true. The following Sunday, we visited another church Baptist Church which was across the Seminary in where Haggai and Mary Habila and the children were members. The church had mixed races, blacks and whites, Asians and other races and seemed to co-exist well together. It was pretty diverse but we did not feel it was our fit. The third Sunday, we visited St. Matthews Baptist Church which was recommended by the Pastor from the first Baptist Church we visited. The St. Matthews Baptist Church was a warm church that welcomed us with joy although some of the church members. They were just one or two black members who were from the Seminary and tow others who were mentally challenged. The spirit of fellowship and loving one another was in the atmosphere. As the first visitors to the church, there was a lounge where after the service, the visitors would be greeted by people, asking who you are and where you came from. The last one to greet us was Dr. Terry Seelow who was an Adult Minister and the Interim Pastor. He was so gracious, loving, kind and welcoming. He really made us feel welcomed and loved. There was a click with us. He promised to visit us at our home to welcome us. That was incredible and Dr. Terry Seelow won our hearts when he paid us a visit at our townhouse during the week.

The first impression is the key and it is very important to any human being. Dr. Terry Seelow asked us if the God's Design, a decoration and furniture team would come to decorate and bring some furniture for us. That was actually the last nail on the box to seal the confirmation for us to declare in our hearts and verbally that St. Matthews Baptist Church would be our home church. We became full members of the St. Matthews Baptist Church and committed to fully support the church programs. The team for decoration and furniture the house did a fantastic job by remodeling our house. St. Matthews Baptist Church had also great programs for children, led by Dr. Joyce Oliver, the minister of the children. She was gifted and had a great passion for the children. David Gerrard, the Minister for Youth, was one the strongest Ministers who led the programs for the Youth with precision, vision and passion. He organized memorable youth camps, basketball teams and games for all ages, for the Children and the Youths. St. Matthews Baptist Church had vibrant church programs. Dr. Terry and his wife, Melissa Early Seelow, were a lovely family that we befriended so much to this day. The search team/committee, finally, got a prospective candidate, Dr. Greg Barr with his lovely wife, Jackie Barr. Dr. Greg Barr was inducted as the Senior Pastor of St. Matthews Baptist Church. Pastor Greg and his wife, Jackie Barr, quickly assimilated into the church family and they were warmly welcomed and they began serving the church and Dr. Seelow concentrated on his original Adult Ministry which he executed very well.

We joined a Sunday School Fish Bible Study Class which had very interesting characters and they embraced us. The Fish Class was our main and major vein in fostering fellowship within our group.

It was composed of families and those who were singles. Some of the members of Fish Class that had great impact in our lives were Lee and Mary Ellen Yates, David and Lynn, Lori Lawrence, Mark Estes, David and Adrienne Eisenmenger, Sejong Ryu, Michael and Beth Wilmes, Rachael Tan, Mu-Chia Nadia Chen, Chris and Denise, Jackie and Debbie, Eric and Lisa, Terry and Melissa Seelow. Dr. Terry Seelow was the Fish Class Teacher. The Fish Class was really dynamic and was instrumental in organizing fellowship gatherings in various homes. I remember we gathered at David and Lynn's house on several occasions and Lee and Mary Ellen Yates' house. Later on, when the Fish Class split and was dissolved, we had to form another class. We had one fellowship gathering at Mark Estes' house and another at the house of Eric and Lisa.

I started at the Seminary in August 2010, however, the Doctorate in Educational Leadership program I was interested in was scheduled to start in fall of 2011. I was taken aback to experience a different culture at the new Seminary. It was different from the other Seminary in Grand Rapids. As a black, I was looked at as a second-class citizen although it was not announced or documented. The prejudice at the Seminary was more visible, more pronounced in action and it was felt in every sector but it was not announced. I could really see that one does not belong here to this kind of Christianity community. Some of the professors and students, and other staff were incredibly good, helpful and kind but the majority of them had bias, prejudice and were not welcoming. It was the kind of homogenous unit principle, the kind of people who belonged to each other with the exclusion of others, systematically. The Seminary was one of the largest Seminary in the world with the largest student enrollment and represented by many different countries. The USA was the first with the most students, followed by the Asians, Africans, Europeans and the rest of the world.

There were some opportunities to work at the campus and I started looking for a job and I could not get the job for more than one and half years regardless of how multiple times I had applied. Blood is thicker than water. There were very few black students given the office jobs but they were recruited as janitors, cleaners, grounds maintenance, etc. Asians were more favored and preferred than the blacks in job recruitments, especially clerical jobs.

One would feel better and comfortable outside the Seminary than inside the Seminary. The secular universities such as Louisville University, University of Kentucky and other secular universities would treat you better as a black person than Seminary. The Seminary is regarded as the most conservative, most evangelical with sound doctrine and spiritually furnished Seminary in the Southern Baptist Convention. It was saved on the verge of being plunged into secularism and liberalism by the renowned and prolific leader and author, Dr. Albert R. Mohler, the conservative, who became the President in 1993 He was able to push out the liberal and moderate faculty members who were dragging the Seminary into the dungeon of depravity. He is a loving and great man of God that I admired for his convictions and passion for the gospel. I came to know Dr. Albert R. Mohler, personally, when I was finally hired by the senior driver, John H. Flores, a very kind man originally from Bolivia, who helped me pass the driving test to be hired by the Seminary. He was the Seminary Senior Driver and the Legacy Hotel, which is the branch of the Seminary and responsible for hiring the drivers for the Seminary. The Manager of the legacy Hotel was Tim Belcher, a great man of God. He had a lovely wife, Mary and their two daughters. I worked well with him until he had a call to plant a church in Hawaii. It was a huge breakthrough to be the Seminary driver. It gave me the opportunities to drive and to interact with the likes of President, Dr. Mohler, the staff, the students and renowned authors such as Dr. A. Carson, John McCarthy, John Piper, David Jeremiah, David Plat, Tabiti Anyabwile, Conwell Mbewe, and many other guest speakers, conference speakers and professors who came for conferences and as visiting Professors. There was only one black Professor out of many. The job exposed me to so many people that I had never imagined I would ever meet personally, and talk to them face to face. However, at Legacy Hotel, one of the branches at Southern Baptist Theological Seminary made it possible and availed that opportunity.

I enjoyed working at Legacy Hotel, as one of the Seminary. I had developed a good rapport with the Seminary President Dr. Albert Mohler and His wife, Mary Mohler because I used to transport them and pick them to and from the airport, several times. I got to pick and drop Dr. A. Mohler and Mary's mothers several times. It was really a privilege and a blessing to know them and to serve them.

One incident that baffled my wife and I was when it was the Fall Festival in 2014 and one of our sons, Blessing, participated at the festival events in a drama and when other participants were recognized and given some awards for participating. Our son was on third position but he was left out and he was told to go and get his award in Africa. That did not sit well with us but we had nowhere to go to complain or report about the behavior of the presenter of the awards. We just consoled our son and encouraged him to stand tall and that he was worthy and that God would reward him one day. Little did we know that the other festival personnel saw and heard what happened. They investigated whose son it was and they were told that it was my son. One day, the Legal Hotel Manager approached me and gave me an Apple gift card of $80.00 to give to my son, Blessing. I was grateful for the gift as a consolation to what they had done to my son. I gave him the gift card and gave him extra money to buy an iPad that he had desired to have. He was thankful for the gesture. God sees! There was another incident when our children were swimming at the Seminary swimming pool and other children who were swimming in the same pool told our children that their parents told them that they were not supposed to play with African children. It was really sad to witness prejudice at the Seminary where love, diversity and understanding about races was supposed to be manifested through love, support, care, tolerance and co-existence.

As an international student, I was supposed to remain enrolled in the Seminary program so that I could not be out of status while waiting for my program the following year. So, I enrolled to study Masters of Divinity in Biblical Counseling, from August 2010 to the fall of 2011, while waiting for the Doctoral program to start. It was a great program. The Biblical Counseling program was good and my professors were Dr. Stuart Scott and Dr. Heath Lambert who were incredible professors. In the fall of 2011, I started my Doctoral program with Dr. Michael S. Wilder, who was the Dean. Dr. Michael S. Wilder was a very kind professor, who loved his students. He was an excellent professor with the passion for the gospel. The course work was very interesting but demanded hard work, resilience, patience, aptitude with diligence and focus. Two years later, I had completed my course work in 2013 and I started to write my dissertation proposal with the topic which I was going to write about to be approved. The dissertation title was "Biblical Response to HIV/AIDS," and I was assigned to a supervisor, however, I spent two years trying to communicate with my supervisor but he was always ignoring my communication. After two and half years of not making any headways, he finally told me that he could no longer be my supervisor because he did not understand HIV/AIDS as an American. It was two and half years wasted because he did not want to admit that he did not understand HIV/AIDS disease and he had no clue of it. He said HIV/AIDS was a problem in Africa and other third world countries not a problem in America. There was nothing I could do except to accept and get advice from the Dean about my next step.

The faculty had to find another supervisor who had knowledge about HIV/AIDS disease. In God's provision, a new Professor, Dr. Danny Bowen, joined the faculty as one of the Adjunct Professors. He was a Medical Doctor, by profession and with a specialized discipline as an esthetician for over 40 years, with incredible expertise and experience. When in the faculty meeting, the Dean, Dr. Michael S. Wilder presented that my dissertation needed a supervisor with knowledge of HIV/AIDS disease and with medical experience. Dr. Danny Bowen showed great interest on the topic of HIV/AIDS because he had worked with doctors without borders overseas and was thrilled to be my supervisor. Dr. Danny Bowen was a kind and compassionate Professor and was willing to work with me through it all. His expertise, experience, passion and enthusiasm in the medical field and theological dogma really brought a fresh start. Dr. Bowen was very smart and very easy to work with and his experience working with diverse peoples made it easier to connect and work together well through the process of my dissertation. When we were getting ready to go to join Northwest Baptist Convention in Greater Seattle, I had to leave even before I graduated. I couldn't wait to complete my dissertation. I was prepared to go and serve the Lord than to waste my time still stuck at the Seminary.

CHAPTER TEN

The Second Great Commission

W hen I arrived in the USA in 2008, one of my dreams was to start a church in the USA as I did in the UK in 2005. In Grand Rapids, Michigan, I organized mostly the Zimbabweans to meet on Saturdays to pray for Zimbabwe's political and economic turmoil and to fellowship as Zimbabwean people. The Zimbabwe Fellowship was taking roots but we had to relocate to Louisville, Kentucky and we could not pursue that fellowship. In Kentucky, they were some few Zimbabweans where we quickly organized ourselves and started the fellowship. Within a year being in Louisville, Kentucky, we had formed a fellowship. We discussed with Kudakwashe Mashindi, one of the friends whom we worked with at Scripture Union in Mutare, Zimbabwe. I was in Mutare Scripture Union and he was stationed in Chiredzi Scripture Union although we had not yet met but we knew each other. When I shared with Kudakwashe that I had organized and formed a Zimbabwe Fellowship in Grand Rapids, Michigan, he got interested and we decided to mobilize people, our friends and form a fellowship group to pray and fellowship together. We sat down with Kudakwashe Mashindi and drafted the plan and the name of the Fellowship. We called it International Christian Fellowship Ministries Inc. (ICFM), as a non-profit organization. We started gathering with many friends for prayers and fellowship and we formed an executive committee. The Executive was as follows: President: Sam S. Mhlanga; Vice President: Roosevelt Fenelus; Secretary General: Kudakwashe Mashindi; Treasurer: Douglas Gonde; Committee member: Sadock Mashindi. We registered the organization with the Secretary of the State Louisville, Kentucky and filed the Articles of Incorporation and By-Laws on October 11, 2011.

The ICFM became vibrant in Louisville, Kentucky as a fully fleshed non-organization and we secured a place to lease for the purposes of meetings, fellowship, prayers and seminars at the College of Scriptures. Mr. Sadock Mashindi was a Professor at the College of Scriptures and it made it easier for us to secure the place which we rented. Roosevelt Fenelus was technical minded and he helped us with technical and computer expertise to develop the website. The International Christian Fellowship Ministries Inc. became like a church plant in Louisville, Kentucky. Some of the church planters around the area thought that it was a church plant and advised me to register it under Kentucky Baptist Association. I had to go through the interviews and the meetings with the Kentucky Baptist Association. I was still at the Southern Baptist Theological Seminary as a student not as a church planter yet. I did not have a call to be a church planter as such, in Louisville, Kentucky. I wanted to plant the church in liberal states to plant the gospel in the states that needed to gospel more. At the Seminary, there was a North American Mission Board recruiting advisory office that was ready to introduce and map out those who wanted to become missionaries, to give advice and to show them the areas of where they need missionaries more. Aaron was the man who directed me to many states that needed more church planters such as Philadelphia, Minnesota, Washington DC, Washington state, and many liberal states that were open. I wanted to plant in Washington DC with various embassies from all over the world as Washington D.C. was the capital city of the USA. I wanted to reach out to the ambassadors in Washington D.C. and evangelize them and to have a multi diverse church.

To that effect, I applied to Capitol Hill Baptist Church, wanting to partner with them as a sending church. I was invited by the Senior Pastor of the Capitol Hill Baptist Church, Dr. Mark Dever, to come and join the interns at his church for one week. I went and spent a week with interns to learn about how they were doing and also to be introduced to the elders of the church and to see the possibilities of being accepted and sent as their church planter and a sending church. I was introduced but Dr. Mark Dever told me at the end of the week that the church had chosen Tabiti Anyabwile to partner with him and to be a sending church for him as he was also intending to start the church there in Washington D. C. He was actually the first to apply to Capitol Hill Baptist Church in Washington D. C. However, it was a good experience to see the church members participating and the Scripture being the central focus in their lives. My vision to plant a church in Washington D. C. was dashed because of lack of support and a sending church. I went back to Louisville, Kentucky after a week at Capitol Hill Church in Washington D. C. When I was back in Louisville, Kentucky, I applied to the Philadelphia Baptist Association but the director there was not responsive to my emails and inquiries. I applied to several states with the help of Aaron who was at the Southern Baptist Theological Seminary in the office of the North American Mission Board. It was now 2013 and I was still trying to find the state that would be willing to call me to be one of the missionaries and plant the gospel.

My friend Haggai and Mary Habila were already church planters in Seattle, Washington state and I shared with him how challenging it was to find a state where I could be a church planter after so much prayer and search for God's will. Haggai Habila advised me to contact Gary Irby, the Director of church planting in Northwest Baptist Conversion. He gave me the phone number and the email for Gary Irby and I wrote Gary Irby and called him also. It was amazing how quickly Gary Irby responded and told me that they would love me to join them in Greater Seattle, Washington. He connected me with Natalie Hammond who was and is still the Administrator of the Northwest Baptist Convention, (NWBC). She was so kind to help me and to send some forms for me to fill to see if I qualified. It was a long process and after submitting all the required documentation, applications, references, and the assessment team invited me with my wife to travel to Seattle, Washington for assessments. It was a breakthrough to be invited for the assessment process by the assessment team to be considered as church planters/ missionaries in the Northwest. We jetted to Seattle on April 28, 2014, with my wife Judith and Joseph for assessment. Natalie Hamond had organized the air tickets for us, booked the hotel, booked the rented car and everything was in order. The assessment began on April 29, 2014 and we spent the whole week being assessed and toured the possible areas to plant the church. We prayed about the area where God led us to plant. We had first chosen Everett city because of the Boeing company that had workers scattered in the area. However, when we toured the city of Kent, we felt that God was leading us to plant the church in Kent and at the airport. We changed from Everett to Kent and it was still fine with Gary Irby.

When we received the good news that we were approved, we were so excited and got ready to relocate to Kent, Washington. I was asked by Gary Irby and Natalie Hammond to design the name of our church plant, the logo, brochure, and the doctrinal and constitution of the church we were going to plant in Kent, Washington. After much prayer and consultations, we decided to call our church plant, Bread of Life International Fellowship (BOLIF). The church name became a legal name for our church even before we moved to Kent, Washington.

However, there were still some steep hills to climb, which was to raise financial support and to find a sending church. Those were challenging obstacles on our way to realize our dreams of becoming missionaries in the Northwest. We visited some churches trying to amass financial support but it was like we were hitting the concrete wall. Being Africans, without the backing of any church or organization, it was a hard nut to crack. We had no one who could put trust in us and fully support us. St. Matthews Baptist Church, our local church in which we had been members for more than six years, was willing to be our sending church but not any financial support whatsoever. It was so sad to see our church refusing to support us financially, and promised to pray for us in support, only. The potential church that had become friendly to us was Redemption Baptist Church, which was located in Southeast Louisville, about an hour drive and the Pastor was my friend, Nick Moore, with his wife Kyndra. They had responded to a call to be missionaries in Zimbabwe and he was preparing to go with his family. I had preached several times in Redemption Church and it was like a family church outside Louisville, Kentucky for us.

I was still a student in 2014 at Southern Baptist Theological Seminary when we were approved to be church planters/missionaries in the Northwest. I was having a new supervisor Dr. Danny Bowen and the main editor of my dissertation was Betsy Fred, an incredible editor with an eagle's eye to notice any errors in my manuscript. While I was busy writing my dissertation, I felt the apt to pursue the missionary journey in the Northwest because I had a conviction that it was time to move on with my journey to life, regardless of the circumstances drawing me back to the drawing board. I had spent two more years than anticipated at the Seminary because of the previous supervisor who had not come out clearly to indicate that he could not proceed with me as my supervisor because of the nature of the topic of my dissertation. My financial account at the Seminary had dried up and it was difficult to pay the rent. The last day of the payment of the rent was like Monday, February March 30, 2014. We prayed with my wife Judith for God to provide for our rent. When we got to the church, St. Matthews Baptist Church, I was praying throughout the service and I had decided in my heart that I would approach and ask Mr. Lee Yates, one of our friends in the Fish Class who really had become our closest friends to help us with the rent. This was the first couple, Lee and Mary Ellen Yates, who came to see Joseph Sam Jr. in the hospital when he was born on July 28, 2012. They loved us and we loved them and we were really good friends and I felt comfortable to approach them to tell them about our plight or crisis.

I was sitting, strategically, at the pews to go straight to Lee Yates and ask him and Mary Ellen to help after the service. Little did I know that God had already spoken to Lee in his heart and he had convened a meeting with other Fish Class members, the selected few, to help us. After the service, I went straight to Lee Yates and I saw him also coming straight to me after the service and motioned to me that he wanted to speak to me. While others were dismissing going home, Lee told me that the selected few of the Fish Class had decided to pay for our rents for the whole year. It was unbelievable to hear the good news. I had not even asked Lee Yates to help us with the rent and God had already spoken to him beforehand. God is faithful and awesome. "You prepare a table before me in the presence of my enemies. You anoint my head with oil, my cup overflows," (Psalm 23:5, NIV) in this case, the devil wanted to tear down what God had built. I was so glad that the Lord had already spoken to Lee Yates and the selected few in the Fish Class. In the morning, I had gone to church with my head down with frustration and anxiety about the rent that I was supposed to pay. However, after the service, I was thrilled and happy and excited, and I exited the church with a big relief and joy in my heart because God had heard our prayer, short as it was. The whole of 2014, the Fish Class paid for our rent and for the living expenses in addition to paying our rent. By March, 2015, when the Fish Class ended their financial support, we had applied for work permits and I was first employed at Big Spring Country Club as an associate. The Manager for the Big Spring Country Club was a member of the St. Matthews Baptist Church and I got the job so quickly while my wife started work at Home of the Innocents. We were now managing our rent and living expenses but at the Big Spring Country Club, it was not a fulfilling job. I actually made a great impact there because six of my associates received the Lord Jesus Christ as their Lord and Savior in their lives. I was able to witness the love of Christ with my colleagues there. I am glad I will be with those friends in eternity with Christ.

I resigned from the Big Spring Country Club because I had got another job at Oxmoor Ford as a Sales and Leasing Consultant. It was a great exposure to the whole world because the car business attracts all kinds of people as everyone needs a vehicle in one way or the other. However, the training was challenging as it was my first time and it demanded a lot of work and knowledge of all types of Ford vehicles, starting from the Fiesta, Focus, Fusion, Mustang, Taurus, C-Max, Escape, Transit Connect, Edge, Explorer, Expedition, F-150 trucks, F-250, and some other models. As a sales and leasing consultant, you required to know all the types of Ford vehicles, all their models, their engine capacities, engine sizes, features, fuel consumptions, gas mileage per mile, environment friendly pollution, price range, credit scores for each client, vehicle protection, vehicle insurance and coverage, financing, leasing, and all the updates of each of the vehicle, including pre-owned vehicles. There were some knowledge tests of all the models of Ford vehicles which one needed to pass every three months in order to be a certified and licensed sales consultant. Oxmoor Ford/Lincoln Company also sold Lincoln vehicles and the sales and leasing consultant was also required to know all the models, their features, engine capacity of all Lincoln models, just as one was expected to know Ford vehicles. The sales and leasing consultant was required to know the Lincoln vehicle models such as Navigator, Aviator, Nautilus, Corsair, Continental, and all the models of MKZ, and other Z's etc. The sales and leasing consultant was trained how to present each vehicle which was on the market to clients who came in looking for the vehicle of their choice and according to what they could afford, complemented by the credit scores numbers. The presentation of each vehicle to a client was one the major processes, using the ten points. The dress code was business. The sales and leasing consultant was given a computer and his/her own office desk to keep the database and all his/her clients names, emails, phone numbers and their address and online sales and leasing were required and monitored by the Sales Manager.

A new employed sales and leasing consultant was given three months of free salary and thereafter, was paid in commission. At Oxmoor/Lincoln Company, a sales and leasing consultant was expected and required to sell at least ten vehicles per month in order to maintain one's status or to sale vehicles with more value in their MSRP, i.e., which is the manufacturer's suggested retail price or the price recommended by the dealership to sell the vehicle. After three months of receiving a free paid salary, it became evident that I was not going to make it because of my accent and there was a high volume of competition as well as the sales and leasing consultants scrambled for clients. It was the survival of the fittest and one needed to be alert and be around for hours and hours to look for the clients or else someone would grab or snatch the clients from you and you would remain, empty handed. It was indeed a miracle and amazing to see many sales and leasing consultants coming in and going away, some being fired, others quitting because of the nature of the work that demanded one's natural talent or learned skills to lure the clients. It was a boiling pot environment. With experience, skills, talents and expertise, some sales and leasing consultants in Oxmoor Ford/Lincoln Company, made good figures. For example, John Safi, was the best sales and leasing consultant who scooped awards as the best sales and leasing consultant of the year for more than five consecutive years. He had great art and skills as a consultant. I was always praying every day for the Lord to keep me in at work so that I could sustain my family. I was constantly praying for the Lord to open the doors in the Northwest so that we could move there quickly because I did not want to work in such an environment that demanded my physical, moral, spiritual and emotional maximum every day. I worked at Oxmoor for two years, and developed relationships with various workmates. I saw myself being one of the best sales and leasing consultants of the year and received a third prize for being one of the best sales and leasing consultants. I received a smoker grill for a third price.

I had become acquainted with the General Manager, the Sales Managers and other Managers. One of the sales managers, Tim Robinson was a Christian and he became my best friend. Some Managers I had befriended were John Bell the General Sales Manager; Brandon Alexander; Billy Grierson the Sales Manager; Kent Thornburgh the Sales Manager; Roderic Lasley the Dealer Trade Manager; Mark Conder the Inventory Manager; Kenneth Coulson the Finance Manager; Robert Anderson the Lincoln Concierge; and Scott Heffernan the Manager, Vehicle Inventory; Betty Aldridge the Special Finance Manager; Jenna Freeman the Assistant Internet Sales Manager. Some of the Sales and Leasing Consultants were Steve Whittaker, Dan Williams, John Safi, George Oakes, Joseph Campbell, Rachael Denise, Allen Alvarez, Cameron Gum, Alex Alsup, Mike McWhorter, and

Nakia Boyd. I worked well with all these incredible people at Oxmoor/Lincoln Company in Louisville, Kentucky.

While I was still in Oxmoor/Lincoln Company, we were still at St. Matthews Baptist Church. Meanwhile, one of my friends who had graduated and had become a church planter in Minneapolis, Dr. Sam Asuma, from Kenya, originally, called me to ask me to come and take over from him as he had some plans to move to another career. It was a difficult decision to make. I had committed myself to go to Northwest and the process was ongoing and I did not want to just abandon what I had started. When I told my friend, Dr. Asuma, that I could not take the position as a church planter in Minneapolis, because I was still in the process of applying in the Northwest and that the process was advanced. He was unhappy with my response because he had wanted me to go and help me. He then asked me to recommend a friend who was honest and trustworthy so that he could go and take over. I told him that I would come back to him soon as I was searching for one. I prayed as to who to approach. I had a friend of mine, Philip Nache, his wife, Jumai Nache, from Nigeria. They were family friends. It was one day when I saw Philip Nache sitting on one of the benches at the Seminary and I called him and told him about the opportunity that had arisen in Minneapolis about a position of church planting. When I told him that I wanted to recommend him to my friend, Dr. Sam Asuma, he was willing to go there as a church planter. I connected him with Dr. Asuma and they agreed for Philip Nache to go to Minneapolis to be a church planter with his family. It did not take long for him to be conducted as the church planter. His assessment and all the procedures did not take long and within a few months, his project tool and approval by NAMB and Minneapolis Baptist Convention was granted. Philip Nache's process took some few months and while my process had taken more than three years. I started to question why my process was taking so long and I started to ask God if it was His will for us to go to Northwest or otherwise.

The same scenario happened also with one of our family friends, Suresh Samangi from India, originally. We were also together at the Seminary and working together at Legacy Hotel as Seminary drivers and in the same church St. Matthews Baptist Church. After graduating, he went to be a church planter in Boston. His assessment did not take long either. Within a few months, his assessment was approved and he moved to Boston with his wife Anita Samangi with their two boys. While they were there, they wanted me to go and join them in Boston as a church planter because they were some positions which were open. He spoke to his Director and the Director visited me to convince me to join them in Boston for church planting. I told him that I had committed myself to go to the Northwest, not Boston. He was also disappointed about my unwillingness to join their state for mission work. I had to seek the face of the Lord and enquired if it was God's will for me and my family to move to the Northwest, Greater Seattle. The Lord kept on confirming that it was His will. But then why was it taking so long and difficult while others it was a matter of some few months. I had to be patient and wait for God's timing, *kairos*.

Our son Joseph was loved by many children at St. Matthews Baptist Church but there was one special young girl who was so kind and loving. On Wednesdays, she would take care of Joseph, play with him and change his diapers every Wednesday. This girl continued for weeks and months without flinching. One day, my wife Judith and I started discussing how awesome the young girl was in taking care of our son, Joseph. When she brought our son, Joseph after playing, caring for him during the Wednesday Prayer Meetings, I asked her name and appreciated her for her care and a loving heart. She told us that her name was Emma Hightower. I said to her, we would like to meet your parents because the orange does not fall far from the orange tree. She told us that she would inform her parents the following Wednesday so that she would introduce us to them. The following Wednesday, she took Joseph to care for him and when she brought him to us, she took us and introduced us to her parents, Brett and Jana Hightower and to her sister Meredith Hightower. We were thrilled to meet Brett and Jana Hightower, the parents of Emma whom they had raised to be an amazing girl who loved children of all kinds and of all walks of life regardless of their race or color of their skins. We are so thankful to Brett and Jana Hightower for raising such an angel whose love permeated to all people at St. Matthews Baptist Church.

We had to get to know Brett and Jana, their lovely children, Meredith and Emma Hightower, deeply. They asked us what our plans and vision were in terms of our future. We were glad to hear them having interest in our future which was really rare to hear such concern from people whom you are different with. We told them that we were looking for a sending church that would support us as church planters/ missionaries in the Northwest. We told them that St. Matthews Baptist Church, which we had been members of for six years, had indicated that they were willing to be the sending church but without any financial support to give us. Other churches that we had approached in the area were also not willing to be sending churches with financial support. We told them that at the Northwest Baptist Convention, they would not create a position request from the North American Mission Board (NAMB) without a sending church with financial support. The churches that promised to support us were Grace Fellowship Community Church in Indiana, Second Baptist Church, in Arkadelphia, and Living Hope Baptist Church. Brett and Jana informed us that their church, Woodburn Baptist Church in Bowling Greens may be willing to be our sending church. A seed of hope was planted in our hearts. Brett and Jana promised that they would speak with their Pastor, Tim Harris about supporting us because their church had a vision of 2020 and of planting ten churches within ten years. We kept the communication going on with Brett and Jana Hightower and they connected us to Pastor Tim Harris. Pastor Tim Harris invited me to come to meet with him at his church, Woodburn Baptist Church in Bowling Green. Pastor Tim was thrilled to hear my vision, my dreams, and my passion. He told me that they had the money for the mission work that had been in the bank without being used for some years without being used and they were willing to partner with us for the mission in the Northwest. Mr. Jack Wright, at the Woodburn Baptist Church, worked together with Brett Hightower, Gary Irby, Tim Howe, Natalie Hammond, Linda Grimes, Steve Bass from NAMB, for the budget to make sure that the project tool has been approved by NAMB and their support.

The puzzle was coming together and I could not believe that God was using these men and women to build the kingdom of God through us. Brett and Jana Hightower were at the center of it all in this puzzle. Their daughter, Emma and Joseph, our son, connected us to be church planters/missionaries in the Northwest. It was incredible and unbelievable how God can work with the children. The Woodburn Baptist Church, in Bowling Green, invited me to come and preach on September 13, 2015 in two services, the morning service and the 11:00 am service and the Youth service. We drove with the family and spent a weekend at Brett and Jana Hightower's home. On Sunday, Woodburn Baptist Church had to hear me preach and decided to embrace us as their own. We became one big family. The Northwest Baptist Convention (NWBC), North American Mission Board (NAMB) and Woodburn Baptist Church (WBC), approved us as missionaries and church planters. We were finally approved to be church planters in the Northwest, Kent City. We were so excited with my family when we received an email stating that we had been approved to be church planters/missionaries, officially, starting on June 1, 2016. Woodburn Baptist Church, Bowling Green was our sending Church. To God be the glory for using Brett and Jana, Emma and Joseph and their daughter Meredith, Pastor Tim Harris and the whole Woodburn Baptist Church who were instrumental and used by God to extend His kingdom in the Northwest through us.

I was still writing my dissertation when I was approved by the North American Mission Board (NAMB), Northwest Baptist Convention (NWBC), and Woodburn Baptist Church (WBC) to move to Northwest, Greater Seattle. Woodburn Baptist Church in Bowling Green, the sending church invited the whole family to come to their church to be prayed for and to have a sending off church service. It was an awesome sending off service we had ever had. Natalie and Gary called me to Seattle to look for the house for the family. Natalie arranged my air flights and a hotel for me to travel to Seattle to find a house where we would be living. I jetted to Seattle and I was given a week to find the house for the family. When I landed in Sea-Tacoma airport, I stayed in a hotel near Kent where we would be planting the church. I consulted Dr. Terry and Melissa Seelow from Louisville, Kentucky, as Mellissa was a realtor at Semonin Realtors to help me find a Realtor in Seattle who could help me to find a house. Dr. Terry and Melissa are very close friends and Melissa consulted with Christian Realtor in Seattle and she found Lorain Maddox for Windermere Real Estate. Lorain Maddox was willing to help me as a Christian Realtor and we moved from one house to another and used her own vehicle and I never paid anything. She was such a great assistance to me. Tim Howe also moved with me from one house to another to find a house for rent. We had few options of houses to select from but the rents were more than double than in Louisville, Kentucky.

With the help of Lorain Maddox, I signed a three-year lease with the landlord in which we agreed that there would not be any increase on the rent in three years. After signing the leasing agreement on May 30, 2016. I called my wife to start packing even before I flew back to Louisville. With the help of Natalie, I hired a 5 Towns Auto Transport & Logistics moving truck and directed them to my home in Louisville, Kentucky. They sent the moving truck to a townhouse in Louisville, Kentucky and my wife and the kids started packing and putting the furniture into the truck on May 31. While I flew back home, in Louisville, Kentucky, Natalie Hammond booked the air tickets for the family to fly to Seattle as church planters/missionaries. Children were very excited to leave Louisville, Kentucky after spending more than six years. We bid farewell to our friends, our church, St. Matthews Baptist Church, the Seminary, Oxmoor/Lincoln Company, and of course, our neighbors and my best friend Elder Keith and his wife, Dayna Brooks. Legacy Hotel at the Southern Baptist Theological Seminary where I used to work, gave us three days to stay at the hotel and then drove us to drop us at the airport. We boarded the plane from O'Hare airport, Chicago to connect to Seattle/Tacoma International Airport. We landed on June 7, 2016 and Randi Boyett picked us with the van from the airport and we met with Gary Irby, who happened to be her father. It was all exciting and Gary Irby took us for lunch at MacDonald to treat in style.

They lent us the van for almost two weeks before our two vehicles were shipped from Louisville, Kentucky. We were also waiting for the 5 Towns Auto Transport & Logistics to bring our furniture and our belongings. We started to get accustomed to Kent City, the shops, the stores, the schools, hospitals, clinics, dental clinics, the churches, restaurants, water utility offices, energy offices, telephone stores, and many social goods that we would need to survive. The summer in Seattle was awesome and gorgeous compared to Louisville, Kentucky, especially for me. The landscape was breathtaking, the mountains were spectacular, the streams of clear water, undulating in the hills in the neighborhood. Although there is a lot of rain in Seattle it brings coolness to the day, without any crazy humidity. Yes, I love Seattle, Washington!

CHAPTER ELEVEN

Planting the Gospel

W e started to settle down in our new home and in the
new City of Kent and our first Sunday service was our
first Sunday on June 12, 2016. Charity begins at home! The seven
of us had our first service at home and we held our first service as
church planters and we prayed for God to guide and lead us in Kent
as church planters and missionaries. We were full of the zeal and
enthusiasm to evangelize and spread the gospel. I actually trained
my family about evangelism explosion III and we divided ourselves
into twos. Our church's name was Bread of Life International
Fellowship (BOLIF). After our first Sunday service at home, we
had our lunch and we headed to Kent station, downtown to start
evangelism outreach for what we had come for, that is to plant the
gospel and the church. We had the church brochures and business
cards to share and distribute to whoever we met in the streets, shops,
stores or restaurants. When we got to Kent Station, downtown, we
went in groups of twos, sharing the good news about Jesus Christ
to anyone we met in the streets and went to shops and restaurants.
Within twenty minutes of our adventure in a new City and excited
to win souls for Christ, we were stopped by the Kent City Security
and they asked us to stop witnessing. Someone had called the Kent

Station City Security telling them that there were people moving around in the city and telling people about Christ Jesus and that they should repent. When they stopped us, we were shocked to the core. We never expected to be stopped as we witnessed for Jesus in Kent Station City. We were used to Louisville, Kentucky where there was freedom of sharing the gospel everywhere without incidents. They took us to their office and directed us to the office of Kent Station City Administrator, Cynthia Boyd. Unfortunately, she was out of the office and the Security gave me her card. They warned us not to share our religion in the streets because it was illegal to share one's religion, Christianity for that matter in the street. They told us that we had to have our own space, or a building where we can freely invite people in and share with them whatever religion we believe but not in the street.

That was a shock to be denied to share God's Word in American, the land of the brave. Well, we could not dispute with them but only to obey the law of the land. We went back to the drawing board to strategize the other methods of evangelism. The following week, I called Cynthia Boyd but she was always out of the office for the following weeks. I kept on calling without backing down until she picked up the phone and we talked at length. She invited me to come to her office the following day to discuss more on the subject and how their laws operate. The appointment was made and I met with her the following day. In the meeting, she gave me some documents that stated the restrictions of public religious gathering that needed to have permission. Cynthia was very kind to me and told me that she was also a Christian. She said that as employees at Kent Station they were following the law and that everyone needed to adhere to it. She asked me if my church could join an annual event at Kent Station called, "Summer is Over at Kent Station" (S.O.A.K.S.) in August. Bread of Life International Fellowship (BOLIF) became a permanent member of the (S.O.A.K.S.) from that day and to other events in Kent. Every year, we pitch up our pop-up canopy table with more than 30 businesses, organizations and schools at Kent Station. People come to our pop-up canopy table and we share with them the love of Jesus with them as they visit each tent. It has given us great exposure to the community and our neighborhood as we plant the gospel to their lives. That was a plus to be known as the City's Administrator and be considered to be part of the city.

The following week, when I was opening the account at Bank of America, I was served by a Manager for Small Businesses, a kind young man who was also Christian. His name was Vernie. I opened an account and Vernie donated $100.00 and deposited it in the account. Vernie also helped me to apply, file and register Bread of Life International Fellowship with the Secretary of State and Business License. By June 20, 2016, Bread of Life International Fellowship was official in the State of Washington. We continued to meet at our home with our children because we did not know anyone. We also attended local churches to see how they were doing and seeking for their support. We first visited Calvary Church in Renton and now it is called Sunset Community Church. The interim Pastor was James Appleby, a humble Pastor and very kind with his lovely wife Marilyn Appleby. We were introduced in the church and the congregation welcomed us warmly. After the church service, Pastor James and Marilyn invited Judith and I for lunch the following day. They encouraged us to visit his friend's church, Sequoia Baptist Church in Kent and the Pastor there was Pastor Brian Duffer. The following Sunday, we visited Sequoia Baptist Church. We were greeted warmly by the Pastor, Brian Duffer even though he did not know us. We also met two couples from Zimbabwe, Mr. Albert and Priscilla Ndlovu and Fanuel and Sokuluhle Malunga who were members of SBC. We were thrilled to meet the Zimbabwe folks. After the service, we introduced each other. It was a sweet surprise to know that they are from my City, Bulawayo. They told us that there were some Zimbabweans around Kent. We organized to meet on a Saturday at Mr. and Mrs. Malunga's home. They called all the Zimbabweans and South Africans, Sudanese, and people from other African countries. We had a sweet fellowship that day and made some connections.

We shared with them our reasons for coming to Greater Seattle and Kent in particular. We told them that we came as missionaries and church planters to start a new church. We invited them to come to our home for church services the following Sunday. We started to have many people coming to our home for church services. One Tuesday, Pastor Brian invited me for lunch and he wanted to learn more about me and my family and the purpose of us coming to Kent. During the lunch, Pastor Brian asked me to share with him my personal needs and church needs. Many times, I have got friends who asked me such questions about my personal needs and the church needs. They would then turn around and say I am begging them for help while they were the ones who would have asked me and I would share with them in honesty and in confidence, hoping that they would keep it a secret but they would share with their friends and families and the word would just spread as gossip. I later developed my personal culture not to share with anyone whenever they ask me to share my personal needs. I told Pastor Brian that I don't usually share my personal needs to people anymore because of the experience I have had with people who were not honest about that question. When Pastor Brian Duffer asked me that question, I was skeptical to disclose my needs to him but with his persistence and honesty, I told him that I was having a balance of my tuition at the Seminary that may prevent me from graduating. When he promised that they would do something and that he would share with his elders at Sequoia Baptist Church, I thought there you go again and regretted sharing it with Pastor Brian. I was surprised when Pastor Brian called me and told me that they would help me to clear my balance and to also give me money for my air ticket to go to Louisville, Kentucky for my graduation. He did not stop there but that his church would support BOLIF on a monthly basis, financially. They also allow us to use their Fellowship Hall for free for our church programs. I appreciated Pastor Brian for being honest and being helpful to my predicaments. Pastor Brian Duffer was different from other people I had met before with empty promises. Sequoia Baptist Church has been supporting Bread of Life International Fellowship (BOLIF) since 2016.

I went back to Southern Baptist Theological Seminary, Louisville,

Kentucky for my oral defense of my Dissertation/Thesis on October 2, 2016. The panelists for my oral defense were my Supervisor Dr. Danny R. Bowen, Dr. Shane Parker and Dr. Michael Wilder, the Dean. After presenting my dissertation chapter by chapter, and they questioned and challenged my dissertation by the panelists, intense grilling, I was finally declared a doctor. I was welcomed in the field of academic scholars and they congratulated me and they wished me the best in my life. It was a thrill and I thanked them for their support, critique, guidance and advice throughout the process. Dr. Danny R Bowen, my supervisor who had experience in the medical field as a doctor in the, was so excited and thrilled to have me as his supervisor and worked together so well. Dr. Michael Wilder, my dean, was also happy and congratulated me for working so hard and coming out with such a dissertation that would help the church all over the world and the communities at large. I came back from Louisville, Kentucky to Kent, Washington to prepare for my graduation and it was set on December 2, 2016. I flew back to Louisville, Kentucky, on December 1, to graduate on December 2, 2016. I saw God's hand in all the process and Dr. Albert Mohler, the Southern Baptist Theological Seminary President, took time on the stage to congratulate me and because we knew each other closely. Dr. Danny R. Bowen, the faculty, friends and all those who knew me, were so excited to see me graduate. Those were the greatest moments in my life to see me graduate with the Doctorate which had never happened in my Gasela-Mhlanga family. The title Dr. Sam S. Gasela Mhlanga is a milestone to my family and my consanguinity in the past, especially my grandfather, Mabuto Gasela who was an evangelist and a missionary in the London Missionary Society at Hope Fountain Mission in the 1950s.

To put everything into the right perspective, 2016 was a foundational year, a year to establish Bread of Life International Fellowship (BOLIF), planting the gospel in the community, in Kent City and to register the church, shared our vision with the community, connected with community leaders, City of Kent Mayor, Elizabeth Albertson, the Police Enforcement, Fight Fires and the

Store Managers and the civil and community leaders to befriend. In January, 2017, after securing a building to rent, BOLIF moved to execute its programs as we had access to the building 24/7. The church grew day by day and within a few months, we had a core group. I drafted the BOLIF constitution, the bylaws, the church structure, the strategic plan, the website, the Facebook page, and the church executive committee. In 2017, we started to conduct core group leadership seminars, evangelism Day Outreach, Children and Youth Day, Neighborhood gathering every last Friday of August, BOLIF Community Services like Clean Up Kent City. In June, we had two events, Homeless Outreach with food and witnessing and a movie for the children in the neighborhood of the church. On July 4th, 2017, we invited many people to celebrate USA Independence Gene Coulon Park in Renton. We had people from various countries in Africa, Asia, the Islands and of course, from here in the USA. On July 29, 2017, we held our first Vacation Bible School (VBS) at Kent Meridian Park with so many children who participated. Mary Dempsey had joined BOLIF and she was good at organizing and teaching children and she was BOLIF Treasurer too. Mary played a very pivotal role in putting in place Sunday School for children and the BOLIF Banking System. Brother Albert Ndlovu and his wife, Priscilla Ndlovu have been our great support in the ministry and in the evangelism outreach. We are so grateful for them, indeed.

BOLIF CHURCH STRUCTURE

Church Chairman

The church chairman shall be elected by the members of the church and shall meet the qualities of an elder/overseer (I Timothy 3:1-7, NKJV).

The chairman shall preside over the meetings if the Pastor is not present except if the Pastor asks him to preside over the meetings even if the Pastor is present. He shall liaise with the Pastor and cannot report any news or announcements without consulting the Pastor first. He reports to the Pastor.

The term of office is annual and can continue for three years if approved by the church of which at the end of the three years, he is eligible to be voted in again for two more years. After serving the additional two years, he cannot be reelected for two years.

Church Secretary

The church Secretary shall meet the qualities of an elder/overseer (I Timothy 3:1-7, NKJV). He shall be elected by the congregation. He shall be someone who is a good communicator and one who knows how to write and be able to disseminate information expeditiously when instructed.

He shall report to the chairman. He cannot disseminate information to the public without the knowledge of the Pastor and the chairman. He shall record all the minutes of all the meetings accurately.

The term of office is annually and can continue for three years if approved by the church of which at the end of the three years, he is eligible to be voted in again if he/she is still in good standing.

The Vice Secretary will perform the same duties of the Secretary and he/she shall act as the Secretary in the absence of the Secretary.

Church Treasurer & Marketing Director

The church treasurer shall be elected by the congregation. The Treasurer shall meet the qualities of an elder/overseer (I Timothy 3:1-7, NKJV).

The treasure shall be someone who has financial background and knows accounting and bookkeeping. He/she shall be someone who is honest and reliable. He/she shall report to the Finance Committee chairman and deacon chairman. She/he is the marketing Director of the church. He/she is the public relationship officer (PR) who represents the church and she/he is responsible for budgeting, financial controlling, balance sheet and organizing audits.

The term of office is annual and can continue for three years if approved by the church of which at the end of the three years, he/she is eligible to be voted in again if he/she is still in good standing.

Administrative & Organizing Secretary

The Administrative Secretary shall be elected/appointed by the church to organize events and meetings. He/she shall have the qualities of a deacon (I Timothy 3:8-10, NKJV). He/she reports to the chairman and Pastor.

The term of office is annual and can continue for three years if approved by the church of which at the end of the three years, he/she is eligible to be voted in again if he/she is still in good standing.

Praise & Worship Music Director

The Praise and Worship Director shall be someone who is gifted in singing. She/she shall be someone who has the qualities of a deacon (I Timothy 3:8-10, NKJV).

She/he reports to the chairman. She/he organizes worship service songs, leads the praise and worship team. She/he can compose songs and lead the worship service every Sunday with the help of others who are musicians also. If she/he is not available, she/he shall assign her/him assistant and shall inform the Pastor and the chairman a week before Sunday. she/he reports to the Pastor.

The term of office is annual and shall continue for three years if approved by the church of which at the end of the three years, he/she is eligible to be voted in again if she/he is still in good standing.

Sunday School Director

The Sunday School Teacher shall be someone who is able to teach and also has the qualities of an elder/overseer. He/she shall be someone who organizes teachers for each department and makes sure that all the Sunday schools run smoothly. He/she is responsible to order Sunday school materials for each class and monitor time and consults the Sunday school teachers for their materials. He/she reports to the Pastor.

The term of office is annual and can continue for three years if approved by the church of which at the end of the three years, he/she is eligible to be voted in again if he is still in good standing.

Marriage & Family Counseling Director

The marriage and Family Counseling Director shall be someone who has the qualities of an elder/deacon (I Timothy 3:1-10, NKJV). He/she shall be someone who is mature and has experience in handling marriage issues well and preferably licensed by the state or city. An ordained minister can also execute the duties of a Counselor. He/she reports to the Pastor.

The term of office is annually and can continue for three years if approved by the church of which at the end of the three years, he/she is eligible to be voted in again if he is still in good standing.

Youth & Creativity Director

The Youth Director shall be someone who has the qualities of an elder (I Timothy 3:1-7, NKJV). He shall be someone who is mature and has experience to guide the youth. He shall be someone who understands youth challenges and be able to give Biblical counsel.

He reports to the Pastor. He is responsible for organizing meetings, camps, seminars and must be active and energetic, able to engage with all the youth in all levels.

The term of office is annual and shall continue for three years if approved by the church of which at the end of the three years, he is eligible to be voted in again if he is still in good standing.

Technology Director

The technology Director must be someone who meets the qualities of a deacon (I Timothy 3:8-10, NKJV). He/she must have a tech background and be able to figure out any technological problems and give solutions. He/she is responsible for all the sound systems, lighting, and equipment. He/she shall be someone trustworthy and reliable. He/she must train assistants to help him/her. If he/she would be absent, he/she must consult the chairman and the Pastor a week before so that arrangements may be made.

He/she reports to the chairman and Pastor. The term of office is annual and can continue for three years if approved by the church of which at the end of the three years, he is eligible to be voted in again if he/she is still in good standing.

Children's Ministry Director

The Children's Ministry Director must be someone who has the qualities of an elder/deacon (I Timothy 3:1-10, NKJV). She/he must be a person who loves children and who can relate to them well. She/he must be someone without felony and must have clear criminal records. She/he must be able to provide relevant materials for all the age group levels. She/he must have the ability to recruit responsible teachers and be able to train and work with all teachers well.

She/he must be able to relate to children with love, care and support. She/he must be able to organize games and understand the learning spans of all children age groups. She reports to the Pastor and the chairman.

The term of office is annually and can continue for three years if approved by the church of which at the end of the three years, she/he is eligible to be voted in again if he is still in good standing.

Evangelism/Missions Director

Evangelism Director shall be someone who has the qualities of an elder (I Timothy 3:1-7, NKJV). He must be someone who is mature with a background of evangelism and discipleship. He must be someone who has the heart for the lost and must love people. He must be able to organize evangelism outreach and be very active in mobilizing people for outreach. He reports to the Pastor.

The term of office is annual and shall continue for three years if approved by the church of which at the end of the three years, he is eligible to be voted in again if he is still in good standing.

Education and Financial Investor Director

The Education Director shall be someone who has the qualities of an elder (I Timothy 3:1-7, NKJV). He/she must be someone who is mature with educational and financial background. He/she must be someone who has the heart for education and an investment knowledge. He must be able to organize seminars for educational and investment seminars, meetings, workshops and be very active in mobilizing people for such. He reports to the Pastor.

The term of office is annual and shall continue for three years if approved by the church of which at the end of the three years, he is eligible to be voted in again if he is still in good standing.

Social & Hospitality Director

The social and hospitality Director must be someone who meets the qualities of a deacon (I Timothy 3:8-10, NKJV). He/she must have a social and hospitality background and be able to connect with people, be able to organize social events, conferences, social gatherings and seminars for the group. He/she shall be someone trustworthy and reliable. He/she must train an assistant, the vice to help him/her. If he/she would be absent, he/she must consult the chairman and the Pastor a week before so that arrangements may be made for any organized events.

He/she reports to the chairman and Pastor. The term of office is annual and can continue for three years if approved by the church of which at the end of the three years, he is eligible to be voted in again if he/she is still in good standing.

Entertainment & College/University Director

The Entertainment & college/University Director must be someone who meets the qualities of a deacon (I Timothy 3:8-10, NKJV). He/she must be at college/university or have graduated less than 5 years and be able to connect with students, be able to organize the current students and former students for seminars, fellowship, prayers, games and be able to connect them to BOLIF. He/she shall be someone trustworthy and reliable. He/she must be able to train others to be assistants to help him/her in organizing the meetings and events. If he/she would be absent, he/she must consult with the chairman and the Pastor a week before so that arrangements may be made for any organized events.

He/she reports to the chairman and Pastor. The term of office is annual and can continue for three consecutive years if approved by the church of which at the end of the three years, he is eligible to be voted in again if he/she is still in good standing.

Catering Director

The Cater Director must be someone who meets the qualities of a deacon (I Timothy 3:8-10, NKJV). He/she must be a specialist in cooking, serving and nutritionists. She/he must be someone who loves to serve and help people, be able to organize events for food competition, catering for small and big catering occasions such as church events, weddings, engagements, graduation parties, baby showers, bachelor's and birthday parties. He/she shall be someone trustworthy and reliable. He/she must train assistants and have a committee to assist him/her. If he/she would be absent, he/she must consult the chairman and the Pastor a week before so that arrangements may be made for any organized events.

He/she reports to the chairman and Pastor. The term of office is annual and can continue for three consecutive years if approved by the church of which at the end of the three years, he/she is eligible to be voted in again if he/she is still in good standing.

Healthy Director

The Healthy Director must be someone who meets the qualities of a deacon (I Timothy 3:8-10, NKJV). He/she must be in a healthy system, as a Dr., Nurse, Clinical Psychologist, Healthy Specialist, Professional Counselor and any health-related professions. He/she shall be someone trustworthy and reliable. He/she must be passionate about people's health and be willing to assist in any way possible, in healthy related issues. He/she must organize health workshops, seminars, organize community service for health for all. He/she should organize mission trips for healthy purposes locally and overseas. He/she must be certified in his/her area of specialty. If he/she would be absent, he/she must consult the chairman and the Pastor a week before so that arrangements may be made for any organized events.

He/she reports to the chairman and Pastor. The term of office is annual and can continue for three consecutive years if approved by the church of which at the end of the three years, he is eligible to be voted in again if he/she is still in good standing.

Attorney/Law Director

The Attorney/Law Director must be someone who meets the qualities of a deacon (I Timothy 3:8-10, NKJV). He/she must be an attorney/lawyer who is active in practicing law or in the process. He/she must be a professional in the law field with a Bachelor of Law of equivalent. He/she shall be representing Bread of Life International Fellowship (BOLIF) in all legal issues and to write petitions, file law-suits or defend or act on behalf of BOLIF or any member who wishes to be represented with agreements and in accordance with the laws of the state. He/she shall be someone trustworthy and reliable. He/she must be passionate about people's legal issues and be willing to assist in any way possible. He/she must organize workshops, seminars on behalf of BOLIF. He/she must be certified in his/her area of specialty.

He/she reports to the Pastor and chairman. The term of office is annual and can continue for three years if approved by the church of which at the end of the three years, he is eligible to be voted in again if he/she is still in good standing.

Church Pastor

The church Pastor shall meet the qualities of the elder/overseer (I Timothy 3:1-7, NKJV) in order to perform his duties as a minister. He must be ordained and must have been at least three years in a theological seminary/college/university from a credible and accredited institution. He should be able to lead and conduct his duties with diligence and faithfulness.

He reports to the board of the elders of the church. His term of office is limitless as he is a full time Pastor only with the exception of unacceptable moral conduct or behavior or if he has become heretic in contrast to Biblical and theological truth that leads to apostasy in which he would be evaluated and charged. If he is found guilty, confession and repentance will be sought by the board of the elders to determine if he still qualifies to serve the church or be discharged of his duties as a Pastor. He is responsible to take care of the congregation in matters of spiritual, moral, and leadership counsel and guidance. He acts as the spiritual father for every member of the church and shall be impartial.

Board of Elders

The board of elders is a spiritual board of the church and every member of it shall have the qualities of (I Timothy 3:1-7, NKJV). They are the highest board of the church, but they report to the congregation. The Pastor is part of the board of elders. The chairman of the church and the Pastor chair the board of elders. It is composed of 1 to more members depending on the size of the church. As the church is autonomous, the elders and the congregation together resolve any conflicts, problems and the challenges of the church but first addressed by the Pastor of the Church. They report to Christ who is the Head of the church and they listen and follow the Biblical counsel (Eph. 5:23, NKJV).

Board of Deacons

The board of deacons shall have the qualities of (Timothy 3:8-11, NKJV). They must be people who are willing to work without complaint and be available to serve all the time. They report to the board of elders and the chairman. They are responsible for the church operations and to make sure that the church and the furniture is in order all the time. They shall choose their chair-person within their board.

The term of office is annual and shall continue for three consecutive years if approved by the church of which at the end of the three years, he/she is eligible to be voted in again if he/she is still in good standing.

Committee Member

The committee member (s) is available to be used by God anywhere and anyhow he or she feels called to do. Other committees may ask her or him to help in anywhere she or he feels comfortable.

Our first Church Chairman was Mr. Fanuel Malunga, the Church Secretary was Mrs. Judith Mhlanga, the Church Treasurer was Mrs. Sukoluhle Malunga and Youth coordinator Blessing Mhlanga, in 2017 to 2018. The summers have been the most active periods with various events we put into place such as Vacation Bible School (VBS, Basketball camps, leadership seminars, park evangelism, Summer is Over at Kent Station (S.O.A.K.S), 4th of July Celebration and BOLIF Retreats. We partnered with Central Baptist Church in Jacksonville, Texas for Basketball, VBS and other events. They had brought seven coaches to conduct our first basketball camp on July 16-20, 2018 and to train and coach our youths and the children in the community. The children who participated were from 1st grade to 6th grades, conducted at Neely O'Brien Elementary School, from 10:00 am to 12:30 pm. For the 7th grade to the 12th grades, it was conducted at Kent Phoenix Academy from 2:00 pm to 4:00 pm. We were so happy with that kind of partnership with Central Baptist Church. We were able to reach out to our community and some children received Christ as their personal Lord and Savior and some of their parents heard the Word being shared, planting the seed to them. The recurring event of Summer is Over at Kent Station (S.O.A.K.S) which gave us the opportunities to meet with the Kent City residents, businesses, schools and other organizations, the City Mayor, City Administrator and many to share the gospel with what we stand for.

MINISTRIES

The following ministries are already established or they are under development and they will be available in the near future.

- **Fellowship** - Meetings for Fellowship, Prayer, Teaching, Worship, Celebrations.

- **Conferences & Seminars** – Conferences and seminars for various events such as leadership, women conferences, youth conferences, men conferences etc.

- **Marriage and Family** - Seminars for courtship, godly marriage, raising of godly children, balancing work and home, family finances, education, preparing for retirement, etc.

- **Health Living-** Physical exams, affordable health insurances, healthy foods and nutrition, affordable clinics and physicians, weight watch, etc.

- **Biblical Counseling-** Couples, youths, divorcees, depression, suicide, anxiety, pre-marital counseling, HIV/AIDS, marriages, etc.

- **Children and Youth** - Culture and traditions, raising godly children, choosing a life partner, parent-child relationships, self-control, etc.

- **Evangelism** - Campus ministry, street evangelism, crusades, etc.

- **Sports & Games-** Basketball, soccer, volleyball, table tennis, cricket, football, tennis, etc.

- **Sunday School** - Adult, Youth, Children classes.

- **Philanthropic Ministry -** To help those who are in need and such as the homeless, orphans, widows etc.

Translations - Interpretation and translation of different languages, e.g., French, Portuguese, Chinese, Korean, Zulu, Swahili, Spanish, Shona, Haitian, etc.

On August 1st, we always have neighborhood gatherings in which we share with each other whatever we have and also to get to know each one in the neighborhood. We had the first neighborhood gathering on August 1, 2018 and it has become a tradition. We also have a tradition to have the BOLIF Retreat as a church, as summer closes down and we approach the fall and then winter. Our BOLIF retreat was on August 18, 2018 at San Juan Island sponsored by our members of the church. Our final event in 2018, was the Financial Investments and Cyber Security and Protection Seminar and we had one of our speakers, Professor Don Makande, on October 20, 2018, from 11:00 am to 3:30 pm.

2019, began promising to be a great year for the BOLIF Church family as Olufunmilayo and her three children, Imoleayo, Ikeoluna, Ibukunoluna, joined our church. The husband, Shadrach Roland Ogunlola, had remained in Nigeria working on his papers to join the family in the USA. With fervent prayer, God finally opened the doors and he was able to join his family. We worked to officiate their wedding in the Church in the USA although they had wedded in Nigeria. It was the first wedding for BOLIF church on April 21, 2019 to be specific. Every member of the BOLIF Church participated with the wedding ceremony and the reception which was spectacular. Mr. Shadrach and Mrs. Olufunmilayo Ogunlola were declared a husband and a wife in holy matrimony. We were also joined by Welislie Mint, originally from Jamaica with his wife from Democratic Republic of the Congo (DRC) and their children. We were also joined by Jackie Wanja with her daughter, Chloe. We had a strategic plan in the previous months to map out the way forward and we filled the BOLIF officer bearers. The BOLIF officers were as follows: Pastor: Dr. Sam S. Mhlanga; Church Secretary: Nomasonto Forgiveness Nxumalo; Treasurer: Dr. Barbara Lucia Sibanda; Social & Hospitality Director: Sibonile Sibanda; Education & Financial Director: Professor Don Makande; Youth & Creativity Director: Shadrach Roland Ogunlola; Organizing & Worship Director: Mrs. Patience Malaba Gach; Sunday School & Hospitality Vice: Mrs. Angela Moyo; Vice Church Secretary & Catering Director: Judith Mhlanga; Entertainment & University/College Director: Natalie Murumbi; Evangelism & Outreach Ministry Director: Qhawelenkosi Blessing Mhlanga; Music Director: Sinqobile Shalom Mhlanga; Technical Director: Thandolwenkosi Prosper Mhlanga; Committee members: Olufumnilayo Roland Ogunlola; and Nkosilathi Emmanuel Mhlanga.

We hear about a natural catastrophe of the Cyclone Idai in Zimbabwe, Mozambique and Malawi that had hit and left many people dead, some were left without their homes, some were injured and displaced. I consulted with family and friends in the diaspora and organized a philanthropic event to raise the donations for the victims and the survivors of Cyclone Idai, an intense Tropical Cyclone which affected the southern hemisphere in Zimbabwe, in Chimanimani and Chipinge and part of Mozambique and Malawi. The storm wreaked havoc and a catastrophic damage and there was a humanitarian crisis for more than 1,300 people who were dead and many more missing having been washed away to the Indian Ocean by the floods. We could not watch the news and do nothing when our own people were in dire need of assistance. I called for a meeting for people from Zimbabwe and Africa and the sympathizers to donate clothes, food and medical stuff. For accountability, we appealed for donations for people to bring to our gathering at BOLIF Church. The monies were directed to the Family and Friends Diaspora group Treasurer, Mr. Hamah Mawindi who did a great job by accounting to every dollar and giving receipts to people. People came in great numbers from Africa, the Middle East and other places to donate. As a result, we were able to send three drums, one in Chimanimani, another in Koppa, a valley where many people were washed away to Indian Ocean with the floods and the third one was sent to Chipinge. The three drums were sent through International Cargo Link which delivered them at the United Baptist Church Head Office through Bishop Austin Mabhena and Rev. Irvin Moyo, Vice Bishop. I was once the Vice Bishop of the United Baptist Church while I was still in Zimbabwe and I knew how transparent and honest the church systems were. We instructed them to send the drums directly to the local community leaders and the local churches to distribute to the needy people. They really did a good job and they took and sent us some videos as the survivors received the donations.

We have an extended family and community that we worked together with under Friends and Family in Diaspora that we formed and also other people that we got connected with although some of them were not part of Friends and Family in Diaspora. The people who participated in contributing and donations to help the survivors in the Cyclone Idai were, Loverage Guzha, Rev. and Mrs. Guzha, Nhial and Patience Malaba Gach, Shalom Sinqobile Mhlanga, Mrs. Angela Moyo, Elijah and Natalie Moyo, Cosmas and Mrs. R. Mafurise, Hamah and Future Mawindi, Elizabeth Makonese, Fiso Sibanda, Nakai and Ms. Bofu, Prosper Thando Mhlanga, Emmanuel Nkosi Mhlanga, Vernie Gonzale Dahl, Latasha Rodgers, Raquel Rodgers, Joseph Sam Mhlanga, Olufunmilayo and Shadrach Roland Ogunlola, Ikeoluwa Roland, Imoleayo Roland, Ibukenoluwa Roland, Ife Grace Roland, Mambo Moyo, Sam and Leah Maina, Mrs. Siyayi Mukungatu, Mrs. P. Mutisi, Marsha Mutisi, Tafadzwa Mapiye, Merrilee Smith, Fortunate Mwanaka, Phetheni Ndhlovu, Sibusiso Ndlovu, Sibonile Sibanda, Barbara Lucia Sibanda, Judith Mhlanga, Charity Mukungatu, Fanuel and Sukoluhle Malunga, Albert and Priscilla Ndlovu, Natalie Murumbi, Nomasonto Forgiveness Nxumalo, Jackie Wanja and Chloe, Simba and Amber Rusike, Catherine and Jeremiah, Professor Don Makande, Rev. and Mrs. Kativu, Tafadzwa Mapiye, benedicta Muneri, Leroy and Milile Nyathi, Mai Makore, Russel and Judith Chinyani, Nyasha Chinyani, Risho and Mother Africa, Gerald and Anna Nkala,

Ann and Shane, Rachel and Qin, Welislie Mint and many others who just became our close friends.

BOLIF held its second basketball camp on July 22 to July 26, 2019 at Millcreek Middle School in Kent and this time the camp was for 1st grades to 6th grades. We had two coaches from Central Baptists Church, Jacksonville, Texas, Coach Darvin Hooker with 35 years of coaching experience and Mel Socia with 8 years of coaching experience. BOLIF provided two coaches, Nkosi Emmanuel Mhlanga and Thando Prosper Mhlanga with basketball skills gained from their schools. The basketball camp was a great success as more than 90 students came from all over Greater Seattle, including some from the City Everett, Renton and Auburn Cities. The basketball camp started at 10:00 am to 12:30 pm with Bible teachings and sharing at regular intervals directed by the coaches and me as a Pastor. Lunch was between 12:30 pm to 1:00 pm. Then from 1:00 pm to 4:00 pm we had basketball free interactions, which the students enjoyed most. We had some visitors from South Africa who assisted us on the Basketball Camp. They were Thoko Nxumalo, Pearl Molotsi and Auntie Connie Mamphudi who were a blessing for their presence. We had two vans from Awakening Church, Bellevue from my close friend, Pastor Jonah Easley and also from Will Forrest. These two Pastors have been supportive ever since. We picked up the children from their home and dropped them after the basketball camp, especially those who needed transportation.

On December 28, 2019, Judith and I celebrated our 25th Wedding Anniversary at Sequoia Baptist Church and we had the privilege to have Pastor Brian Duffer to officiate our 25th wedding anniversary. Our children participated and led the occasion with the members of BOLIF. It was a time of reflection and introspection of our past twenty-five years together with God having blessed us with five beautiful children. The time flies, it was like yesterday when we wedded. We were so grateful for all the years we had pulled together even if we had faced numerous challenges on the way. The BOLIF, SBC, and friends supported us in making the 25th wedding anniversary a success.

We had our BOLIF Retreat at Mount Rainier. Some of us managed to climb to the top of the mountain at 6,800 feet. We ended 2019 with a high note as we prepared to start a New Year of 2020. We started the year with our Evangelism Core Group Training to prepare for the year to witness for Christ on January 25, 2020. Covid-19 started to blow out the BOLIF Strategic Plan for 2020. We had planned to launch our second campus/church in Tacoma on August 30, 2020 but all our plans were dashed aside because of the covid-19 pandemic. We had to postpone it to August 1, 2021. By March, 2020, as the lockdown was issued by the Washington Governor Jay Inslee health guidelines and the close down of stores, schools, churches and public transport, including airplanes, we also followed the guidelines and closed our church. It was hard but we survived the challenge and we started meeting on a zoom platform for Sunday Services, Wednesday Prayer Meetings, Friday Meetings and Saturday Women Prayer Meetings. The church members continued to be committed and we were joined by others who had never had time to fellowship with us. We had to navigate and be part of the global network that was reaching out to the world. We started to connect with the United Baptist/UK which I had started in the UK in 2005 and were now able to connect with them because of the zoom. I was able to preach for them and the Pastor there, Pastor Edward Mutema and another UBC Pastor in the UK, Ngoni Chindondondo, were able to connect and preach for us. We continued the zoom platform connection from March and July, 2020. Some of our BOLIF members felt that it was becoming more challenging to meet online and we called for the meeting to discuss and at the end of the meeting, we had a vote as others wanted us to go back to church and meet in person while others were afraid to contract the covid-19 pandemic.

The vote favored those who said they wanted to go back to meet at the church in person. The members were left with the choice either to attend the church services with those who wanted in person services. Others remained with the option to attend the services through the zoom. We all agreed that for Wednesday Prayer Meetings, Friday Youth Meetings, and the Saturday Women Prayers Meeting would remain on zoom platforms except the Sunday services, especially those who wanted to meet in person. On July 5, we reopened or in person

Sunday services. We followed all the health guidelines issued by the Governor, to wear masks all the time in the church, observing the social distance of six feet apart, taking and recording temperatures for each person in attendance, washing hands and sanitizing hands all the time. Those health guidelines we have observed and I am glad that we never had convid-19 infected members during our meetings to worship the loving God. The lockdown unlocked a lot of opportunities, personally. I had to spend more time with my family and with my God and seeking His will. For many years, I had wanted to publish my books but I was not able to with many efforts and endeavors. However, with the lockdown, I managed to focus on writing and publishing my books. I managed to breakthrough by God's grace and published my six books in both 2020 and 2021. To God be the glory!

CHAPTER TWELVE

Unfinished Business

The ministry continues with the amplitude to see what the Lord has in store for us as a family and the church. We are in 2021 and the covid-19 pandemic made us adjust how we operate, worship, work and fellowship to make it new normal. As we start a second campus in Tacoma, BOLIF-Tacoma, on August 1, 2021, we anticipate and look forward to another adventure with the Tacoma community as we plant the gospel, mandated by God in (Matt. 28:18-20, NKJV). One of the Mission I was working under signed a five-year contract on June 1, 2016, to be a missionary/church planter in Kent, Washington, and the five-year contract expires in 2021. After the contract expires, one is on his own, in the ocean on his own peril, just as Jonah was thrown from ship into the sea (Jonah 1:10-16, NKJV). Fortunately, God had prepared a great fish to swallow Jonah, His prophet, for three days and three nights he was in the belly of the great fish. God ordered the great fish to spit Jonah on the dry beach on the third day. Jonah was running away from the Lord's mission to go to Nineveh. I am not running away from the commission that the Lord commanded me to accomplish for His will and purpose. I pray that God will send a whale to swallow me and vomit me on the dry land on the other side where I will continue to spread the word of God until my last breath.

In 2018, I was admitted at the University of Washington to study Medical Anthropology and Global Health, (PhD), to pursue a research program on Human Diseases, Treatment and Prevention. It was a non-matriculated PhD and the courses were intriguing, indeed. I wanted to understand human health issues which are connected to their spirituality. I was also admitted at Walden University to study Clinical Psychology-Forensic, (PhD). I wanted to understand the human psych how it functions and also to understand how the psych and the spirituality connect and work in congruence. I am in my second year. In 2020, I was enrolled to be licensed as a certified Biblical Counselor with the International Association of Biblical Counselors and I will be graduating soon. All these scholastic adventures are in pursuit of knowledge to understand human needs, holistically, physically, mentally and spiritually. These are some unfinished businesses that are set before me to accomplish before I retire in this world. The ambitions are great and I remain optimistic, hopeful and faithful, yearning to please God and fulfill what God had brought me to do on this planet earth. My hope and prayer are to have a Gasela International Counseling and Leadership Center (GICLC) in the USA, Zimbabwe and South Africa for counseling and leadership development. "Where there is no vision, the people perish...," (Proverbs 29:18, KJV).

My life has been an incredible journey, introspecting where I am coming from and what I have been blessed with. It is amazing how God has provided, guided and led me through thick and thin with my family background. I confidently declare, "Ebenezer, thus far the Lord has helped me," (I Samuel 7:12, NIV). The Lord has protected me from harm and danger, the Lord has provided for me and my family, the Lord has led me to pastor, teach and train His servants in the church. The Lord has guided me through His Spirit, to make good decisions for His church, my family and for myself. God has been faithful to me and His love, mercy, grace, kindness, gentleness surpluses my weaknesses and "Surely goodness and mercy shall follow me All the days of my life; And I will dwell in the house of the Lord Forever," (Psalm 23: 6, NKJV). The Lord watches over me and He sees me, "The eyes of the Lord are on the righteous, And His ears are open to their cry," (Psalm

34:15, NKJV). My daily prayer is to be always faithful to God and to be a vessel to bring the blessings to all sinners, the hurting, the suffering, those who are desperate, depressed, the lonely, the abandoned, those who are forgotten, the homeless, the orphans and fatherless.

I pray that my memoir/autobiography will inspire many people to depend on the Lord and to let Him guide their steps, daily. My prayer is that my children, Qhawelenkosi Blessing, Sinqobile Shalom, Thandolwenkosi Prosper, Nkosilathi Emmanuel and Joseph Sam Jr. Nkosana and of course, my lovely wife, Judith, will remain under God's protection and watch. To the whole Gasela-Mhlanga family, scattered all over the world, to remain united, committed to the things of the Lord and to each other, to be a blessing to our communities and above all, to be godly for God's glory. To the BOLIF church family, I pray that we all remain faithful to the Lord, loving one another like in the early church (Acts 4:32, NIV) until the second coming of our Lord Jesus Christ. To all my friends, thank you for being my friends and I am who I am because I am standing on the shoulders of the giants, you!

CONCLUSION

My observations and analysis on the three states that we had lived in America, Grand Rapids, Midwest States; Louisville, Kentucky, Southern States and Greater Seattle, Northwest States; one would say, the prejudice in Midwest States is not visible, not audible and not pronounced. In the Southern States, the prejudice is visible, audible and pronounced. The church is even promoting it more than the secular. In the Northwest States, the prejudice is under the skin not on the surface or visible but is it loaded in the work systems, both religious and secular systems.

This memoir/autobiography is the first part of my life. The second part of my memoir/autobiography will complete the journey of my entire life on earth. This memoir/autobiography has been a deep reflection of myself as to where I was born, by whom, and the people who stood on the way to cheer me up as the cloud of witnesses. This has brought me a deep sense of responsibility, accountability, my duty, my allegiance, my passion and my aspiration to be a better version of Christ. A dark cloud fell me and my family when my mother, Josephine (Nee Nyathi) Gasela Mhlanga passed away on November 10, 2019 after long illness. She was the pillar of my life who taught me to love people and to be kind to every human being on earth. She raised me, cared for me and supported me all the way. She loved me, my wife, our children and the ministry. I will always be grateful to her and thank God for allowing her to live to see her grand-children and to remain my encourager, comforter, advisor and mother. In the family, she was the world. May her soul rest in eternal peace till we meet again as she was a prayer warrior and loved the Lord, dearly. No matter what all the obstacles on my life journey has been, I was and still under the radar of God, guiding my steps, inspiring me to keep on pushing forward, to keep on believing in Him, to keep the faith and to keep on loving, exuding the love of Christ, His goodness, His grace, His mercy, His kindness and sacrifice, regardless of all the challenges I faced. To God be the glory!

REFERENCES

(https://en.wikipedia.org/wiki/Mzilikazi, accessed, November, 23, 2020).

(https://www.sahistory.org.za/people/king-mzilikazi, accessed, November 26, 2020).

(https://www.britannica.com/biography/Mzilikazi, accessed December 2, 2020).

(https://www.sahistory.org.za/people/king-mzilikazi, accessed, December 5, 2020).

(https://zimfieldguide.com/matabeleland-south/hope-fountain-mission, Accessed December 7, 2020).

(https://en.wikipedia.org/wiki/Lancaster House Agreement, Accessed on December 10, 2020).

(Wikipedia, https://en.wikipedia.org/wiki/Abel Muzorewa, Accessed on December 13, 2020).

(https://www.britannica.com/topic/Robert-Mugabe-on-Zimbabwe-1985189/The-Lancaster-House-Negotiations, Accessed on December 15, 2020).

(https://en.wikipedia.org/wiki/Henry Venn (Church_Missionary_Society, Accessed on December 30, 2020).

Printed in the United States
by Baker & Taylor Publisher Services